W9-ARD-617

The Economics of Age

The Economics of Age

Michael J. Brennan
Professor of Economics, Brown University

Philip Taft
L. Herbert Ballou University Professor of Economics, Brown University

Mark B. Schupack
Associate Professor of Economics, Brown University

W · W · Norton & Company · Inc·

New York

First Edition
Library of Congress Catalog Card No. 67-11089

Published simultaneously in Canada by
George J. McLeod Limited, Toronto
Printed in the United States of America
1 2 3 4 5 6 7 8 9 0

Contents

PART I. The Young and the Old

1. Age: An Economic Variable 3
2. The Aging Problem: An Historical Perspective 12
3. Research on Aging 26

PART II. Industrial Employment by Age

4. Demand, Supply, and the Older Worker: The Market Approach 43
5. Hiring Practices and the Older Worker 59
6. Union-Employer Contracts and the Older Worker 74

PART III. Age and Geographic Mobility

7. Factors Affecting Mobility by Age 95
8. The Migration Evidence 107

PART IV. The Age Structure of Occupations

9. Age and Occupational Choice 119
10. Occupational Change: The Data 131
11. Occupational Regression Analysis 160
12. Predicting Occupational Employment 179

PART V. Toward a Public Policy on Aging

13. The Analysis of Public Policy 203
14. Issues of Public Policy 220

Preface

In recent years the economic behavior patterns of various age groups have received increasing publicity. In respect to the youngest members of the labor force, monetary returns to education and the status of school dropouts have been emphasized. Of more pressing social importance for the immediate future are the income and employment problems faced by older workers. As a consequence, research efforts concerned with economic differences among age groups have been directed primarily toward an explanation of poverty levels of income and poor employment prospects of older and aged workers. However, these effects have been fragmentary or highly questionable from a methodological viewpoint. The aim of this study is a more comprehensive analysis of economic problems associated with age than has heretofore been undertaken.

Certainly, previous studies have not provided comprehensive answers or unambiguous causal interpretations of observed behavior. Neither can this study pretend to offer final answers to the many facets of age and economic status. Too little is known about the causal interrelationships. More important is the fact that too little accurate data are available for direct tests of hypotheses.

A dual attack on the problem is adopted: (1) direct surveys (on employers practices and the provisions of union contracts), and (2) theoretical models designed to measure statistically the relative importance of those variables exerting a systematic effect upon the phenomena to be explained. In seeking answers to some questions a focus upon older workers as such was deemed most appropriate. For other questions the approach reflects a conviction that the entire age spectrum of the labor force must be analyzed in order to derive meaningful answers about the economic status of any one age group. Thus, although older and aged workers face the most serious employment problems, the boundaries of our inquiry extend beyond the older worker.

If older workers are described as those 45 years of age and over, a useful distinction can be drawn between those 45–64 and those 65 and over. Typically, those below 65 are active members of the labor force (although a nonparticipation problem begins to emerge at the 45–54 age bracket). Therefore, the relevant questions are those related to the income and employment status of this group *vis-à-vis* the status of younger members of the labor force. For those 65 and over the problem is one of labor force participation. This age group has received the most attention. Aside from isolated productivity studies, little is known about the forces determining the status of the 45–64 age group. One contribution of this study will be an analysis of those below ordinary retirement age in terms of demand and supply factors affecting their income and employment.

Three aspects of employment and earnings by age are investigated: industries, regions, and occupations. Part I points out the need for reaserch in this area. It also provides a discussion of the historical evolution of the aging problem and a critical review of existing literature.

In Part II income and employment problems are approached from the perspective of different industries in the economy. The employment status of older workers, and that of other age groups as well, is appraised within the context of market forces and institutional practices that affect age groups in different ways or to varying degrees. Age groups within a given industry are compared, and comparisions are made among industries for each age group. Our objective is to identify the common factors operating across industries to produce employment patterns by age and to determine the extent to which industries differ in their hiring practices with respect to age.

Part III centers upon geographic migration, differences in mobility by age (including those beyond 65 years of age), and the effects of migration upon the distribution of income and employment by age. In Part IV investigation of occupations is undertaken in order to determine what factors explain the age structure within each occupation and the extent to which different occupations provide employment opportunities for older workers. Finally, in Part V, the main conclusions are used as a basis for discussion of public policies with respect to different age groups.

No economic study of aging attempted to date is as comprehensive. Of course, among other difficulties, we are limited by incompleteness of empirical data. At some future date economists will doubtless look back on studies such as this and point out their crudity. In the meantime, however, public and private action is necessary. Society cannot wait for the future economists. Our hope is that this contribution will help in the formulation of more enlightened and effective social action.

M. J. B.
P. T.
M. B. S.

January 1967

Acknowledgments

THE AUTHORS wish to thank the Ford Foundation for support of their research on the income and employment problems of older workers from which this book emerged. We also wish to express our gratitude to Miss Marion F. Anthony and Mrs. Sally Deslauriers who typed the major portion of the manuscript.

Professor Philip Ross of the University of Pittsburgh aided us in the assembly of material bearing on employer and union practices with regard to older workers. Chapter 12 is based upon a paper prepared jointly by Professor Mark B. Schupack and Dr. A. Kunstman of the Netherlands School of Economics. We appreciate his permission to include excerpts from that paper in Chapter 12.

John Wiley and Sons, Inc. has graciously granted permission to quote from Henry Sheldon's *The Older Population of the United States.* The Princeton University Press has also cooperated by permitting us to quote from Clarence Long, *The Labor Force Under Changing Income and Employment.*

Finally, we wish to acknowledge the cooperation of numerous persons who supplied information and opinions on the employment status of different age groups when interviewed. Among these persons are: Tyner Brown of ACF Industries; David A. Hartman of Acme Markets, Inc.; R. A. Wrenzler of Air Reduction Co.; A. R. Coombs, John E. Groves, and Daniel Y. Poling of Allegheny Ludlum Steel Corp.; Francis J. O'Connell of Allied Chemical Corp.; W. H. Davis of Aluminum Co. of America; Robert B. Parker of

American Brake Shoe Co.; E. J. Mitchell of American Can Co.; Clayton Du Bosque of American Machine and Foundry Co.; William S. Walker of American Metal Climax, Inc.; E. L. Cushman and W. W. Webb of American Motors Corp.; Maxwell E. H. Pyle of American Newspaper Guild; John R. Corbett of American Smelting and Refining Co.; J. B. McCarthy of The American Tobacco Co.; A. Bruce Campbell of Ametek, Inc.; Douglas Munroe of The Anaconda Co.; B. Watts of Automatic Radio Manufacturing Co., Inc.; Charles Raymond of BIF Industries, Inc.; John Deady of Boston Building Trades' Council; Earl Page of Grinnell Co.; James Rigney of Brown and Sharpe Co.; James A. Brooks and M. Maki of The Budd Co.; Lawrence Johnson of Cabot Co.; M. C. Strittmatter of The Celotex Corp.; W. A. Bechill, Donald M. Irwin, and Sidney W. Salsburg of Chrysler Corp.; Eileen Ahern, W. A. Locke, Eugene Rabbit, Peter Snyder of Continental Can Co., Inc.; Harold Dillabough and J. Harold Lenz of Ex-Cell-O Corp.; Rogers I. Marquis of Federal-Mogul-Bower Bearings, Inc.; W. K. Carothers of FMC Corp.; Malcolm Denise and Donald E. Scriven of Ford Motor Co.; Melvin R. Darrow of Fruehauf Trailer Co.; H. L. Marx, Jr. of General Cable Corp.; Earl R. Bramblett and Louis G. Seaton of General Motors Corp.; John H. Weeks of The Glidden Co.; John G. Ozar of Graham Manufacturing Co.; Donald Hardy of Harris Intertype Co.; Carl S. Carlson, William Dameron, and Albert Epstein of International Association of Machinists; Robert W. Munson of the International Brotherhood of Bookbinders; Jack Mackie and James Noe of the International Brotherhood of Electricians; R. A. Maxwell and Lawrence W. Downie of Kelsey-Hayes Co.; D. E. Lemmon of Koppers Co.; Kenneth Kelly of the Massachusetts AFL-CIO; Art Gertsen of Olin-Mathieson Chemical Co.; R. B. Parran of Pittsburgh Plate Glass Co.; William T. Dodd of the Plumbers' Union; Frank Weikel of Reynolds Metals Co.; Edwin C. Brown of the Rhode Island AFL-CIO; F. Crawford Williams of Sealol, Inc.; Robert Eldridge and Walter H. Maynor of the Sherwin-Williams Co.; Stephen F. Byrd of Sinclair Oil Corp.; C. W. Robison of Thompson Ramo Wooldrige, Inc.; Henry Polichetti of Trifari, Krussman, and Fishel, Inc.; Kenneth Bannon, Arthur Huges, Charles E. Odell, Leonard Schiller and Nathan Weinberg of the United Automobile, Aircraft, and Agricultural Implement Workers of America; J. M. Dry of United-Carr Fastener Corp.; Joseph T. Kennedy of the United Mine Workers of America; Ben Fischer, Marvin Miller, and Lawrence Spitz of the United Steelworkers of America; John McConnell, President, University of New Hampshire.

PART I

The Young and the Old

CHAPTER ONE

Age: An Economic Variable

IN THE past half century great strides have been made in the economic progress of the American people. The work day has been shortened, pay checks enlarged, and drudgery greatly reduced. The economy produced about 104 billion dollars worth of goods and services in 1929. Today the value of national production is in the neighborhood of 700 billion dollars. Not only the quantity but also the quality of consumption has changed. Electrical appliances, air travel, housing, and recreation are enjoyed in an abundance hardly conceivable even thirty years ago.

Yet, in a society of affluence there exists a stubborn strain of poverty. The prosperity manifested by the economy as a whole does not extend to each of its members. Elegant television sets display filmed documentaries on tenant farmers with incomes of 500 dollars a year, or Negro slum dwellers, or the aged whose "golden years" are marked by inadequate diets and emotional frustration. Aware of prevailing inequalities, society now seeks ways to permit more of its citizens to share in the benefits of mass production.

The Emphasis of Economic Research

Economic research responds to needs dictated by events. During the great depression of the 1930's, and in the following decade, economists grappled with the problem of business cycles. High on the list of research priorities was the task of identifying the causes of fluctuations in national income and employment. During a severe business slump the issue of allocating national income is bound to recede into the background, for the shortage of aggregate demand leaves little to allocate. It was during this period that the Keynesian theory was introduced, debated, and tested. As a consequence, great advances were made in the knowledge of what produces depressions and how these depressions can be counteracted. Systematic use of monetary and fiscal policy was developed as a powerful tool for maintaining a stable and high level of total employment.

After World War II inflationary pressures demanded attention. Of course, the analysis of causes and controls was founded upon a modification of the same aggregate theory that explained lapses from full employment. Then—since much insight into short-run fluctuations had evolved, since postwar recessions were relatively mild, and since international political events shifted emphasis to comparative growth rates between East and West (the Sputnik episode)—the phenomenon of long-run growth emerged as a central theme of economic research. Even assuming that an economy can maintain near full employment with stable prices, there remains an important question of the rate at which national output increases over time.

The approach most frequently adopted in studies of fluctuations and growth is that of an aggregate economic model in which labor is treated as a homogeneous factor of production. In effect, all workers are regarded as identical in productivity. Certainly economists are not unaware of the actual diversity in the labor force. But the necessity for simplification has led to a focus upon capital accumulation, expansion in the size of the total labor force, and technological change as determinants of economic progress.

More recently, a stress upon "human capital" as a source of growth has given birth to investigations of the economic effects of education, labor mobility, changes in the structure of occupations, and differences in productivity by color, age, and sex. Technological innovations may be regarded (at least partly) as qualitative improvements in the material capital stock, rendering the stock of capital more productive. Likewise, improvements in the quality of the total labor force generate greater productivity and expanded output from a labor force of a given size. These qualitative improvements can be traced to education, on-the-job training, better diets, medical care, etc. The human-capital orientation has two aspects.

First, it entails a swing of emphasis from aggregates, such as the total labor force, to the components of those aggregates in terms of groups with different opportunities and productivities. Where earnings are related to productivity, an existing unequal distribution of skills leads to an unequal distribution of earnings. Workers lacking opportunities and skills help create the phenomenon of poverty in the midst of plenty. Second, an improvement in the quality of the labor services these groups offer will help ameliorate social problems at the same time that it stimulates the over-all growth rate of the economy.

Workers differ in many respects: innate mental and physical abilities, educational attainment, age, color, sex, and access to capital ownership. Returns to education have been analyzed. So too have racial discrimination in hiring practices and differences in productivity by sex. Nevertheless, insufficient attention has been given to the age structure of the labor force. Even less attention has been given to the economic effects of a changing age structure over time.

Some Observations

In the United States both the number and the proportion of older workers have been increasing steadily. In 1900 less than 18 per cent of the total population was 45 years of age or older, whereas by 1960 that percentage had risen to 29.3. The American labor force shows a similar transformation. At the beginning of the century 24.4 per cent of the labor force was 45 years of age or older; sixty years later 37.6 per cent was 45 years of age or over.[1] Moreover, there are good reasons to believe this aging trend will continue in the future.

Variability of economic characteristics with age is apparent from examination of Tables 1-1 through 1-3. Employment status for males by age groups 30 years of age and over are recorded for 1950 and 1960 in Table 1-1. The first column demonstrates that, compared with younger groups, workers 50 years of age and over in 1950 constituted a significantly greater percentage of the age population not in the labor force. Of those not in the labor force, only 1.4 per cent of the age group 30–49 reported they were unable to work. In

[1] Cf. *Historical Statistics of the U.S., Colonial Times to 1957,* Series A 22–23, U.S. Department of Commerce; *Historical Statistics of the U.S.,* Series D 13–25, *Ibid.; Statistical Abstract,* 1960, *Ibid.*

contrast, 13.3 per cent in the 50–74 age group reported they were unable to work. It is clear that nonparticipation occurs well before the ordinary retirement age of 65. Moreover, health problems, though certainly more important for the older workers, account for only 13 per cent of their nonparticipation.

Table 1–1. PER CENT DISTRIBUTION, EMPLOYMENT STATUS OF MALES, 30 YEARS OF AGE AND OLDER BY AGE, THE UNITED STATES, 1950 AND 1960

	1950		*1960*	
	(1)	*(2)*	*(3)*	*(4)*
Age Group	*Not in the Labor Force* *Per cent of total population in the age group*	*Unemployed* *Per cent of the age group in the labor force*	*Not in the Labor Force* *Per cent of total population in the age group*	*Unemployed* *Per cent of the age group in the labor force*
30–34	6.1	3.7	4.2	3.8
35–39	5.4	3.5	4.2	3.6
40–44	5.7	3.6	4.6	3.7
45–49	6.8	4.0	5.6	4.0
50–54	9.4	4.2	7.8	4.3
55–59	13.3	4.6	12.3	4.8
60–64	20.6	5.2	22.4	5.1
65–69	40.2	5.5	56.2	5.9
70 and over	71.7	3.9	78.2	4.9

Sources: U.S. Census of Population, 1950, U.S. Summary, Table 118; U.S. Census of Population 1960, U.S. Summary, Table 194.

A similar picture of labor force participation appears in 1960, as shown in column 3, except that the percentages not in the labor force for the two extreme upper age groups are even larger. Unemployment data for those in the labor force are recorded in columns 2 and 4. Again, the percentages vary with age, the older groups showing somewhat greater unemployment. A notable exception is the age group 70 and over still in the labor force; these older workers display relatively low unemployment statistics.

The fact that income varies with age is shown in Table 1-2. In both 1950 and 1960 per capita income rises with age, within the age span 20–44. For older ages per capita income declines with age. The last column provides an indication of how the distribution of income by age has been changing over time. Given that national income expanded over the decade 1950–1960, the largest percentage increases in per capita income occurred for those in the intermediate age groups. The youngest age group (20–24) and the oldest age group (55 and over) exhibit the smallest increases. Thus, the youngest and oldest groups have suffered *relative to* the intermediate age group.

Table 1–2. PER CAPITA INCOME BY AGE, THE UNITED STATES

(MEDIANS FOR THOSE WHO EARNED INCOME)

Age	*Per Capita Income, 1950 (dollars)*	*Per Capita Income, 1960 (dollars)*	*Per Cent Increase 1950–1960*
20–24	1,521	2,202	44.8
25–34	2,295	3,827	66.8
35–44	2,539	4,249	67.3
45–54	2,453	4,009	63.4
55–64	2,097	3,299	57.3
65 and over	955	1,282	34.2

Source: U.S. Census of Population, 1960, U.S. Summary, Table 219.

There appears to be an "income problem" at both age poles of the labor force: those entering and those approaching departure. For several reasons a relatively low income at the youngest ages is to be expected. Experience normally enhances productivity and earnings; promotions occur only after some time on the company payroll; apprenticeships and on-the-job training (with the consequence of a lower income) are customary at this age. To the extent that low income in any given year is the result of these "natural" processes, the youngest age group is not experiencing an income problem. However, the relative income of the youngest has declined over the decade. Probably this decline reflects the effect of delayed entry into the labor force because of extended education. If a greater proportion of the young remain in school longer, thus expanding their earnings in later years, the income of those entering the labor force at an earlier age is more heavily weighted by dropouts from school.

The relative decline in income at the upper ages presents a more serious social problem. Not only does income decline beyond the age of 44; the rate of increase over time also declines. Moreover, the oldest group shows the smallest rate of increase. Any income-earning problems created by school dropouts among the young are carried along through the age groups with the passage of time to be added to the other factors that produce the income distribution by age.

One final piece of evidence is symptomatic of some causes underlying the diversity of income, employment, and labor force participation by age. Table 1-3 shows education related to age in 1960. The

Table 1–3. YEARS OF SCHOOL COMPLETED BY AGE, THE UNITED STATES, 1960

Age	*Median School Years Completed*
25–29	12.3
30–34	12.2
35–39	12.1
40–44	11.8
45–49	10.6
50–54	9.7
55–59	8.8
60–64	8.6
65 and over	8.3

Source: U.S. Census of Population, U.S. Summary, Table 173.

number of school years completed declines steadily with age, reflecting in part the difficulties encountered by older workers in maintaining their job status in an economy undergoing rapid technological revolutions.

These data refer to the entire population and labor force in the United States. But when the data are broken down to smaller levels of aggregation, diversity by age persists. For example, within a given occupation variations of earned income by age show much the same pattern as that revealed for the entire labor force. Variations in income and employment by age are observed in different degrees for regions within the U.S., for industries, and for both males and females by color. The evidence clearly points to age as an economic variable. By no means can the labor force be said to be a homogeneous resource input in the productive process. Instead, various age groups are essentially different resource inputs, each with its own productivity characteristics—in turn leading to a distribution of income and employment by age that is creating demonstrable social problems.

The Public Concern

Quite understandably, past activities and studies have concentrated upon the economic, social, and medical problems of older workers. In 1935 Congress established a national system of old-age insurance for workers 65 years of age and over retiring from active employment. The National Health Survey of 1935–1936 revealed that of those people suffering from some form of long-term disability or illness, one half were over 45 years of age. As a result, more attention was directed toward the older population. The Bureau of Labor Statistics surveyed employer attitudes toward older workers in 1938. In the middle forties a committee to examine the social effects of aging was sponsored by the Social Science Research Council. Several other foundations soon followed with large grants for inquiries into the personal and social adjustments to old age. At the same time various public and private agencies embarked upon studies in gerontology and geriatrics.

In 1950 President Truman called for a National Conference on Aging. The conference, sponsored by the Federal Security Agency, brought together over 800 interested researchers and administrators. A broad program of action was outlined from the distillation of their ideas. At the community level, programs were established to cope with one or more aspects of the aging problem: senior citizens' organizations of a recreational or social nature, efforts to provide health facilities and better housing for older people, and adult education. Commissions on Aging were initiated in several states, and legislation provided encouragement and support for local activities. Similar developments occurred at the federal level of government. Research in the welfare of the older population became an integral part of the Old Age and Survivors' Insurance and the federal-state old age assistance program. Many agencies of the federal government—especially the Department of Labor and the Department of Health, Education and Welfare—placed a more pronounced emphasis upon the economic adjustments that accompany advancing age.

President Eisenhower established a Federal Council on Aging in 1956, integrating the activities of the various agencies that administer aging programs within the federal government. In addition to the coordination of current programs, the council was to explore the scope of federal objectives and to develop a broader range of remedial measures.

Today, President Johnson's anti-poverty program is intimately connected with the economic problems and prospects of different age groups. Major emphasis is placed upon the young among economically deprived groups, but some account is taken of the aged as well. Rather than viewing the solution to poverty as a question of doles, the anti-poverty program attempts to help people help themselves by making them aware of opportunities and encouraging them to acquire skills and efficient work habits. The job corps consists of camps operated by private corporations and nonprofit institutions but centrally administered in Washington by the Office of Economic Opportunity. The camps provide an environment in which poor young people live, go to school, learn work habits, and develop skills.

A second feature of the anti-poverty legislation is the Community Action Programs. Community schools have been established to provide adult education for the poor (academic subjects, sewing, cooking, financial management). These schools also provide tutorial services for elementary school children and training in reading awareness for preschool children. The aim is to bring the poor child up to the standard of other children in his grade or to give the child from a poor family the start necessary for proper academic performance. In addition to community schools, the Community Action Programs attempt to train the young for work by means of the Neighborhood Youth Corps and Drop-in Centers. They are designed to attract school dropouts back into an environment where they begin to appreciate the function of work and the satisfaction of carrying out tasks successfully. They also act as referral agencies for various training programs.

Directed more specifically toward assistance for the aged is Medicare. Medical insurance is provided at minimal cost for those 65 years of age or over. Coverage includes hospitalization expenses in excess of 40 dollars for up to sixty days. For extended hospitalization between sixty and ninety days, a contribution of 10 dollars per day is allowed. A voluntary companion insurance is also offered at a cost of 3 dollars per month. Physicians' fees in excess of 50 dollars are covered up to a maximum of 80 per cent of the total fees. All participants in the Social Security System are eligible once they reach the age of 65 regardless of current income.

These, and similar programs, have recognized the economic waste entailed by structural unemployment. More important, they have publicized the human deprivation associated with the statistics on employment status. To the extent that aging trends, in the face of changing technology and production methods, are related to poverty, the social problems are significant indeed. The anti-poverty program attacks the causes of economic hardship primarily at the earliest ages, before entry into the labor force. On the other hand, assistance, such as Medicare, to the older population applies to those who normally have left the work force. However, the available evidence strongly suggests that income and employment problems set in well before retirement age, around 45 or 50 years of age when most workers of that age are still active members of the labor force. Unless more is known about the effects of age, it is unrealistic to suppose that well-conceived and well-executed public policies can be achieved in the future.

CHAPTER TWO

The Aging Problem: An Historical Perspective

A RELATIVELY low income among the youngest members of the labor force is a less serious social problem than low income among the aged for two reasons. First, growth of income is to be expected as a worker approaches middle age (due to the acquisition of experience and upgrading on the job). Second, in cases of those whose low income is not attributed to this "natural" process, the remedial *economic* measures are more clear-cut. The young are more flexible and trainable than the old, once favorable psychological attitudes toward education and work are developed.

Compared with the present, there was far less of an "older worker problem" in 1890, for example, when the first reliable labor force statistics were collected. The existence of a large group of older people, many in economic distress, is the result of a slow but persistent change in the age composition of the population and the labor force since 1890. These changes have taken place in most of the industrialized countries of western Europe and North America, but only those in the United States will be discussed in detail. A comprehensive view of the present situation requires an outline of the changes that have occurred over the past seventy years and some of the causes that appear to have produced these changes.

Population and Labor Force Trends

The American population has been growing progressively older for a long period of time. One measure of this aging trend is found in the median age of the white population. It was 16 in 1800 and rose to 19 in 1850; the median age was 23 in 1900 and 31 in 1950. Another indication of this same pattern is that 4 per cent of the population was over 60 years old in 1850 whereas 12 per cent was as old in 1950.

More detailed data are available for a comparison between 1900 and 1950. The age distribution of the entire population at these two dates shows that in 1950 there was a smaller percentage of the population below 30 years of age and a greater percentage for each age group above 30, with the difference in percentage increasing with age. An increase in the proportion of older people between 1900 and 1950 occurs for foreign-born only, for females only, and for whites only. Changes for the last two groups are very close and could be explained by small differences in fertility and/or mortality rates. The change for immigrants resulted from the pattern of immigration during this period. A great number of young people immigrated just before and just after 1900, and very few thereafter. Aging of the foreign-born population reflects a decline in one former large source of young people.

There is general agreement that the major cause of an increase in the proportion of older people in the population was a decline in fertility rates over time, rather than changes in mortality rates.[1] The actual effect of a lower mortality rate depends upon which age group benefits most from reduced mortality. If mortality is reduced only for older people beyond the childbearing age, then the median age of the population will increase, as will the proportion of older people in the population. If, however, the decreased mortality is mostly at very young ages, the effect will be to increase the numbers of children a few years later and decrease the age of the population. Insofar as mortality rate changes have affected the median ages of populations in the past, the latter effect seems to have predominated. That is, declining mortality rates operated in the direction of making populations younger.

Falling birth rates have counteracted and outweighed the impact of lower mortality. Birth rates have been declining since the first part of the nineteenth century in the United States and since the

[1] Cf., e.g., Henry D. Sheldon, *The Older Population of the United States* (New York: John Wiley and Sons, Inc., 1958) and Joseph J. Spengler, "Aging Populations" in *Employment, Income, and Retirement Problems of the Aged*, Juanita M. Kreps (ed) (Durham, N.C.: Duke University Press, 1963).

latter part of the century in the rest of North America and Europe. The rate dropped from 55 per 1000 in 1820 to 32 per 1000 in 1900 and to a low of 18 per 1000 in 1933. It has since risen slightly to 24 in 1950. While mortality and immigration may have added substantially to the *number* of older people, it was a falling birth rate that caused an increase in the *proportion* of older people in the population.

Population analysts disagree as to the future age structure of the population. Henry D. Sheldon,[2] for example, predicts that the next few decades will bring an enlargement in the number of older people but little, if any, increase in the proportion of older people. He argues that medical discoveries are unlikely to raise life expectancy very much further in the near future and that forecasts of fertility suggest the rate will remain high enough to prevent further aging of the population. Joseph J. Spengler,[3] on the other hand, agrees with the prediction regarding mortality but argues that birth rates will fall due to excess population pressure. He foresees a rise in the proportion of older persons in the next several decades.

Whether or not aging continues, the number and proportion of older people in our population has certainly been growing over time. This phenomenon does not necessarily cause economic problems. However, the changing age composition of the population has been accompanied by a large reduction in the fraction of older people who consider themselves part of the labor force. Thus, not only has there been an increase in the absolute number and proportion of older people, but an even greater increase in the number unemployed.

Income figures indicate that only those older people who remained in the labor force were able to make an income above any generally accepted poverty level. In 1951, the median income of people 65 and over in the labor force was 2,121 dollars; those not in the labor force had a median income of only 774 dollars. A poverty standard against which this income might be compared can only be a matter of judgment. Some crude computations indicate that perhaps one third to one half of persons over 65 had incomes which were below an acceptable level. The difference between poverty and above-poverty levels of income seems to rest on whether or not the head of the family is employed. The burden of the older people is not age per se, but rather the low income brought about through non-

[2] Henry D. Sheldon, *op. cit.*, pp. 17–22.
[3] Joseph J. Spengler, *op. cit.*, pp. 36–38.

participation in the labor force.

As indicated in the previous chapter, a relatively high rate of nonparticipation begins to appear at about 45 years of age. But in long-run changes over time the decline in labor force participation for those 65 and over is most striking. In 1890, 73.9 per cent of the males over 65 years of age were in the labor force.[4] By 1960, this participation rate dropped to 30.5 per cent. When combined with a large growth in the number of older males, it can be seen that the number of unemployed men over 65 rose from 0.3 million in 1890 to 5.1 million in 1960, a rise of 1,700 per cent.

During this same period, the labor force participation of women over 65 remained about the same, 10 per cent, during a period when the participation of women of other ages nearly doubled. Combining the figures for males and females, there were 1.3 million unemployed people over 65 in 1890 compared to 13.1 million in 1960. The growing burden on the rest of the economy is unmistakable. This, in part, is what is meant by the development of an "older workers' problem."

No other age group has displayed this strong decline. For male workers 55–64 years old there was a decline from 89.0 per cent labor force participation in 1890 to 82.7 per cent in 1960. The decline was very slow and the level is still high compared with those 65 and over. For the 45–54 age group, there has been almost no change since 1890, a 93.9 per cent rate of participation at the beginning of the period and 93.3 per cent at the end. This is only slightly below the approximate 96 per cent participation rate maintained by younger age groups beyond school age.

We can thus characterize employment and income problems associated with age as beginning to appear at the 45–54 age level. The effects at this age level are not yet very great. By the next age level, 55–64, there are significant increases in unemployment. The economic status of this age group is deteriorating over time, but at a slow rate. The group over 65 years of age has experienced catastrophic increases in unemployement over time until the rate has reached a tragically high level today.

Economic Change and Its Effect on the Labor Market

The remainder of this chapter is devoted to a discussion of simultaneous changes in the American economy that have contrib-

[4] Clarence D. Long, *The Labor Force Under Changing Income and Employment* (Princeton, N.J.: Princeton University Press, 1958) p. 287.

uted to the trends in employment and labor force participation by age. We hesitate to call them major causes of the older workers' problem for two reasons. First, accurate data are not available to test the quantitative importance of these factors over half a century or more. The extent of the impact of each factor remains unmeasured. Second, some of these changes are included in studies of aging reviewed in the following chapter, and on the basis of admittedly crude statistical data they do not seem to be major causal factors. Nevertheless, it is likely that they have exerted some effect upon income and empolyment changes by age.

It is convenient to think of these forces as operating on the demand side or the supply side of the labor market. On the demand side they operate to determine changes in the amount and type of work offered to older workers. On the supply side they affect the ability or the willingness of older workers to perform the work made available to them.

Occupational Composition of the Labor Force

One of the largest changes in the occupational composition of the labor force since 1890 is a substantial decrease in the proportion of farmers. In 1950 the number of farmers was no more than in 1880, about 4.3 million. The percentage of the labor force in farming was 40.5 per cent in 1880 and only 14 per cent in 1950. The change in numbers of farmers was not constant thoroughout the period; the number rose to a peak of 6.2 million in 1920, and then declined to the 1880 level.

Farming is one of the major occupations in which an older worker should have a good chance of remaining at work. A farmer can, within a wide range, determine the amount of work he does and the conditions under which it is done. He need not follow the relatively rigid routine needed in most nonfarming jobs. He can adapt his working environment to his changing personal requirements as he ages. If farming does indeed provide a major source of employment for older people, employment they could not obtain elsewhere, then a large decline in the number of farming jobs available contributes to the older workers' problem.

Labor force participation rates for older workers do indeed appear to be higher for farmers than for the nonfarming segment of the population. In 1890 the farmers over 65 years of age showed a participation rate of 76.5 per cent compared with a rate of 66.6 per cent for the urban sector of the population. By 1950, however, the participation rate of farmers had declined even more than the rest of the population so that theirs was only slightly higher than the urban population, 44.1 per cent compared with 40 per cent. The farm rate is computed as the percentage of men living in a rural area who are working. But during this period there was a large out-migration from rural areas to urban areas. Farmers who stop working are likely to move to the city resulting in a raising of the apparent farm labor participation rate and lowering of the apparent urban rate. Since data are not available for judging the true relative participation rates for farmers after removing the influence of migration, the quantitative effect of a decline in farming upon the total participation rate of older workers remains an uncertainty.

The percentage of employed persons in nonagricultural self employment has also decreased over time. The attractiveness of such occupations for older persons is based upon the same reason given for farmers: a worker is allowed to adapt his working conditions to suit his personal needs as he ages. Consequently, a decline in these occupations constitutes a shrinkage in employment opportunities most suitable for older workers.

Along with changes in the agricultural and self-employed sectors of the labor force, other aspects of the occupational structure have been changing over time. One suggested cause for the older workers' difficulties stems directly from this shifting. As the relative demand for different types and levels of skills changes, older workers are simply unable to adapt themselves to these changes as rapidly as are the younger workers. As they are forced out of obsolete occupations, older persons fail to find positions in other occupations and retire from the labor force.

The occupational composition of the labor force has been changing since 1900. There are substantial reductions in the farming and unskilled occupations and increases in the professional, clerical, and semiskilled occupations. There is also evidence that the occupations of older people differ substantially from the occupations of the labor force as a whole.[5] In a 1952 survey, older workers were overrepresented among farm occupations and underrepresented among managers and semiskilled operatives compared with the work force

[5] Peter O. Steiner and Robert Dorfman, *The Economic Status of the Aged* (Berkeley, Calif.: The University of California Press, 1957) pp. 38–55.

as a whole.

The above composition of older workers was based on the occupation they reported in the special survey as being the occupation they engaged in for the longest period during their life, i.e., what they would call their normal or regular occupation. When their current occupation is considered, another disadvantageous shifting pattern is observed. Compared to their longest occupation, their current occupation shows underrepresentation in farming (a shift in accord to the way the rest of the labor force is moving), craftsmen, and operatives (contrary to the rest of the labor force) and overrepresentation in labor and service occupations. The overrepresentation in labor and service occupations is not only contrary to the movement over time of the rest of the labor force but represents a downgrading in skill and income compared to what the older workers could attain in their younger days.

Employers' Job Requirements

Related to the changing occupational composition of the labor force are changes in the technological structure of the economy, both in the types of products produced and the way in which they are made. Advancement in technology may force workers to change employers or to change jobs within the same firm, even though their occupation as usually measured has not changed. Any shift, even if still within the same occupation, can put the older worker at a disadvantage relative to younger workers. The young are more mobile and adjust more readily to technological change. On a more detailed level, even the same job may change when new machinery and processes are introduced. Unless the older worker possesses the physical, mental, and psychological aptitudes needed for a more complex production operation, he will have to accept downgrading or unemployment.

A number of surveys have shown that many firms do have hiring policies which, in one way or another, discriminate against older job applicants. There are a variety of forms that such discrimination can assume and a number of factors that lead to discrimination. Aside from automation and technological displacement, some firms have substituted female workers for older males. If females are willing to work for less (partly because their income is a supplement to the household income) and if they can perform work with at least the dexterity of older males, then their labor services are less costly to an employer. Another practice that has undoubtedly exerted some effect is forced retirement at earlier ages. Only quite recently have retirement benefits approached even half of preretirement earned income.

Once unemployed, for whatever reason, an older person faces more difficulty in obtaining a new position. When seeking additions to their work force, firms are inclined to discriminate against older applicants on the ground that they are too costly. Even if older workers do not expect a higher wage because of experience, their pension cost to the firm exceeds that of a younger person. Pension plans normally guarantee a predetermined retirement income. The remaining employment life of an older person and his corresponding contribution to the retirement fund is far below the amount he withdraws upon retirement. As a consequence, he will not be hired or he will be denied retirement income. One government study revealed that one third of private pension plans exclude workers hired at age 55, and over half exclude those hired at age 60.

Seniority rules have provided some protection against unemployment and the ensuing difficulty of finding reemployment. However, seniority provisions have not protected a worker against layoff when the entire operation of a plant or a department is suspended or when a job is abolished following a downswing of general business activity. The older workers then enters the ranks of the unemployed. During a depression many older people will leave the work force after a fruitless search for scarce jobs. Employers, emphasizing the need for efficiency, will tend to give the few available job openings to the younger, stronger, relatively better educated sector of the labor force. As the economy enters a general upswing and approaches prosperity, labor shortages will encourage older workers to remain in the labor force and encourage employers to hire workers at productivity standards somewhat below those required during a business slump. Nevertheless, over the entire cycle the older workers as a group are subjected to a net loss in employment.

This phenomenon was demonstrated during the deep depression of the 1930's and the prosperity of the 1940's. The drop in the labor force participation of males 65 and over was larger during the 1930's than for any other decade since 1890, from 58.3 per cent in 1930 to 41.5 per cent in 1940. During the 1940's participation rose slightly, to 41.6 per cent in 1950. But this was only a short-run condition caused, in part, by the wartime shortage of younger male workers and provided only a brief interruption in the continuing decrease in labor force participation over the long run. The participation rate in the prosperous 1940's was still a good deal below the rate of the prosperous 1920's.

Retirement Income

A second set of factors operate on the supply side of the labor market to affect the ability or willingness of older workers to perform the work made available to them. One such factor is the magnitude of pension or retirement income. Retirement benefits have expanded over time, and the temptation to retire and live on these benefits does affect the supply of older workers on the labor market. For those who can afford to retire comfortably, of course, withdrawal from the labor force presents no economic hardship. Therefore, a part of the decline in labor force participation—to the extent that nonparticipation is voluntary and that it is adequately funded—cannot be regarded as a serious economic problem.

As society became more industrialized and people shifted from rural to urban areas, the need to provide for the older person during his retirement became more important. The style of living, the size of families, and their greater geographical dispersion made dependence upon younger and economically active members of families uncertain. The urban family, exposed to the uncertainties inherent in an enterprise economy, was not always able to save for the long rainy day brought about by enforced "leisure" or retirement. It took a long time before it was generally recognized that failure to save was not necessarily the result of extravagance or avoidance of work, and that, with longer life expectancy, many industrious and thrifty persons would not be able to accumulate sufficient funds to support them during their last years. Members of the family, fraternal organizations, churches, private charitable institutions, the poorhouse, or the government would have to provide part or all of their support.

The problem of providing for the maintenance of retired workers and their dependents was recognized, but few practical steps were taken to meet this need, except through private charity and public assistance providing only low levels of maintenance. In the 1870's, the first industrial pensions were introduced by a number of railroads. Over the next three decades pensions were established in other industries, but they were limited largely to managerial and other white-collar employees. The blue-collar, or manual worker was largely neglected by these programs, and prior to the 1930's the great mass of industrial workers had no coverage under any formal pension program.[6]

Beginning in 1900 a number of unions initiated pension programs, but again the great bulk of union members were not covered. As union members constituted a small fraction of the labor force, even complete coverage of unionists would still have left the major part of the labor force without any protection. Agitation for some type of state assistance to indigent older people, many of them industrial workers, led to the enactment of laws in the 1920's. The qualifying standards were severe, and only a few states adopted mandatory laws; others gave the county the option of accepting the old age pension or some other system of relief for the aged.

After the downturn of business in the early 1930's, public pressure for government intervention or better government relief increased. Families without a working member could not spare even a pittance for an aged relative or parent. Because of the economic catastrophe, the argument against government intervention in the field of social welfare was seriously weakened. As a result, the federal government enacted a comprehensive social security law that included provisions for grants-in-aid to states on a matching basis for expenditures for old age assistance up to a maximum for each person. A system of compulsory old age annuities was established and subsequently revised to include survivors' benefits, which were lacking in the first version. The law has been revised a number of times. In 1939, for example, benefits were extended to survivors of fully insured claimants. In addition, the dollar value of benefits has substantially increased. The taxable base has also been raised from 3,000 dollars, in the original law, to 6,600 dollars at present.

Another important trend has been the development and expansion of private pension plans negotiated under collective bargaining agreements. As noted previously, pensions were established for industrial workers in the 1870's. While a number of industries adopted such programs, only 3 million workers were covered by health, welfare, and retirement benefits in the summer of 1948.[7]

[6] *The Older American Worker,* Bureau of Labor Statistics, U.S. Department of Labor, June, 1965.

[7] *United States Bureau of Labor Statistics Bulletin No. 908–17,* p. 3.

Wartime tax and wage controls stimulated interest in pensions and other types of welfare programs, and the number of covered industrial workers expanded. While union representatives could include such programs on their list of demands, the obligation of the employer to bargain on this demand under the requirements of the National Labor Relations Act was not made clear. The issue was decided affirmatively in a case involving the United Steelworkers of America and the Inland Steel Company.[8] The latter had established a limited pension program in 1936 and argued that pensions were not a bargainable issue. However, the view was not accepted by the National Labor Relations Board. When the United States Court of Appeals Seventh Circuit upheld the decision of the board, demands for pension programs greatly increased.

Retirement systems are now widespread. The majority of plans contain compulsory retirement clauses, with the retirement age set at 65 years in more than 50 per cent of the plans. Within recent years, influenced largely by high unemployment in certain mass production industries, employment contracts have included *regular* early retirement provisions which allow workers to retire before the established retirement age with a reduced pension. *Special* early retirement provisions have also been established in a number of mass production industries. Under the special provision workers can retire at an age as low as 55 years and with given years of service, at the employer's request and with mutually satisfactory financial conditions. Until age 65, the claimant will receive a larger than normal benefit because of ineligibility for Old Age and Survivors' Insurance.

The growth of retirement benefits provides more opportunity for departure from the labor force at age 65, or even earlier. A natural question follows. Have these benefits been of sufficient magnitude to exert a major influence upon the observed decline in labor force participation by the aged? Although there are several obvious cases in which greater retirement income motivated a decision to retire earlier than had been planned, available evidence suggests that this factor is not of primary importance in the aggregate.

First, large numbers of older workers dropped out of the labor force during the 1930's when there were few pensions available, and large numbers reentered the labor force during the 1950's de-

[8] *Inland Steel Company v. National Labor Relations Board* 170 F. 2nd 247, 1949.

spite the growth in pensions and social security benefits. Clearly the availability of pensions must have been a secondary consideration.

Second, a special census survey in 1952 indicated that certainly fewer than 11 per cent of the retired people over 65, and probably closer to 2 per cent of the retired, were retired because they wanted to be retired, and, by implication, lived on the pension and social security benefits available to them. Surveys conducted by the Social Security Administration lead to the same general conclusion. Part of the reason for this reluctance to retire is that most pension or social security benefits are quite low compared with employment income. Until retirement income can compare favorably with employment income, the mere availability of retirement income will be unlikely to have a strong effect upon labor force participation of older people. If the future brings a sizable expansion of retirement income relative to employment income, however, its effect upon labor force participation will likely become significant indeed.

Health

In terms of how unemployed men report their condition, poor health is by far the most important reason given for their not working. This has been true in every recent census tabulation; the special survey of 1952 showed that about 60 per cent of the unemployed over 65 years of age gave poor health as their reason for retirement. Certainly there are physical changes associated with aging, even in an apparently healthy person, which will adversely affect working ability. Aging also increases the probability that a person will have an illness preventing his participation in the labor force. Poor health is undoubtedly a determinant of relatively low labor force participation among the aged. Nevertheless, the responses to questionnaires must be interpreted with caution. On the basis of census surveys one cannot infer that poor health is the major factor causing a long-run decline in employment on the part of older persons.

First, little is known about the reliability of answers to the question about why a person retired. The response of poor health may be a cover for a variety of other factors, including inability to find work or unwillingness to accept the work offered. Second, and more important, there is no evidence that the health of older people has deteriorated in the last 70 years. It is only a *change* of general health conditions over time which could account for the *change* in labor force participation of older people. Since medical care has improved remarkably over time, it has been argued that younger and middle aged people in relatively poor health survive to become older people who drop out of the labor force. Certainly the argument is reasonable, but there is no accurate evidence to substantiate this point of view. In fact, a Dutch study implied that rising standards of living and health care have led to better health at every age.

As a consequence, one can only conclude that poor health is a cause of relatively low labor force participation by older workers, but its importance as compared to other causal factors remains inconclusive. Medical research should help to provide more information in the future.

Education

The final supply factor is education. A person with a relatively small amount of education, measured as number of years of school completed, will possess relatively low qualifications for any given job. One exception may be jobs requiring purely manual operations. But these are typically the lowest paying positions. If older people have less education than younger people, they will have more difficult employment problems simply because they are worth less to any prospective employer than a more highly trained younger man. The older man might still be hired and paid what he is worth, i.e., a lower wage than a younger worker. Even though the older worker may be willing to accept a lower wage just to obtain the job, there is a great deal of social pressure, including that from trade unions, against such discriminatory wages. The usual result is that the older worker will not be hired.

Because of a rapid rise in the general level of education in the last several decades, the older person of today is more poorly educated than younger members of society. In 1900, young and old had almost the same educational attainment. Men over 65 had about four fifths as many school years completed as younger males. By 1950, this ratio fell to two fifths, very low indeed. The reason for this difference is that educational standards rose very little in the decades before 1900 and very rapidly since that time. Since each succeeding generation was offered more and better educational opportunities, the gap in educational attainment widened.

In the labor market, older workers found themselves at a disadvantage compared with their younger contemporaries in terms of the educational qualifications they could offer to employers. The difference in educational attainment by age is correlated with the relative decline in labor force participation by age. Inability to compete effectively enforces other pressures leading to unemployment or withdrawal from the labor force.

CHAPTER THREE

Research on Aging

WHY DO workers of different ages manifest contrasting income and employment traits? This question has stimulated much research, most of which has been centered upon older workers. Older workers face greater difficulties in obtaining or retaining remunerative employment, and sources of nonwage income are not adequate to provide a minimum standard of living.

There are many possible causes for the patterns of income and employment by age that we have observed in the previous chapters. It is the function of research to sort them according to their relative importance, and to discover the mechanism by which they operate upon employment and wage levels. Unless this objective can be achieved, research cannot serve as a reliable guide for the formulation of policies intended to ameliorate the conditions of low-income groups in the economy.

The purpose of this chapter is twofold: to suggest a general methodological framework suitable for answering relevant questions, and to examine past studies in the light of this framework. Some past efforts approach the procedures indicated by the framework. Most others, however, while providing some information, are not designed in a way that provides answers to the questions most important for policy decision making.

A Method of Approach

Ordinarily, economic research consists of a theoretical description of group behavior and a comparison of the theory with empirical evidence. Assumptions incorporated in the theory may be verified or refuted directly by empirical observations, but propositions deduced from these assumptions are more likely to be amenable to empirical tests. If such predictive propositions are confirmed by the "facts," they are accepted as a satisfactory explanation of the phenomena under investigation. If not, the theory is regarded as unsatisfactory. Then, it is either discarded or revised on the basis of the evidence, depending upon the extent and nature of its explanatory errors.

Underlying this approach is the assumption that there are systematic forces at work in the economy which can be described by theoretical models and quantified by observation (usually by statistical estimation). If this assumption is not accepted, we must relinquish hope of discovering regularities in the economic system. Since such regularities have been confirmed in other aspects of the economy, there is no reason to suppose they are not also present in the aging process.

In addition to the selection of variables that bear upon the questions posed, the research design should provide empirical approximations to these variables and measures of their relative importance. Not all variables can be precisely identified and their interaction specified—either because the interactions are too complex or because suitable empirical data are not available. Nevertheless, the more completely the model describes behavior the more useful the results are likely to be. Careful theoretical analysis is needed to direct the empirical investigation and to provide a meaningful interpretation of observed behavior patterns.

In the economics of aging the variables to be invoked and their causal interdependence are of primary importance—and of primary difficulty. Yet it is this part of the research design to which least attention has been given. To demonstrate how the general methodological framework may be applied, a list of factors affecting participation in the labor market by workers of any age can be set out. Each factor can be classified as belonging to the demand or the supply side of the labor market, or as affecting the interaction of demand and supply. As it turns out, these factors are also those that have been considered by one or another study concerned with the problems of older workers.

Briefly, the demand factors implied in this connection include labor productivity, retraining potential, accident rates, labor turnover rates, absenteeism rates, the cost of providing group insurance and paying for disabilities, institutional hiring practices, union work rules, changing demand for final products reflected in a changing industrial composition, changes in technology, and the amount of unemployment prevalent.

Factors influencing the supply function of workers include demographic factors affecting the age distribution of the population, the health of persons in various age groups, nonwage income, the amount and nature of migration taking place, and the willingness and ability of relatives to support the older people. In addition to supply and demand factors, consideration might also be given to changes in the basic institutional structure of the labor market. In particular, one must note the rigidities and imperfections introduced primarily through the change from an essentially competitive market to one in which unions and collective bargaining play a large part.

This list is, of course, not exhaustive. However, it probably does include most of the major factors at work in the market. They are not independent of each other. Nor are they simple concepts; many have complex subfactors that combine to yield a single effect.

No previous study has begun with the idea of a market and developed a complete theoretical description of the effect of age upon employment. In an important sense, it is impossible to do so now because we know too little about the components of the market and how they interact. Given this imperfect knowledge, comprehensiveness is a matter of degree (accounting for more or less of the factors and their relative quantitative importance). Thus, the methodological framework indicates that efforts should be made to account simultaneously for more factors than previous studies have encompassed.

Not all past studies will be evaluated. Those discussed will be the major ones that have been completed and are representative of the approach adopted in many others. Nor is a complete bibliography called for. Extensive bibliographical information is available elsewhere.[1] For our purposes it is convenient to divide previous studies

[1] A somewhat different evaluation of current literature can be found in Mark B. Schupack, "Research on Employment Problems of Older Workers," *The Gerontologist*, Vol. 2, No. 3 (September 1962), pp. 157–163. For bibliographical information see Nathan W. Shock, *A Classified Bibliography of Gerontology and Geriatrics* (Stanford, Calif.: Stanford University Press, 1951). Two supplements were issued in 1957 and 1963. Current bibliography information can also be found in each issue of the *Journal of Gerontology*.

into two types: (1) those explaining observed phenomena, and (2) those determining the presence or absence of particular factors.

Studies Explaining Observed Phenomena

The most comprehensive explanation for the cause of older workers' problems has been carried out by Clarence D. Long as part of his larger study of the labor force.[2] He notes the great decline in the labor force participation of older workers since 1890—not only in the United States but also in Canada, Great Britain, Germany, and New Zealand. Starting with the fact (his dependent variable, or phenomenon to be explained) he attempts to assess the various explanations offered as causes of the decline.

Long discusses the following possible causes:

(1) Older workers have always had a higher rate of labor force participation in rural areas than in urban areas, but the trend since 1890 is for population to shift from rural to urban areas.

(2) Changing composition of the population with respect to color and national origin has influenced labor force participation by age.

(3) There has been a marked rise in the availability of Old Age and Survivors' Insurance, private pensions, and similar means of providing for retired people.

(4) Rising personal disposable income induces more people to leave the work force.

(5) Larger firms are more likely to discriminate against older workers in their hiring practices and thus, with the recent rise of large firms relative to small ones, the older worker participation falls.

(6) There has been a decline in the number of self-employed people, including farmers. Since these people are not normally affected by hiring and retiring practices of firms, their decline would signal an increase in the numbers of older people who have to leave the work force.

(7) Increasing technological progress can cause a decline in the employment of older workers since either (a) their skills have become obsolete and they are unable to keep up with the changes around them or (b) the shifting industry structure causes displace-

[2] Clarence D. Long, *The Labor Force under Changing Income and Employment* (Princeton: Princeton University Press, 1958), General Series No. 65, National Bureau of Economic Research.

ment of those in the declining industries who now have to move to the new and growing industries. Older workers have a harder time than younger ones in making this sort of shift.

(8) There is a connection between total unemployment and the numbers of employed among the older workers. The higher the general level of unemployment, the lower becomes the percentage participation of older workers.

(9) Hiring and firing rules of firms generally are constructed in such a way that they discriminate against hiring workers past middle age or retaining presently employed workers over 65 years old.

(10) Older workers' productivity is now lower than it previously was, forcing them out of the labor force.

(11) Since older groups have much less average education than younger age groups, due in large part to the trend toward universality of education in recent years, they are forced to leave the labor force.

(12) Older workers have been displaced by younger women.

By presenting evidence contrary to these assertions, Long either rejects or discounts the importance of the first eight items.[3] He rightly argues that discriminatory practices, item (9), are merely symptoms of more basic underlying causes; there remains the question of why discriminatory employment practices have been adopted. All of the information cited to support the validity of item (10) is drawn from other studies on productivity related to age, a topic to be covered in the next section of this chapter. Credence is given to item (11), but it is to item (12) that the role of major cause is assigned.

> Women—better trained and better suited for the jobs, and often willing to work for less—may well have out-competed males in the job market and made employers ready to pass rules against older workers (which to so many have appeared to be the real force in compelling early retirement). In addition, the earnings of the women could have helped finance longer schooling for the young males and earlier retirement for the older ones. This pressure exerted by the women does not exclude independent reasons for the withdrawal of males. . . . But it is our hypothesis that the prime mover was the influx of female workers, and that their displacement of the male worker helps explain the stability in overall participation.[4]

[3] *Ibid.*, pp. 161–179.
[4] *Ibid.*, p. 32.

What is the relationship between Long's study and the framework suggested in the previous section? Factors affecting the decline in the percentage of older males employed are examined as possible *major* causes. No market theory is explicitly presented, but a market model is implied. Observed employment is the result of interacting demand and supply forces. Each of the twelve "variables" operates upon these forces to determine employment. Conception of the problem in this way generates a very fruitful pattern of thinking: collection of data is related to the search for explanations that help to answer basic research questions and provide a basis for policy action.

Nevertheless, two fundamental difficulties limit the usefulness of the study:

(1) Long does not try to assign to the factors varying quantitative amounts of blame for the labor force decline. He attempts to find a major cause of the decline. Consequently, if a factor did not cause a major part of the observed phenomenon, it was dismissed. But all had some effect on labor force participation; added together they might very well account for a major portion of the observed changes. Long's procedure is somewhat analogous to looking for *the* cause of the business cycle. There is no one cause. Rather, many factors operate with varying intensities.[5]

(2) The data are far too aggregated to allow quantitative conclusions. Even the effects of any one factor can be obscured within the very broad groupings of the data used. For example, Long compares changes in the size of industries and changes in the percentage of older workers for the nine major industrial groups.[6] There is no correlation among the nine groups. Does this mean that relative growth of an industry is not a relevant factor in causing changes in older workers' participation? Nothing can be told from the data presented. Within each of the nine large groups are many subgroups, some growing and others declining. It is entirely possible that the growing subgroups show a relatively small increase in the percentage of older workers while the declining industries show a much larger increase.

[5] It is well known that in regression analysis simple correlations between two variables may not be significant, but combining several variables in a multiple regression may produce significant relationships. The complexity of several variables acting at once upon the dependent variable must be explicitly taken into account before the true relationship can be observed.

[6] C. D. Long, *op. cit.*, p. 172.

Little can be said about Long's major conclusion that younger women are a prime force in displacing the older workers. It does not seem possible that an answer to this question can be given without analyzing the increased supply of women workers as one of the factors influencing the demand for older workers. Thus, Long's study does not provide the analysis necessary to measure the effects of the increased supply of women workers on the demand for older workers.

Henry D. Sheldon has suggested one promising way to generate better data.[7] He computed survival rates between 1940 and 1950 for workers who were over 65 in 1950. The survival rate is defined as the fraction of workers in a certain occupation who were, say, between 55 and 65 years old in 1940 and who survived in that occupation until the 1950 census (when they were then between 65 and 75 years of age). His division of the labor force into 158 occupations is far more detailed than the 12 major occupational groups utilized by Long. One important aspect of the older workers' problem is a low survival rate: too few workers in the upper age groups are surviving in their occupations from one decade to the next. Similar results were found in English data by F. L. Clark.[8]

Clark and Sheldon ask a question related only indirectly to the main question of income and employment status. They wish to know what occupations provide relatively good employment opportunities for older workers. Sheldon clearly points out that one cannot conclude anything about this question by looking solely at the percentage of older people in a given occupation at a moment of time.[9]

[7] Henry D. Sheldon, with Clark Tibbits, *The Older Population of the United States* (New York: John Wiley and Sons, Inc., 1958).

[8] F. Le Gros Clark and Agnes Dunne, *Ageing in Industry* (New York: Philosophical Library, 1956).

[9] Two major studies that include the use of such misleading data are Harvey C. Lehman, "Jobs for Those over Sixty-Five," *Journal of Gerontology*, Vol. 10, No. 3 (July 1955), pp. 345–357; and Charles A. Pearce, "Employment Status of Older Workers," *Industrial Bulletin* (Monthly news magazine of the New York State Department of Labor), (January 1949), pp. 34–40. One study that attempts some explanation was Carl Raushenbush and Abraham J. Berman, "Occupational Patterns of Older Workers, 1940 and 1950," *Making the Years Count* (Albany N.Y.: New York State Joint Legislative Committee on Problems of the Aging, Legislative Document No. 32, 1955), pp. 55–79. British data were considered in the National Advisory Committee on the Employment of Older Men and Women, *First Report*, (London: H.M.S.O., 1953); and K. F. H. Murrell, S. Griew, and W. A. Tucker, "Age Structure in the Engineering Industry," *Occupational Psychology*, Vol. 31, No. 2 (July 1957), pp. 150–168. While these studies are of some interest, they all observe

The fact that an occupation group contains a relatively high percentage aged 65 and over does not necessarily imply that the occupation is one in which the probability of retirement with increasing age is low; or, on the other hand, that it offers employment opportunities for older persons. Among blacksmiths, for example, the proportion 65 and over was 35 per cent higher, and the proportion 55 to 64, 106 per cent higher, than the corresponding proportion in the total male population 14 years old and over. Yet, the number of blacksmiths 65 and over in 1950 constituted only about one-fourth of the number aged 55 and over in 1940, and only the most imaginative would list blacksmithing among the opportunities for postretirement employment. In short, the concentration of older persons in a given occupation group is a function not only of low attrition rates or high entrance rates at the upper ages but also of past trends in the size of the group.[10]

In other words, the time element cannot be ignored if we are to analyze changes which take place in labor force participation with increasing age. In terms of the question asked by Clark and Sheldon, we must find occupations that not only have a relatively large number of older workers but that also have relatively high survival rates at the upper age groups. Sheldon found only two occupational groups satisfying this condition: charwomen, janitors, and porters; and elevator operators. "Generally speaking, the gains in the number of older persons in these occupations reflect the downward occupational mobility incident to aging and suggest also the limited opportunities for older persons."[11] Clark suggests that many more people will be retired from relatively strenuous jobs, but they will still be able to take less demanding jobs. Indeed, there will be more seeking light jobs than there will be light jobs available.[12]

Neither Clark nor Sheldon has done much to explain the pattern of survival rates observed. The major conclusion of the previous section was that a causal explanation should have been the goal of their studies. Sheldon's analysis is much like Long's with fewer factors considered. Clark has not attempted an explanation. Again, the beginning of a fruitful research procedure has been developed, but more must be done.

---

the dependent variable in an incorrect manner, as explained by the citation from Sheldon quoted in the text.

[10] H. D. Sheldon, *op. cit.*, p. 74.

[11] *Ibid.*, p. 78.

[12] F. Le Gros Clark, *Age and the Working Lives of Men. An Attempt to Reduce the Statistical Evidence to its Practical Shape* (London: The Nuffield Foundation, 1959).

A major study of reasons for retirement was conducted by Peter O. Steiner and Robert Dorfman.[13] They utilized data about persons 65 and older from a sample survey of about 3,000 families, each with at least one person over 65. The sample was collected by the U.S. Bureau of the Census during April, 1952. Retired persons were asked the reasons for retirement. Information assigning varying importance to the factors triggering a decision to retire might lead to an explanation for the increased number of older people who now consider themselves permanently unemployed or retired. Although full assessment of the factors would require comparison with the part of the labor force still at work, this form of inquiry could provide most of the desired explanation. People who left the work force are observed and the relative quantitative importance of their reasons for leaving is invoked as an explanation.

Unfortunately, data collected in the fashion indicated have deficiencies that preclude drawing definitive conclusions. Four major problems of interpretation arise:

(1) The events recorded in the survey took place at many different points of time. Some of the retirements may have occurred just before the census taker arrived; others may have taken place ten or even twenty years earlier. But the research problem arose in the first place because the rate of retirement had been increasing too rapidly *over time*. Observations that compound market phenomena of many different time periods fail to reveal the effects of causes operating over time.

(2) Another consequence of the inability to sort out different time periods is the distortion that arises in the composition of the sample of people observed. A random sample of retired people at a

[13] Peter O. Steiner and Robert Dorfman, *The Economic Status of the Aged* (Berkeley, Calif.: University of California Press, 1957). Another large study of this type was conducted among people collecting social security pensions: Margaret L. Stecker, "Beneficiaries Prefer to Work," *Social Security Bulletin*, Vol. 14, No. 1 (January 1951), pp. 15–17; "Why do Beneficiaries Retire? Who Among Them Returns to Work?," *Ibid.*, Vol. 18, No. 5 (May 1955), pp. 3–12, 35–36. Two similar studies were done for British retired workers: Ministry of Pensions and National Insurance, *Reasons Given for Retiring or Continuing at Work* (London: H.M.S.O., 1954); L. Moss, "A Sample Survey of Older People and Their Employment in Great Britain in 1950," *Old Age in the Modern World* (London: Livingston, 1955) pp. 353–360. A survey of those who retired from a large corporation with a pension, a selected group of people, was made by John J. Corson and John W. McConnell, *Economic Needs of Older People* (New York: Twentieth Century Fund, 1956), p. 40.

moment of time is not a random sample of retirement events. In so far as mortality rates differ among different groups of people, and in so far as they are related to any of the factors we wish to observe, a sample like Steiner and Dorfman's will contain distortions. People who retire for health reasons or from very strenuous occupations may have less of a chance of appearing in the sample than those who retire in good health from less taxing occupations. Although information about mortality rates is incomplete, there is evidence to suggest that the rates do differ substantially among occupations. Thus the observations are not valid representations of the phenomena to be explained, i.e., the dependent variable has not been accurately observed.

(3) Answers people give to the investigator may not be valid reflections of the reasons why they are unemployed. This is particularly true of people who claim ill health as the reason for their retirement. Steiner and Dorfman note the trouble.[14] But Sheldon casts even more doubt on the validity of any simple answer to the question, "Why did you retire?"[15] Since "ill health" is an especially suspect answer, and since Steiner and Dorfman conclude that ill health is a major cause of excessive retirement rates, the explanation cannot be embraced with confidence.

(4) While early retirement and involuntary unemployment result from interactions of demand and supply in the labor market, only the supply side of the market has been observed.

One other piece of analysis was undertaken by Steiner and Dorfman. The occupational distribution of people over 65 (or their previous occupation if they were retired) was compared with that of the entire work force. Large discrepancies between the two were found. From this they concluded that a major difficulty of the older worker is the possession of skills that do not match those in general demand in the economy. However, even if the differences in distribution could be interpreted to mean this, the method of data collection is defective, as noted in points (1) and (2) above. In addition, changing technology, demand patterns, and the development of career lines will always make the distribution of older workers somewhat different from that of younger workers. The question which they did not ask is this: How much will such

[14] Steiner and Dorfman, *op. cit.*, p. 43, n. 4.
[15] Sheldon, *op. cit.*, pp. 43–47.

shifting contribute to unemployment among older workers? Again, conclusions regarding the quantitative importance of this factor relative to others cannot be drawn because only a portion of the market has been considered.

Surveys conducted among unemployed workers in general have the advantage of observing all age groups and, at least in theory, of being useful for tracing the development of patterns that culminate in the major problems of older workers. Studies conducted so far are too limited in scope to provide much information, however.[16] The sample observed is usually from a very small geographical area and is restricted to persons who have contact with a U.S. Employment Service Office. It is not random or representative in any broad sense. The questions asked refer mostly to personal characteristics of the worker. They do not probe for fundamental economic factors that might affect supply and demand relationships. The proper questions must be asked before data will be collected in a manner conducive to obtaining meaningful answers.

Studies Determining the Presence or Absence of Particular Factors

In these studies a particular factor is selected, and an effort is made to discover whether the factor has a different effect upon different age groups. The answers are typically of the yes-no type. For example: yes, the older worker is less productive; no, he does not have more accidents. Whereas studies discussed in the previous section begin with observations of unemployment or labor force participation, many of these studies attempt explanations without quantitative observation of the ultimate phenomenon to be explained. As a consequence, they are not directly related to the methodological framework presented earlier. They even appear to ask questions different from those suggested as most fruitful for causal explanations and policy action.

The literature in this area is extensive. Selected factors include

[16] The two major studies are by the United States Department of Labor, Bureau of Employment Security, *Older Worker Adjustment to Labor Market Practices* (Washington: GPO, September 1956), BES #R151; and "The Philadelphia Older Workers Study—A Summary," *Economics and Business Bulletin* (Philadelphia: Temple University School of Business and Public Administration), Vol. 9, No. 2 (December 1956), pp. 1–55. The BES study covered seven cities, the Temple study covered only Philadelphia.

productivity (both in the psychology laboratory[17] and in manufacturing firms[18]), accident rates[19], absenteeism[20], health[21], relative costs of fringe benefits and pensions[22], changing amounts of

[17] The major work directly related to older workers' total productivity has been done by A. T. Welford, *Skill and Age: An Experimental Approach* (London: Oxford University Press, 1951); *Aging and Human Skill* (London: Oxford University Press, 1958). One good summary of much other laboratory work is by Oscar J. Kaplan, "Psychological Aspects of Aging," *Annals of the American Academy of Political and Social Science,* Vol. 279 (January 1952), pp. 32–42.

[18] The most comprehensive studies using actual production figures were two reported by the Bureau of Labor Statistics, *Comparative Job Performance by Age: Large Plants in the Men's Footwear and Household Furniture Industries* (Washington: GPO, November 1957), BLS Bulletin #1223; *Comparative Job Performance by Age: Office Workers* (Washington: GPO, February 1960), BLS Bulletin #1273. Some British studies have tried a new, and probably more promising approach. They directly observe the jobs being done by different age groups in a plant. Their aim is to detect the types of work which will prove difficult for the older workers. Examples are by R. M. Belbin, "Older People and Heavy Work," *British Journal of Industrial Medicine,* Vol. 12, No. 4 (October 1955), pp. 309–319; and I. M. Richardson, "Age and Work: A Study of 489 Men in Heavy Industry," *ibid.,* Vol. 10, No. 4 (October 1955), pp. 309–319. The most detailed analysis of job activities was done by S. Griew and W. A. Tucker, "The Identification of Job Activities Associated with Age Differences in the Engineering Industry," *Journal of Applied Psychology,* Vol. 42, No. 4 (August 1958), pp. 278–282.

[19] For two conflicting conclusions, see Max D. Kossoris, "Relation of Age to Industrial Injuries," *Monthly Labor Review,* Vol. 51, No. 4 (October 1940), pp. 789–804; and William M. Gafafer, Rosedith Sitgreaves, and Elizabeth S. Frasier, "Studies of the Duration of Disabling Sickness: III. Duration of Disability from Sickness and Non-Industrial Injuries among Male Employees of an Oil Refining Company with Particular Reference to the Older Workers, 1933–1939," *Public Health Reports,* Vol. 57, No. 4 (January 23, 1942), pp. 112–115.

[20] Max D. Kossoris, "Absenteeism and Injury Experience of Older Workers," *Monthly Labor Review,* Vol. 67, No. 1 (July 1948), pp. 16–19; BLS Bulletin #1223, *op. cit.;* Rashelle Goldberg, "Wanted: More Facts, Fewer Opinions on Absenteeism," New York Legislative Document No. 32, *op. cit.,* pp. 92–95.

[21] A survey of a number of these studies is given in Faculty Committee, Graduate School of Public Health, University of Pittsburgh, "From the Point of View of the Worker, Is It Likely to be Better for Him to Continue in Employment as Long as He is Able to Work or to Retire at a Given Age?", *Criteria for Retirement, op. cit.,* pp. 61–118.

[22] See the discussion of "Panel 5—Insurance and Pension Costs as a Barrier to the Employment of Older Workers," *Proceedings of the Second Conference on the Problem of Making a Living while Growing Old: Age Barriers to Employment,* (Philadelphia: Temple University and Pennsylvania Department of Labor and Industry, September 1953), pp. 136–156; and the more technical discussion of Jack M. Elkins, "Pension Costs and Older Workers," *Industrial Bulletin,* Vol. 37 (September 1958), pp. 3–7.

assets held[23], costs of retraining[24], effects of union activity[25], and the effects of business cycles.[26]

A great variety of empirical results were found. Some showed that a particular factor such as productivity differs with age; some showed no difference. Some found a factor important in the minds of those questioned so that it was prominently mentioned; others found the reverse. If one begins with the concept of interacting demand and supply forces, such diversity is not surprising. For many factors operate simultaneously, and certain factors are important under some circumstances but not under others. Studies that concentrate upon a single factor alert the researcher to the possibility of including that factor in a causal model. But the studies themselves establish no connection between a poor employment status for older workers and observations on the factor being studied. That is, they give little hint of the mechanism by which various factors interact or of the relative quantitative importance of each factor in determining employment and income by age.

Even if these studies are viewed as a means of selecting relevant variables that influence demand and supply, two main difficulties remain to plague the investigator.

First, the data are often inadequate. Data problems are perpetually present, of course, but in several studies of this type they

[23] Edna C. Wentworth, "Economic Situation of Aged Insurance Beneficiaries: An Evaluation," *Social Security Bulletin,* Vol. 17, No. 4 (April 1954), pp. 13–22, 26; Lenore A. Epstein, "Economic Resources of Persons Aged 65 and Over," *ibid.,* Vol. 18, No. 6 (June 1955), pp. 3–19, 32–33.

[24] Two British studies have been done: A. M. N. Shooter, A. E. D. Schonfield, H. F. King, and A. T. Welford, "Some Field Data on the Training of Older People," *Occupational Psychology,* Vol. 30, No. 4 (October 1956), pp. 204–215; and D. G. Entwisle, "Aging: The Effects of Previous Skill on Training," *ibid.,* Vol. 33, No. 4 (October 1959), pp. 238–243.

[25] Melvin K. Bers, *Union Policy and the Older Worker* (Berkeley, Calif.: University of California, Institute of Industrial Relations, 1957); Albert J. Abrams, "Barriers to the Employment of Older Workers," *Annals of the American Academy of Political and Social Science,* Vol. 279 (January 1952), pp. 62–71.

[26] The depression of the 1930's was studied by John G. Darley and Donald G. Paterson, "Employed and Unemployed Workers, Differential Factors in Employment Status," *University of Minnesota Employment Stabilization Research Institute,* Vol. 3, No. 6 (September 1934), entire issue; and D. L. Palmer and J. A. Brownell, "Influence of Age on Employment Opportunities," *Monthly Labor Review,* Vol. 48, No. 4 (April 1939), pp. 765–780. The effect of the labor shortage of the 1940's was discussed by Miriam Civic, "Perspective on Older Persons," *The Conference Board Business Record,* Vol. 8, No. 8 (August 1951), pp. 400–402.

are so serious as to cast doubt upon the validity of the final results. For example, laboratory studies may not be transferable to a real world production situation, answers to questions asked of management or the worker may disguise or distort the true reasons for differentiation by age, and data concerning the health of workers (even comprehensive physical examinations) are very difficult to convert into a quantitative measure of health.

Second, and more fundamental, is the effect of time upon the work force being studied. The younger and older age groups must be similar in all respects except for the factor whose effect is being evaluated. This control is rarely imposed.

In productivity studies, for example, groups of older and younger workers in a plant, or several plants, are compared. Usually their productivity is found to be quite close, and the inference is made that age does not affect productivity. In fact, however, the older workers are probably still on the job *because* their productivity does not differ from that of younger workers. If their productivity had declined, as did the productivity of many others who entered the plant with them years earlier, they would have been displaced.

This same absence of a control group is operative in areas other than productivity. Older workers have lower accident rates than younger workers. Part of this is due to selection of older workers who are employed, but some is also due to different exposure rates. Only younger workers are put on many jobs with high risks involved.[27] On many intelligence tests older workers appear to be distinctly inferior. A reverse time effect may be taking place here. There has been a secular rise in general education and experience in taking the types of psychological tests that are used in experiments. Thus the younger persons have a large advantage over the older ones regardless of the relative inherent intelligence possessed by the two groups.[28]

As some writers have recognized,[29] the kind of data needed for successful studies of this type can be obtained only by following a fixed group of workers over time under closely controlled condi-

[27] Max D. Kossoris, "Relation of Age to Industrial Injuries," *op. cit.*, p. 792.

[28] Harold C. Reppert, "Older Worker Testing and Placement, Psychological Testing of the Older Worker," *Proceedings of the Third Conference on the Problem of Making a Living While Growing Old: Age Barriers to Employment* (Philadelphia: Temple University and Pennsylvania Department of Labor and Industry, December 1954), p. 80.

[29] Faculty Committee, University of Pittsburgh, *op. cit.*, p. 88.

tions. Only in this way can the observations be made on workers who are strictly comparable in every respect except age. However, studies conducted over long periods of time are costly, and controls are difficult to maintain under changing social and economic conditions. Probably a substitute method must be found to allow for the effects of time if reasonably valid interpretations of data are to be made.

PART II

Industrial Employment by Age

CHAPTER FOUR

Demand, Supply, and the Older Worker: The Market Approach

FOLLOWING THE methodology suggested in Chapter 3, in the present chapter a demand-supply model of the labor market for male workers is applied to each of several industries. The model is based upon a theoretical formulation assigning different productivities to different age groups. In the past, production functions or physical input-output relationships have essentially treated labor inputs as homogeneous, so no distinction was made with respect to different ages. A production function that allows for varying productivity with age provides a basis for interpreting observed differences found in the statistical evidence.

The labor demand functions are derived from the production functions in order to ascertain the extent to which age plays a pervasive role across industries with different production techniques and product demands. Introduction of labor supply functions yields the complete model. By relating age to a labor-market mechanism our objective is to identify the effects of age upon aggregate market behavior, and to measure the relative quantitative importance of various causes generating employment and earnings differentials by age.

The basic evidence is comprised of statistical aggregates. Empirical coefficients of the demand and supply equations are compared to uncover regularities affecting employment and income opportunities of different age groups. However, some of the statistical series are weak. As a consequence, the conclusions drawn from this evidence may be questionable. In order to test these conclusions further, and to shed more light on employment conditions, direct surveys of employers and analyses of union-employer contracts were undertaken. These results are reported in Chapters 5 and 6.

The Theoretical Framework

For a single firm in a given industry, capital inputs are assumed to be fixed.[1] Let the firm's production function be of the Cobb–Douglas variety in $I + 1$ variable labor inputs:

$$(1) \qquad x = \gamma \prod_i a_i^{\alpha_i} b^{\beta} \qquad \begin{matrix} i = 1, 2, \ldots, I \\ 0 < \alpha_i < 1 \\ 0 < \beta < 1 \\ 0 < \epsilon < 1 \\ \sum_i \alpha_i + \beta + \epsilon = 1 \end{matrix}$$

where γ, α_i, β and ϵ are positive constants. The variable x denotes output and a_i signifies labor inputs of males in the ith age group. It follows that the larger is α_i the greater is the productivity (marginal physical product for any given labor input) of the ith age group. Because at least one study[2] has hypothesized that the influx of females into the labor force is the prime cause of displaced males, especially older males, the variable b represents female labor.

Demand for the firm's output, assumed relatively price elastic, is given as:

$$(2) \qquad x = \delta p^{-\frac{1}{\lambda}} s^{\theta} \qquad \delta > 0, 0 < \lambda < 1, \theta > 0$$

where p and s denote respectively the product price and a "shift parameter" related to the demand for industry output, with δ, λ, and θ positive constants. Under the condition that the wage rate for each type of labor is given to the firm, profit maximization yields $I + 1$ equilibrium equations which, when solved for each a_i in

[1] In another version of this approach capital was assumed to be variable. However, the data show a high correlation between capital and output, used as a proxy for s in equation (2), so the elasticities of employment with respect to these two variables could not be separated in the regression equations. Since the empirical inferences are no broader under variable capital, the theoretically simpler assumption of fixed capital was adopted.

[2] C. D. Long, *op. cit.*, p. 32.

terms of the other variables, give I demand functions for males by age:

$$(3)\quad A_i = \frac{1}{1-(1-\lambda)\,(1-\epsilon)}\Big\{\omega_i' - [1-(1-\lambda)\,(1-\epsilon-a_i)]\,W_i - (1-\lambda)\sum_j a_j W_j - (1-\lambda)\,\beta\,W_f + \theta\,\lambda\,S\Big\}$$

$$i = 1, 2, \ldots, I$$

$$j = 1, 2, \ldots\, i-1, i+1, \ldots, I$$

$$\omega'_i = \mu' + [1-(1-\lambda)\,(1-\epsilon-a_i)]\,a'_i + (1-\lambda)\sum_j a_j a'_j > 0$$

$$\mu = (1-\lambda)\,\delta^{\lambda}\gamma^{(1-\lambda)} > 0.$$

With w_i representing the wage rate for males in age group i and w_f the wage rate for females, all upper-class Roman letters designate natural logarithms of the variables, and primes the logarithms of constants.

Certain relationships among the elasticities emerge to establish the effects of productivity and product demand upon employment by age. Between any two age groups k and q the ratio of the wage elasticity of demand for group k to that of q is:

$$(4)\quad \frac{e_{wk}}{e_{wq}} = \frac{1-(1-\lambda)\,(1-\epsilon-a_k)}{1-(1-\lambda)\,(1-\epsilon-a_q)} \lessgtr 1 \qquad \text{as } a_k \lessgtr a_q.$$

The ratio of cross elasticities of demand is:

$$(5)\quad \frac{e_{ck}}{e_{cq}} = \frac{a_q}{a_k} \lessgtr 1 \qquad \text{as } a_k \gtrless a_q.$$

Finally, both the pure expansion elasticities and the cross elasticities with respect to the wage rate for females (percentage change in employment with respect to the percentage change in s and w_f respectively) are identical for any two age groups:

$$(6)\quad \frac{e_{sk}}{e_{sq}} = \frac{\theta\lambda}{\theta\lambda} = 1$$

$$(7)\quad \frac{e_{fk}}{e_{fq}} = \frac{\beta}{\beta} = 1.$$

Although the percentage changes are identical, the absolute changes in a_k and a_q do depend upon a_k and a_q. In particular, the larger a_k is relative to a_q, the larger will be the change in a_k compared with a_q in response to a given change in either s or w_f.[3]

These elasticities reflect the way in which productivity and the firm's growth rate operate upon demand to help determine employment and earnings by age. To elaborate their economic significance suppose for simplicity that the kth age group consists of "older" workers and the qth age group consists of "younger" workers. A firm for which a_k is smaller than a_q will employ fewer older than younger workers.[3] Morever, the firm's demand for older labor will be less wage elastic than its demand for younger labor. As population and the labor force expand, but the proportion of older workers increases, thus enlarging the supply of older labor and tending to reduce its wage rate, expansion of employment opportunities for older workers will be restricted by the magnitude of a_k relative to a_q. Of course, older workers are not new entrants into the labor force. The process of persistent restriction of older-worker employment can work itself out over the course of business cycles. In a downturn seniority rights are often not sufficient to protect the jobs of older workers. When a firm is expanding in the upturn, older workers displaced elsewhere may find great difficulty in being hired. The interviews with personnel officers reported in Chapter 5 have indicated that as a rule they are reluctant to hire older workers when they are making additions to their work force.

At the same time, the smaller a_k is relative to a_q the more sensitive will employment of older labor be to changes in the wage rate of younger labor. Anything reducing the supply of younger labor in the

[3] The argument is carried out for s but applies *mutatis mutandis* for w_f as well. Since

$$\frac{\partial a_k}{\partial s}\frac{s}{a_k} = \frac{\partial a_q}{\partial s}\frac{s}{a_q}, \text{ then } \frac{\partial a_k/\partial s}{\partial a_q/\partial s} = \frac{a_k}{a_q}$$

, i.e., changes in a_k and a_q depend directly upon the equilibrium amounts of a_k and a_q employed. In turn, a_k and q_q (prior to the change in s) depend upon the constant terms ω'_k and ω'_q in (3) and relative wage rates. It can easily be shown that $\omega'_k \lesseqgtr \omega'_q$ as $a_k \lesseqgtr a_q$. With regard to wage rates, it can be shown that for $a_k \lesseqgtr a_q$, then $a_k \lesseqgtr a_q$ unless $w_k/w_q \lesseqgtr a_k/a_q$; for $a_k = a_q$, $a_k \lesseqgtr a_q$ as $w_k \gtreqless w_q$. Taking account of both the constant terms and wage rates, it is to be expected that gross wage rates (including fringe benefits) by age do not differ in direction and magnitude sufficiently to offset differences in ω' and ω' due to differences in relative productivity. This expectation is confirmed by the empirical results reported in the third section.

firm's factor market (such as migration out of the region or delayed entry into the labor force) and operating to raise the wage rate of younger labor will have a significant impact in shrinking employment opportunities for older labor in the firm.

An increase in the supply of females (perhaps willing to work for less than males) generates the same percentage change in employment of all males regardless of age. Therefore in a firm for which $a_k < a_q$, the numerical increase in older male labor will be smaller than the increase in younger labor—assuming both are complementary inputs with female labor. As the firm continues to enlarge the number of females in its work force, the difference $(a_q - a_k)$ becomes greater. As a consequence of lower productivity on the part of older males, expansion in the supply of female labor will increase the female-male labor ratio by more for older than for younger males.

Finally, and probably most important, at given wage rates growth in the firm's output in response to expanding product demand will create fewer new jobs for older than for younger workers. For (as shown in footnote 3) with $a_k < a_q$, the firm will employ fewer older than younger workers. When product demand and thus labor demand increase, the same percentage increase in the employment of both entails a smaller numerical increase of older workers. If the supply of older workers is increasing, employment opportunities do not keep pace with the number available for employment.

On the industry level, member firms may display a predominance of $a_k < a_q$. If such an industry is expanding (contracting), there will be a greater increase (decrease) in the employment of younger than older labor. Any industry for which there is a predominance of $a_k > a_q$ will show just the reverse effects. An economy characterized by expanding industries of the former kind and contracting industries of the latter kind, on even a relative basis, makes the employment and income problems of older workers more drastic over time. However, to the extent that the economy is comprised of rapidly expanding industries for which $a_k > a_q$ such problems are ameliorated.

The Model and the Data

Labor demand and supply equations were estimated from cross-section data on each of fourteen two-digit manufacturing industries for 1959. The theoretical framework provides a foundation for the industry demand equations, assumed for simplicity to be identical in form to equations (3). However, the unobservable variable s is replaced by an observable variable based upon value added for the industry, and the number of female workers is substituted for the unobservable wage rate for females. Three age groups were selected: 14–24, 25–44, and 45 and over.[4] The labor demand equations for each industry appear as follows:

$$(8)\ A_i = \psi_i + \sum_{j=1}^{3} \phi_{ij} W_j + \rho_i F + \pi_i X \qquad i = 1, 2, 3$$

A_i = log of employment of male workers in the ith age group (Source: Census of Population, 1960).

W_j = log of gross average hourly earnings for production workers in age group j (Sources: Annual Survey of Manufactures, 1959–1960; Census of Manufactures, 1958; and a series of Bureau of Labor Statistics Reports).

F = log of employment of female workers (Source: Census of Population, 1960).

X = log of "expected" annual industry output (value added in millions of dollars) estimated by a distributed lag on five past annual outputs in order to reflect industry growth or decline as well as the current level of output (Source: Annual Survey of Manufactures, 1955–1959).

To adjust for the effects of different populations of a given age among states, to adjust for inequality in the age spreads utilized, and to facilitate interindustry comparisons A_i is defined empirically as the log of an index. The index was computed as the number of males in age group i employed by the industry divided by the total number of males in age group i employed in the entire state and multiplied by 100. The variable F is similarly defined as the log of the ratio of females employed in this industry to all employed females in the state, multiplied by 100.

Data are not available on wage rates according to age. Thus, hourly earnings for each age group by state and industry had to be constructed. The Annual Survey of Manufactures provides average hourly earnings per production worker by state and industry. This

[4] Actually, several different models were employed, the largest using five age groups: 14–19, 20–24, 25–44, 45–54, 55 and over. Because very few of the coefficients differed significantly between the first two groups and between the last two groups, the set was collapsed to three age groups.

rate was treated as a weighted average for the three age groups, where the weights are the number of workers in the age group as a percentage of the total of all employed workers. From a series of Bureau of Labor Statistics Reports data are available on minimum entrance rates and standard job rates.[5] It was assumed that all workers 25 and over receive the standard job rate and that workers 14–24 receive the minimum entrance rate in all states and industries. With the average, the weights, and the spread between minimum and standard rates known, hourly earnings by state and industry for the three age groups are determined.

These hourly earnings do not include supplementary employer cost (fringe benefits contributed by the employer). Volume I, Chapter IX of the 1958 Census of Manufactures records such contributions by state and two-digit industry. Legally required payments—Old Age and Survivors' Insurance, unemployment insurance, and workmen's compensation—are easily reduced to an hourly basis. The remaining and largest category, other employer payments or allocations, were assumed to represent pension contributions. The problem is to impute shares of these totals to the age groups. In order to do so, let C denote the observed total and assume:

$$C = \sum_{i=1}^{3} C_i E_i$$

where E_i is the total number of all male and female employees in the ith age group, and C_i is the payment per worker in the ith age group. E_i is also observed. To determine C_i assume only that the yearly contribution is determined so as to attain some (unknown) fixed sum P at the retirement age of 65. Then a constant yearly sum C_i set aside and lent at the long-term interest rate r must pay back P at the end of that term:

$$P = C_i (1 + r)^{65-m_i} \qquad i = 1, 2, 3$$

where m_i is the median age for the ith age group. This system of four linear equations in four unknowns gives C_i and P. The C_i's are reduced to an hourly basis and added to the previously computed figures to yield gross hourly earnings by age.[6]

[5] For sources, see Bureau of Labor Statistics, *A Directory of Industry Wage Studies and Union Scale Studies, 1950–60,* U.S. Department of Labor, 1961.

[6] A similar model was estimated on the assumption that workers of all ages are paid the same (the average) hourly earnings. This assumption ignores

In the supply equations, interstate migration was assumed to be zero. Labor supply for each age group is a function of its own wage rate, wage rates in other manufacturing employments within the state, and alternative earnings in nonmanufacturing within the state:

$$(9) \qquad A_i = \tau_i + \sigma_i W_i + \eta_i Q_i + \xi_i E_N + \nu_i E_F \qquad i = 1, 2, 3$$

Q_i = log of the mean of the average hourly earnings for the ith age group in all manufacturing industries other than the one in question (Source: same as W_j).

E_N = log of annual earnings per employed person in nonmanufacturing and nonfarming relative to the industry in question (Source: Census of Population, 1960).

E_F = log of annual earnings per employed person in farming relative to the industry in question (Source: Census of Population, 1960).

If workers transfer jobs on the basis of relative expected incomes, use of the wage rate rather than income in other manufacturing industries assumes implicitly that income differences within manufacturing are reflected in relative wage rates. The variable E_N represents an effort to capture the effect of income prospects in the service trades, wholesale and retail trades, and similar employments. With respect to production workers the professional and financial occupations were assumed to be noncompeting groups. Hence, from all wages and salaries earned in the state were deducted earnings in all manufacturing, the professions, finance, and farming. This residual on a per-employed-person basis was divided by earnings per employed person in the industry to which the model was applied. Inclusion of E_F as a separate variable incorporates the hypothesis that farm-nonfarm migration motivated by relative earnings differs significantly among age groups.

Several attempts were made to measure the aggregate impact of labor unions on labor supply by age, but each attempt proved to be a failure. A variable was sought to measure "union strength" as a determinant of supply. Union membership as a percentage of employment was inadequate for a variety of good reasons. Foremost among these reasons is the fact that membership alone does not

---

higher pension costs for older workers. As the theoretical framework would predict (see footnote 3), the constant term and the demand elasticities as compared to those reported here were somewhat larger for the oldest group and smaller for the younger groups.

Table 4–1. ESTIMATES OF THE STRUCTURAL PARAMETERS, 1959 [1]

Age Group	Demand Equations: Constant Term	Demand Equations: Coefficient of W_D [2]	Demand Equations: Coefficient of F	Demand Equations: Coefficient of X	Supply Equations: Constant Term	Supply Equations: Coefficient of W_S [2]	Supply Equations: Coefficient of Q	Supply Equations: Coefficient of E_N	Supply Equations: Coefficient of E_F
Food and Related Products (43 observations)									
14–24	2.2447	–0.2429	–0.1361	0.3408	2.3181	0.3437	–0.1821	–0.5094	–0.3614
25–44	2.3708	–0.1903	–0.0574	0.4645	2.7276	0.2590	–0.1232	–0.3220	–0.1311
45 and over	1.8096	–0.1471	–0.2106	0.2845	1.8727	0.2856	–0.0787	–0.1011	–0.0573
Apparel and Related Products (28 observations)									
14–24	1.8038	–0.6136	–0.3012	0.7472	1.2987	0.6083	–1.2583	–0.7118	–0.1642
25–44	1.7441	–0.6849	–0.1318	0.8404	1.3924	0.4906	–1.1388	–0.5936	*
45 and over	1.0043	–0.3423	–0.3994	0.8108	0.7475	0.5184	–0.6027	–0.2191	*
Lumber and Wood Products (32 observations)									
14–24	1.5997	–0.3233	*	0.4509	3.8040	0.1416	–0.5322	–0.3681	–0.2508
25–44	1.4758	–0.2448	*	0.4072	4.5754	0.1500	–0.4740	–0.4260	–0.1616
45 and over	1.4007	–0.0993	*	0.3090	4.1316	0.0906	–0.3301	–0.2477	*
Chemicals and Allied Products (35 observations)									
14–24	1.3634	–0.3746	–0.0596	0.4950	0.6616	0.8452	–0.7414	–0.6249	–0.1204
25–44	1.2008	–0.4587	*	0.4133	0.6194	0.9050	–0.7706	–0.5180	*
45 and over	1.0007	–0.2611	–0.1214	0.3405	0.4604	0.7500	–0.5936	–0.3688	*
Fabricated Metal Products (32 observations)									
14–24	1.2111	–0.3638	*	0.6185	0.6356	0.2416	–1.1147	–0.3816	–0.2463
25–44	1.5418	–0.2704	*	0.7890	0.9240	0.2054	–0.8663	–0.2492	–0.1075
45 and over	0.9254	–0.1806	–0.1018	0.5007	0.4233	0.1673	–0.4408	–0.1604	*

1. The multiple correlation coefficient ranged from .74 to .92 with a mean of .84.
2. W_D and W_S denote the age group's own wage rate in the demand and supply equations respectively.
* Not statistically significant at the 5 per cent level.

determine the ability of a union to control labor supply. Another index of union strength was tried: union membership as a percentage of employment by state and industry weighted by union assets per member relative to the U.S. average and multiplied by 100. The rationale underlying this approach was that financial assets per member in addition to membership would reflect union power in the labor market. However, the coefficient of this variable was significantly different from zero for only three of the fourteen industries. Even where the coefficients show statistical significance, common-sense interpretation is questionable. At this point it appears that union effects are intractable to the type of systematic analysis employed here.

The model presented in (8) and (9) consists of six equations in six endogenous variables, the *A*'s and the *W*'s. All other variables are assumed to be exogenous. The overidentified model was estimated by ordinary least squares and two-stage least squares with very similar results. The parameter estimates presented in the following section are those obtained by two-stage least squares.

The Results

Fourteen industries were chosen on grounds of completeness and reliability of the sample data. Significant multicollinearity was found in the case of five industries, so the separate effects of the different variables could not be distinguished. Rather than obscure the results by presenting a vast array of figures for the remaining nine, the results for five industries are shown in Table 4-1. The five are, however, typical of the general patterns appearing in the other four.

The coefficients of wage rates of other age groups in the demand equations (the effect of the wage rate of one group upon employment of another) are omitted from the table because they showed no discernible pattern, even with respect to their signs, and almost half of them were not significantly different from zero at the 5 per cent level. Of course, all other coefficients do vary a great deal among industries. In searching for patterns that persist across industries, it is notable that the oldest group consistently shows the smallest wage coefficient in the demand equations, with mixed orderings for the other two age groups. From the data used here and from other studies [7] it is evident that there exists a wide dispersion of wage rates among states within an industry. Based upon the cross-sectional sample, the results indicate that in low-wage firms employment of older males is not much greater than in high-wage firms, especially as contrasted with the other two groups. Alternatively, in high-wage firms employment is not much less, due perhaps to seniority provisions in work contracts. Since pension costs are built into the wage rates, giving a higher rate with greater age, the relatively low-wage coefficient taken together with the smaller constant term for older workers suggests lower productivity (see footnote 3). At the very least, if older workers in manufacturing do possess superior productivity, it is not sufficient to offset these costs. This inference must be interpreted with caution, however, for in the "crafts" where acquired skill is a very important factor in productivity, the nonstatistical evidence of Chapters 5 and 6 shows that greater age is not a significant determinant of employment.

The coefficients of F indicate that females do tend to displace males in some industries. Nevertheless, their impact is by no means uniform among industries, and the data revealed no effect in some. In food, apparel, and to a lesser extent chemicals, the oldest males are most affected by female employment, with the youngest second in order, and the intermediate age group least affected. Again, these results are not independent of productivity by age. For even if females are willing to work for a wage less than that paid to males, displacement of males hinges upon their productivity compared to that of females.

Coefficients of the final demand variable, X, also display a pattern with respect to age. Firms showing the largest expected output (or "growth") employ the least number of older workers, with the exception of the apparel industry. In three of the five industries, the intermediate age group had the largest coefficient, while in two of the five it was the youngest group that exhibited the largest increase in employment with respect to X. Only in the apparel industry does the youngest worker group have the smallest expansion coefficient.

In the supply equations not much can be said about the coefficients of W_S. In three cases the oldest group showed a slightly

[7] L. Chimerine, "An Econometric Analysis of Regional Wage Differentials in Manufacturing," Ph.D. Thesis, Department of Economics, Brown University (June 1965) (unpublished).

smaller coefficient, but generally the orderings are mixed. The remaining three sets of coefficients can be taken as indicators of mobility by age (aside from interstate geographic mobility). With few exceptions the youngest males are most mobile. Indeed, for two industries they show the only significant farm-nonfarm mobility. The intermediate age group is less mobile, and the oldest group without exception displays the least mobility.

Table 4-1 organizes the parameter estimates by industry. To test for the effects of age, each coefficient was separately arrayed by age and industry (giving twenty-seven estimates for three age groups and nine industries) and subjected to an analysis of variance. In addition to the five industries of Table 4-1, the study included furniture and fixtures; stone, clay, and glass; electrical machinery; and transportation equipment. If an estimate was not significantly different from zero at the 5 per cent level, it was treated as having a value of zero.

The object is twofold: (1) to determine if there is a statistically significant variance in each coefficient by age as well as industry, and (2) to measure the relative magnitudes of the effects exerted by age and industry on a given coefficient. For each coefficient the null hypothesis is that all estimated values emanate from normal populations with the same mean and variance, i.e., that class membership (age or industry) exerts no influence and observed differences are pure sampling effects.[8]

For the industry effect, the null hypothesis was rejected at the 1 per cent level of significance for all but the coefficient of X, and that at the 5 per cent level. For the age effect, the null hypothesis is rejected at the 1 per cent level for the coefficients of W_D, Q, and E_N, and at the 5 per cent level for F, X, and E_F. The hypothesis could not be rejected at the 10 per cent level for the coefficient of W_S.

Given that there is statistically significant variance by age and industry, let e_{ik} denote the estimated value of a coefficient. Then, the following hypothesis is adopted:

$$e_{ik} = e_i + e_k + u_{ik}$$

e_i = effect of age i on e_{ik},
e_k = effect of industry k on e_{ik},
u_{ik} = a random variable, normally distributed with zero mean.[9]

[8] See M. G. Kendall, *The Advanced Theory of Statistics* (London: Charles Griffin and Co., 1946), Vol. II, p. 182.

[9] *Ibid.*, p. 218.

There is a total of twelve maximum-likelihood estimates for each coefficient—three e_i's and nine e_k's. As might be expected, industry effects outweigh age effects. Since we are interested primarily in the effects of age, only the e_i's are recorded for each coefficient in Table 4-2.

Table 4–2. EFFECTS OF AGE CLASSES ON COEFFICIENTS

Age Group	W_D $e_{ik} < 0$	F $e_{ik} < 0$	X $e_{ik} > 0$	W_S $e_{ik} > 0$	Q $e_{ik} < 0$	E_N $e_{ik} < 0$	E_F $e_{ik} < 0$
14–24	−0.0526	−0.0398	0.0221	0.0271 *	−0.0909	−0.0890	−0.1217
24–55	−0.0487	0.0000 *	0.0650	0.0098 *	−0.0253	−0.0294	0.0384
45 and over	0.1055	−0.0652	−0.0871	0.0136 *	0.1163	0.1186	0.1014

* Not significant at 5 per cent.

Only the directional ordering and the spreads between entries in a given column are relevant. If e_{ik} is positive, the larger algebraically is e_i, the greater is the effect attributable to membership in age group *i*. Similarly if e_{ik} is negative, the smaller algebraically is e_i the greater is the effect. For example, differences are slight between the 14–24 and 25–44 groups in the coefficient of W_D. However, for the 45 and over group the contribution of age is to make the coefficient smaller negative (closer to zero) and substantially less than the other two groups. In the coefficient of *X*, membership in an age group also affects the coefficients across all nine industries. The orderings indicate that the intermediate age group has the largest employment-output coefficient, with the youngest group second in magnitude, and the oldest group substantially smaller than either of the other two. Vertical comparison of the entries of each column confirm the inferences drawn from interpretation of Table 4-1.

Conclusions

At the outset of this chapter two questions were raised. First, do the economic variables that affect employment and earnings exert a significantly different impact upon different age groups in the labor force? If so, what is the order of their quantitative importance? Second, is there a pure age effect connected to each variable that operates across industries with different product demands and production techniques? On the basis of the statistical evidence utilized, answers to both questions are affirmative.

In expanding upon the answer to the first question, it should be noted that in Chapter 3 the need to consider several variables operating simultaneously was emphasized. Together the variables determine the employment and income status of each age group. Following this methodological guide, demand and supply variables were selected on the basis of economic theory and incorporated in a multiequation model of the labor market for each industry. The estimated coefficients of the variables form the criteria for comparing the relative strength exerted by each variable. Because of differences in the units in which the variables are measured (units that affect the magnitudes of the coefficients) the regression coefficients are not used directly. Beta coefficients, regression coefficients standardized for various units of measurement in the variables, provide direct comparisons of relative impact.

From comparison of the beta coefficients of each equation, some general conclusions seem permissible. On the demand side of the labor market, employment of females does affect adversely the employment of males—with the oldest, the youngest, and the intermediate ages affected in that order. Female labor has been substituted for male labor by industrial firms, but not uniformly across all male age groups. Older workers are most severely affected, with the youngest males second in order. The intermediate age group, experienced but still young enough to be competitive, are little affected by substitution of females.

However, as a variable explaining male employment by age, female employment is not as quantitatively important as either gross hourly earnings or expansion of output by firms. Underlying both of these variables are greater supplementary employer costs with more advanced age (primarily pension costs) and productivity differentials by age. Since the variable X is quantitatively more important than W_D, an inference that pension costs are of prime importance is hazardous to say the least. A positive relationship between productivity and age between ages 14 and, say, 45 or 50, and an inverse relationship between productivity and age thereafter appears to be of equal or more importance.

It is not only labor demand variables that generate the pattern of employment and earnings by age. On the supply side of the market, the beta coefficients indicate that E_N and Q are predominantly the two most important supply variables, with W_S and E_F less important in that order. This suggests that comparative wage rates among industries and earnings in manufacturing relative to earnings in the "service" trades play a more significant role than farm earnings within the state relative to earnings in manufacturing.

That is, higher earnings offered by a manufacturing industry do attract more labor from other employments within a state. A decline in earnings on the farm compared to earnings in manufacturing does result in an increase in labor supply to manufacturing. But more important than farm versus manufacturing earnings are comparative earnings among different manufacturing industries and comparative earnings between manufacturing and service employments. When expansion of a given manufacturing industry provides more jobs and better pay, the additional labor is drawn most heavily from other manufacturing industries and from service (nonfarm and nonmanufacturing) employments. Similarly, a relative decline in jobs and pay in one manufacturing industry causes an increase in the supply of labor to other manufacturing industries and to the service trades. On the whole, in choosing and changing employment workers compare annual earnings among industries offering the most closely related types of work.

Moreover, and of special significance for our purposes, different age groups react to comparative annual earnings in different degrees. It is the young (ages 14–24) who are most responsive to better financial prospects in alternative employment. This holds true for farm-nonfarm mobility as well as mobility within manufacturing and between manufacturing and service employments. The intermediate age group (ages 25–44) is less responsive, and the oldest age group still in the labor force (ages 45 and over) is least responsive. Therefore, since older workers are less mobile within a state, since they are most reluctant to take advantage of higher earnings in alternative employments, this immobility contributes to their relatively low position on the income scale.

Table 4-2 has focused upon pure age differences rather than on the quantitative importance of different explanatory variables. In both the demand and the supply equations, with the exception of the variable W_S, the oldest males show the greatest effect of age in the labor market. The effect of age was shown to hold across industries generally, even though these industries experience different growth rates. In the demand equations this effect operates to make demand less wage elastic, displacement by females greatest, and expansion of employment with respect to output least. Wage elasticity is the percentage change in employment that results from a given percentage change in the wage rate. Thus, a reduction in the gross wage rate of older workers (including supplementary employer costs) would not lead to a significantly large increase in their employment. In the supply equations pronounced immobility is apparent among manufacturing industries, and between manufacturing and other employments. The youngest males also show some interesting characteristics. Demand elasticity seems little different from the intermediate age group, but there is greater displacement by females and smaller expansion of employment with respect to output. In the supply equations, the youngest group is shown to be the most mobile of all. It would not be surprising if its employment and earnings opportunities are more favorable compared with other age groups in nonmanufacturing. Later analysis of occupations sheds some additional light on this possibility.

Prospects for the oldest workers certainly do not appear very bright for a variety of reasons. It would be helpful to have time series in order to establish definitely whether their employment status in terms of these variables is deteriorating over time. Unfortunately, none are available for the kind of breakdowns necessary to make industry-by-industry comparisons. A model almost identical to the one used here was estimated for the year 1949, but no definite changes over the ten-year interval could be discerned. Perhaps the time span is too short. The growth rates of the nine industries (measured by average percentage change in value added per year) were computed for the interval 1947–1960. A significant positive rank correlation was found between industry growth rate and the difference between the X coefficient for the intermediate age group and the oldest age group; it therefore seems that the income and employment problems of older workers are becoming more severe over time. Certainly the evidence does not point to an improvement in their prospects.

CHAPTER FIVE

Hiring Practices and the Older Worker

WITHOUT EXCESSIVE oversimplification the statistical evidence can be summarized in a few sentences. On the demand side of the labor market, declining productivity with advancing age, greater pension costs, and to a lesser extent substitution of female workers lessen the demand for older males. On the supply side increasing immobility with age prevents a proportionate rise in the income of old and young alike. However, the degree of aggregation in the statistics and the weakness in some of the series might lead one to question the interpretation of the statistical patterns observed. It is important, therefore, that the inferences drawn from the data be tested further in order to determine if they can be supported using a smaller level of aggregation and a different methodological approach.

In particular, two empirical limitations of the estimated model should be underscored. No statistics on wage rates by age are available, and no reliable measure of the influence of labor unions could be devised.

Hourly earnings for each age group had to be constructed from indirect data and assumptions regarding minimum and standard job rates, as explained in Chapter 4. Assignment of a higher gross wage to older workers (inclusive of pension costs) *may* overstate the effect of pension costs and thereby understate the effect of other demand variables. Employment statistics encompassed all workers in each age group. But an older employee of long standing will have contributed a much greater share to the pension fund than an older person seeking employment in an industry. The two types cannot be separated statistically. As indicated in footnote 6 of Chapter 4, a similar model was estimated under the assumption that workers of all ages are paid the same gross wage rate inclusive of pension costs. The general conclusions regarding demand by age were not significantly affected. Nevertheless, in order to isolate (at least partly) the phenomenon of re-employment for an older worker once he is displaced from a job and in order to help determine whether the conclusions regarding labor demand by age are the result of a statistical artifact, further investigation is called for. Only in this way can the reasonableness of the inferences drawn from the statistical evidence be tested.

On the supply side of the labor market the conclusions regarding interindustry mobility are supported by analyses of regional mobility and occupational mobility that follow in Parts III and IV. One possibly important factor, the effect of labor unions upon labor supply and job protection by age, could not be captured by the aggregate statistical evidence. Measures of union strength showed no discernible influence upon the employment of different age groups. This outcome is not surprising. In previous economic studies labor union behavior has proved intractible to the type of systematic analysis utilized in the previous chapter. However, one cannot deny that unions have some influence upon the employment and earnings of different age groups. An evaluation of that influence is warranted.

Because of these considerations, two additional investigations were undertaken. Direct interviews with employers revealed their attitudes toward the hiring of older workers. The purpose was to assist in evaluating the inferences regarding demand for labor of different ages drawn from the aggregate statistical evidence. These results are reported in the present chapter. In Chapter 6 attention is centered upon the provisions of union-employer contracts in an effort to uncover if, how, and to what extent labor unions do affect employment conditions for workers of different ages.

The Survey Design

Since older workers face the most serious employment problems, interviews with employers emphasized workers in approximately the 40–65 age span. It was felt that a central theme was needed in order to focus questions and to allow expansion of discussion beyond those questions. Seniority appeared to be the logical choice of a theme, for seniority rules may provide some job protection. On the other hand, they may hinder re-employment of an older worker once he loses a job. The question of how seniority affects earnings leads naturally to consideration of other factors that influence the demand for older workers by employers. Consequently, whether or not seniority was felt to be a major determinant of employment for older workers, other determinants were soon brought into the picture.

Seniority protects an older worker during the time he is attached to a job. As long as he can meet average standards of performance he is protected against displacement by workers with less tenure who may be capable of more than average productivity. Even when a specific job is terminated, union-employer agreements provide a variety of seniority rights, including preferential treatment on job bidding elsewhere within the plant and offers of transfer and relocation at other plants. But the protection that seniority gives is automatically extinguished when, for any reason, employment is permanently ended. No longer protected by seniority, does this system prevailing in a firm where he seeks employment aid or hinder the reabsorption of the permanently separated worker?

The view that the existence of seniority may hamper the re-employment of permanently displaced older workers is shared by personnel officers and union officials, but quantitative evidence for this view is difficult to find. Statistical verification is lacking, although evidence does exist that older workers as a group are likely to face greater difficulty in finding jobs than those in the lower age groups. The problem facing an attempt to collect evidence on this question is that ordinarily workers above certain ages might face greater difficulties in gaining re-employment irrespective of the existence or absence of seniority. The task therefore is to isolate the effect of seniority systems from other causes which make re-employment of older workers more difficult. It is extremely difficult if not impossible to design an investigation which would measure this factor.

It was decided to interview the heads of personnel and industrial relations departments in thirty-eight firms located in Boston, Providence, New York City, Philadelphia, Pittsburgh, Cleveland, and Detroit. Aside from several in Providence, each of which employed several hundred employees, the majority of covered firms employed more than a thousand people.

Personnel officers do not appear to be in agreement on the effect of seniority upon the re-employment possibilities of older workers, nor whether different policies would be followed if formal seniority systems were nonexistent. Some claim the seniority system has little or no influence on the hiring of older workers, but others insist that it is a barrier to rapid absorption of the unemployed older worker. A third group holds that the seniority system, added to other costs related to age as well as the lower adaptability and the reduced employment horizon of the older worker, tend to discourage the re-employment of some groups among older unemployed workers.

Little or No Effect: The Reasons

Many personnel officers did not feel that the existence of a seniority system hinders the re-employment of displaced older workers. Nearly all agreed, however, that the older worker faces a serious re-employment problem. Two officers of a national oil company employing more than 14,000 workers were of the view that the seniority system on balance was a great boon to older workers. It protected them against layoffs in favor of younger workers. While they agreed that seniority would generally adversely affect re-employment of older workers, they believed that such situations were untypical and should not be regarded as very significant. Workers over 40 years of age would, in their view, find re-employment difficult if they found themselves permanently displaced, but they did not believe that this difficulty could be related to seniority. Fear of reduced productivity, higher workmen's compensation costs, lessened flexibility, and the frequent difficulty of finding a "proper slot" for the older worker were more significant factors, they believed, in limiting re-employment.

A multiplant firm with properties in Boston and Chicago, the former one unorganized and the latter dealing with an independent union and a seniority plan, did most of its hiring through referrals from those already on its payroll. Consequently it did not normally test the market in either of the communities in which it operated. Age itself, the vice president in charge of personnel said, would not affect hiring policy in general, but the company would shy away from hiring unskilled workers in higher age groups. Younger people are better suited for heavy "bull" work, and one cannot disregard the age factor any more than one would fail to take into account other attributes which affect the suitability of the work applicant. The company took another view of the employment of older-age workers for skilled and semiskilled jobs. As skill was, in these cases, the important component sought by the firm, there could not be any objection to the employment of older workers unless the strength and endurance required on a job were too taxing.

Officers of a company employing more than 9,000 workers doubted that seniority is an impediment to re-employment. They believed that workers acquire transferable skills, even though operations are not uniform within plants. They indicated that the desire to avoid experienced men might be based upon the fear that such workers might have developed union loyalties, and that they would be more susceptible to the appeals of the organizer than younger workers. In this instance, the view that older workers will not be rehired for plain unskilled work was reiterated. "Where strength and endurance are predominant factors, the older worker is not in a good bargaining position."

An official of a company operating in several industries employing about 8,000 workers expressed the view that older workers do have transferable skills, but he would nevertheless prefer to hire those in the lower age group, "as most companies do." He held the view that older workers are likely to face increasing difficulty in finding jobs once they are permanently separated because of changing technology. It is easier to train younger men not only because of their greater adaptability but because they are likely to have a higher level of plasticity in the sense that they have not acquired deeply ingrained work habits. He also believed that younger workers are more durable and possess more education. However, in specific jobs where experience may be important, older workers may be preferred. As the company operates in a number of industries, it tends to adopt hiring policies tailored to the particular needs and conditions surrounding a plant. Younger workers or those in higher-age brackets will be hired if necessary, but the policy of recruiting younger workers is generally preferred.

A contrasting view was given by a personnel officer of a company employing more than 9,000 employees with headquarters in New York City. Whenever changes touching the employability of older workers are contemplated by this firm, those likely to be affected are notified in advance. On the other hand, this company does not hire semiskilled or skilled men on the open market when they are available in the plant or are on layoff. However, the view was also expressed, and it was shared by others, that technical changes had eliminated to a large extent the need for great amounts of strength and durability.

Personnel officers in a Cleveland, Ohio, company did not believe that seniority affected hiring of older workers in any significant degree. Seniority exercised no influence upon the particular company's hiring policy. Pensions were the important influence in the employment of older workers, according to two officers of this firm, and the employment manager of the company regarded pensions as the greatest barrier to hiring of older workers. He also claimed there were firms in the area who would not hire new help above the age of 37 years. He cited his experience when he tried to place a number of employees laid off because of the discontinuance of the manufacture of one of their products. So that the laid-off group would not face barriers in seeking re-employment, firms in the area were informed that the workers were laid off because of lack of orders and not due to their low ability or failure to cooperate. He said that a number of firms would not hire men above the age of 44 years, and that some used the mid-thirties as the outer limits for hiring. In one respect seniority may act as a barrier to rehiring, but not necessarily upon the worker permanently detached. A worker on layoff may retain recall rights at a particular plant for one or more years. His pension rights may not be vested, and they may depend upon willingness to accept recall when it is offered. Under such circumstances a worker may leave his new job so as to protect his pension rights at the old plant. Whenever an employer faces this kind of situation, he is likely to be cautious in hiring those attached to another job. This situation is likely to affect workers irrespective of age, but it may be more common among older workers who have had a better opportunity to build up pension rights.

An eastern producer of metal products and automotive bodies and trucks employing over 16,000 workers claimed that seniority in its industry did not affect hiring of older workers. Workers will be hired in large numbers at a given time, and not many specialists outside of maintenance are employed in the industry. Up to the age of 55, experienced workers will find no barrier to hiring. The personnel officer of the company turned the issue around, and claimed that older workers are, in some instances, anxious for layoffs and that there are cases when the older man would prefer to be laid off as supplementary unemployment benefits and unemployment compensation might provide him with a considerable part of his wage.

A jewelry plant employing 600 workers at the peak of the season explained it had no objection to hiring older workers. The list of hires in the last two years contained the names of workers between the ages of 40 and 64 years. In discussing the effect of age upon hiring, it was observed that in a seasonal industry such as jewelry the demand for labor rises and declines sharply, and does not as in some other industries tend to be uniform throughout most of the year. Consequently, the employer's choice of workers is, to a large extent, limited. He must hire those who are available, and cannot wait to select more carefully. Consequently the possibility of age discrimination is reduced considerably. In the jewelry industry, the lightness of the work is also a factor in the employment of older workers. Manual dexterity is important, and age does not appear to be significant in productivity.

The personnel director of a leading mining company placed the problem of hiring older workers in a somewhat different light. The difficulty of hiring an older worker is that he is likely to expect higher pay than a younger worker. The older worker is not likely to be acquainted with current techniques and has a shorter working life. The problem was envisaged as one requiring constant training so that the work force is able to use the up-to-date methods. He suggested that it was essential that training be carried on during the period of employment instead of waiting for a time of layoff or permanent separation to learn new skills.

Two personnel officers of a steel company employing over 50,000 employees felt that age of hiring does not involve a single problem. In fact, they agreed that it would be unwise to hire too many high school students in a plant. Stability would be reduced considerably if the work force were heavily weighed in favor of younger people. Instead, a few younger workers could be hired, if they were "salted" with older ones. In contrast to the view of some personnel men that foremen wanted younger workers hired, they believed that supervisors also seek those who have experience in living, especially plant living. They also emphasized that companies are not completely free to hire at advanced levels even if their plants are not unionized. The effect of outside hiring upon morale must always be considered. The union formalizes and strengthens the seniority system of layoffs and promotions and thereby reduces the opportunities for outside hiring, but it by no means is the only influence in this direction.

What is obvious from these opinions, as well as others not cited, is the predominant stress upon obstatcles to re-employment of older workers. Except in rare instances, expression of the view that seniority systems do not significantly affect re-employment was followed by an explanation of other factors believed to be more important. Few denied that greater age creates special difficulties for the reabsorption of displaced older workers, even though seniority does not add to these difficulties.

Restricts Re-employment: The Reasons

The assumption that senority may hamper or at least reduce the re-employability of older workers is based upon a belief that as a worker ages his strength, flexibility, and adaptability tend to diminish. Such diminution makes him less desirable as a purely unskilled worker, and he is therefore less attractive occupationally than the younger worker who can perform more effectively the task which depend upon strength and endurance. It is further argued that in the course of time, the worker acquires skills and experiences which have some economic value, even though they are not of the same kind and complexity as the apprenticeable arts. The training requirements of the apprenticeable arts are sufficiently long and involved so that plant-wide and department-wide seniority systems cannot impede the hiring of a worker of such grades on the open market when he is needed. In addition, general recognition also exists among the work force that the training of an apprenticeable tradesman takes a relatively long time, and no demands for promotion to this class from semiskilled or unskilled employees are likely to be made. A somewhat different situation is said to prevail within the semiskilled and unskilled groups. The experience and training which an older worker carries with him, while normally real, is not as easily identifiable. Workers who have an interest in promotion will not concede that the older worker has a sufficiently recognizable skill to warrant his employment at a new job above the entry grade level. In other words, the special skill of an artisan or craftsman, as he is called, will be recognized by the work force, and no question on his being hired at his skill level would be formally or informally raised. A different response is likely in the hiring of an experienced semiskilled worker whose greater ability is not as easily recognized. While the hiring of semiskilled and unskilled workers, above the entry level, would likely be resented where a formalized seniority system does not exist, this same hiring would be challenged by unions where they have a voice in the administration of shop rules. Thus, formalized seniority adds to the re-employment difficulties of older workers.

A Midwestern producer of bearings and other metal products employing almost 8,500 workers was interviewed, and the issues were discussed with the vice president in charge of labor relations and the heads of four plants in different parts of the country. A system of seniority, in their opinion, raises serious hiring difficulties especially for the older worker. Seniority prevents the firm from hiring for a particular "spot." It is not possible for a company to hire a worker for a light job with the assurance that he will hold that particular place. For the worker may, in the case of a cutback in personnel, be pushed into a grade requiring the use of strength and endurance. In other words, under a seniority system, the employer must consider not only the job to which the worker is initially assigned, but the others he may be required to fill through the operation of the seniority system. This tendency is accentuated by the "bumping" system which sometimes is an accompaniment of seniority.

The personnel people also expressed the view that the older worker is likely to be less productive, and his greater average stability may be offset by higher pension costs and proneness to injury. The claim was made that older workers are more prone to injuries causing hernias or back trouble and that they are not likely to recover as readily. Whether such views can be statistically validated is not significant so long as the belief is a basis of policy.

Officers of a Midwestern firm employing 7,500 workers were convinced that the more inflexible and broader the seniority system, the more difficult it will be to hire older workers. It is especially true when the seniority system specifies in detail the procedures to be followed in layoff, recall, and bidding for other jobs. Under these circumstances the older applicant is not likely to be hired at his skill; at least, it will be more difficult to place an older worker. The discussion on the effect of seniority elicited the observation that seniority will discourage mobility between jobs as soon as a worker begins building his pension until the minimum time needed for vesting. Between hiring and vesting time, the worker cannot carry his pension with him. After he has worked some time and a pension has been accumulated, the worker will tend to remain on the job until his pension is vested, and that factor will tend to reduce mobility and opportunities for employment.

The personnel officer of a chemical firm employing more than 12,000 workers in a number of plants was of the opinion that seniority is likely to inhibit outside hiring, especially in the absence of expansion. As a rule, giving better jobs to those outside the work force will create resentment among workers on the payroll. The insistence upon promotion from within is obvious from observing some clauses in union contracts on "procedures for filling new jobs in the production department." A new job was defined as one not listed and which "will require a training program of three (3) weeks or more." A typical clause: "Departmental seniority and competency shall entitle employees to first consideration for promotion as opportunity shall offer . . . " It is certainly desirable for firms to offer opportunities for advancement of workers in their employ, but it is obvious that such arrangements may adversely affect the hiring of those outside the plant. In view of the effect of increased pensions and a number of other adverse factors in the re-employment of older workers, the internal promotion programs which are designed to open wider opportunities for members of the firm's work force tend to increase the difficulties of re-employment of older workers.

An officer of a company employing 26,000 workers in the metalliferous mining and smelting industry believed that formal bargaining systems tend to increase the difficulties of re-employment for the older worker. The difficulties are the result of hiring procedures followed by many large companies. Hiring is usually at the tail end of the scale (laborer, etc.) and the skill and experience of the older worker cannot be purchased. He gave an example from the situation which confronts some of the plants operated by this firm. A furnace man who has quit his job or been laid off permanently could not, as a rule, obtain employment at this grade. He would have to be hired at a lower rank, and it might take him fifteen years to work up to the grade he held on his last job. In the view of this personnel man, a trained furnace man would be good as a furnace man, but he is likely to be inferior as a laborer.

However, he attributed the difficulty to the formal and informal systems of seniority that exist in industry. As for productivity, he did not believe that the older man is less productive than his younger competitor. In fact, the older worker's lower absenteeism, regularity, his greater conservatism and willingness to accept discipline may normally make the older worker a greater asset. He regarded the fringe benefits as an impediment: pensions, health and welfare plans, and especially workmen's compensation costs tend to make the older worker less desirable at the unskilled job levels. In jobs utilizing the older worker's experience, he would, if possible, be hired more readily. There is, however, a difficulty in engaging him which is not inevitably related to the presence or absence of union organization in a plant. For purposes of maintaining morale and keeping the better workers attached to the firm, promotions to better jobs must be available, and training must be provided if some of those on the payroll apply for a higher rated job vacancy. While there is a tendency to promote from within the plant's work force in the absence of formal seniority systems, formal systems of seniority tend to be more restrictive and tend to harden more easily. It is easier to bend an informal system without facing a grievance. A firm that seeks to hire outside of the seniority system must make a very good case for not taking a worker from the list. A company will first have to exhaust the bids and then show that those who seek the job will have little chance to qualify.

Officers of a manufacturer of paint products were also of the opinion that seniority tends to discourage the hiring of older workers. The older artisan craftsman has no problem in finding a job. His skills are clearly defined and identifiable, and he is in a different position from the skills which are based largely upon experience. The example given was the hiring of a shader, one who requires knowledge of the difference in paint color. Shading is a skill acquired over time, and shaders are usually helped by an assistant. Under the seniority provisions of the union contract with the company, a shader could not be hired from the outside. Instead someone already employed would be offered the job. The idle shader who might have been hired at this level would not normally be employed for less skilled work. Nor is a worker who had occupied a relatively skilled position likely to accept an unskilled job in the industry. He might be forced to downgrade himself, but the belief was expressed that it would be easier psychologically to work at an unskilled task in another industry rather than in the industry in which a particular worker had been employed in a skilled capacity.

Affects Re-employment of Some: The Reasons

Aside from skilled versus unskilled workers, several employers expressed the view that seniority affects different categories of labor in different ways. In a plant producing mine safety appliances and employing, in different seasons, between 150 and 600 workers during the year, the employer operates a seniority system although the firm is not organized. This particular firm found that the seniority system did cause some difficulties in hiring, but, on the other hand, the personnel director did not find women between the ages of 35 and 55 years of age inferior workers or that their normal employment was affected by seniority. He believed it was necessary to employ women and there was danger that efficiency would diminish if the plant were filled with older people. Nevertheless, he found older workers a steadying influence, and their presence in a plant of some advantage.

The head of the industrial relations division of a metal trades firm was of the opinion that a semiskilled older worker is likely to face considerable difficulty in obtaining a new post or a job as good as the last one held if he becomes permanently unemployed. He attributed the situation to the constant change in skill requirements and in the tendency to hire younger people. He regarded the situation as more serious for white-collar workers than for those in manual employments. One of the reasons is that older blue-collar workers are protected, in many instances, by seniority systems and cannot be as easily released as those employed in clerical and administrative tasks. In the case of technical changes affecting the workers in the shop, attempts are likely to be made, at least under a union-management arrangement, to layoff the displaced on the basis of length of service. The white-collar employee is not protected as frequently by a union contract. He therefore is likely to face serious difficulty in gaining a new job. He is normally not acquainted with the new types of equipment and procedures, and is likely to be less trainable than a younger employee. The grade and salary which an older worker is likely to require would also be greater.

An expanding firm offered the view that as the company was

growing the issue of re-employment and layoffs would normally not arise. The personnel officer was, however, reasonably certain that older workers seeking employment face greater obstacles than younger ones who have some industrial experience. Interestingly enough, he also believed that it was the white-collar worker who may in fact face the greatest difficulty in finding new employment.

Conclusion

The opinions reported here are also representative of those expressed by officers of other firms among the thirty-eight. The approach to hiring older workers appears to be largely pragmatic, if one excludes firms which have informal age limits on hiring. Hiring of older workers is based largely upon estimates of their ability to perform given tasks more effectively than lower age workers. Among the reasons given restricted re-employment of older workers are cost of pensions, adverse effects upon workers' morale, unfavorable attitudes of foremen, less flexibility and training potential, more limited work horizons, and seniority systems. As far as the employer is concerned he avoids hiring older workers for specific jobs because he believes they are not as qualified to perform the task in question at least as effectively as those of lower age groups. Such a conclusion may be based upon prejudice, or it may be founded on observation. It means that the employer believes that certain conditions surrounding a particular job are such that an older worker would be handicapped to the extent that productivity would be lower or that certain work-connected costs would be too high.

Whether or not the opinions are based upon fact, to the extent that these beliefs determine hiring policy they do exert an impact upon the re-employment of older workers. Evidence on the effects of seniority and on hiring practices according to age groups is provided by the experience of one firm. When production expanded after a cutback, those recalled under seniority provisions showed a relatively high average age. But hirings of new employees were restricted to the younger age groups. The company operates a number of plants in the United States. In 1963, the company recalled 247 employees; their ages ranged from 29–78 years with an average age of 51. Ten workers were newly hired; their average was 27 years. During the same period, the company exhausted its recall list at another plant in the same general area but in a different labor market. The 229 newly hired at this plant averaged 32 years of age.

At another plant the forty workers recalled averaged 48 years of age, and two newly hired workers averaged 37 years of age. A greater age difference appeared between those recalled and those who were newly hired at the firm's Chicago plant. Those recalled from the layoff lists averaged 52 years of age. Those newly hired who were employed after the recall list was exhausted averaged 28 years of age. For the four plants employees recalled from layoff averaged 51 years of age; newly hired employees averaged 31 years of age; the composite average age for both groups was 40 years.

Seniority operates in two ways. To some extent it protects the job status of older workers. The chances of layoff are lessened. If an older worker is temporarily laid off by a firm, his chances of recall to the same firm are greater. However, in many instances there is no recall. When an older worker is displaced and seeks employment in another firm, the presence of a seniority system in that firm seriously hinders his chances of finding employment there.

Of course, the thirty-eight firms included in the interviews do not determine a uniform set of hiring practices in the economy as a whole. Morever, the employers interviewed are not in complete agreement regarding the effects of seniority systems. The interviews do, however, reveal information not obtainable from aggregate statistics. More striking than the opinions expressed about seniority is the consensus that older workers are less attractive job applicants than younger workers. Aside from seniority systems, the explanatory factors cited most often are higher employment costs and lower productivity. Employment costs include both greater pension costs and higher workmen's compensation costs. Factors such as less strength and endurance, reduced flexibility and adaptability, and difficulty in adjusting to changing technology are nothing other than symptoms of lower productivity as compared to younger workers. In addition, fear of morale problems in the work force, e.g., resentment of those already on the payroll, imposes another constraint upon the hiring of older workers.

Such qualitative evidence cannot be used to decide the quantitative importance of different demand variables affecting employment opportunities by age. For example, it cannot be said that relatively low productivity on the part of older workers is more important than supplementary employment costs. Neither can it be said that substitution of female labor is less important than either of these. Noteworthy, however, is the fact employers did not mention frequently the substitution of females (possibly because they do not wish to publicize the phenomenon). Noteworthy too is the frequent and unsolicited mention of productivity and employment costs, which emerged as the two most important demand factors in the aggregate statistical analysis. In this sense the interviews support and lend credence to the inference drawn from the model and the statistical estimates of the previous chapter.

CHAPTER SIX

Union-Employer Contracts and the Older Worker

UNIONISM AND collective bargaining influence hiring policies. To the extent that they do so, the employment contracts resulting from collective bargaining may be expected to affect favorably or adversely the employment status of older workers. Opportunities for younger employees are no less affected by practices regarding job tenure and seniority. No clear effect of unionism upon labor supply (and thus upon employment) of different age groups could be uncovered in the statistical data. However, the absence of an identifiable pattern in the statisical series is undoubedly traceable to the extreme difficulty—perhaps the impossibility—of measuring the effect of unions. As a consequence, examination of clauses related to job tenure in union-employer contracts was undertaken.

In part, it is the seniority system that determines a worker's ability to maintain his job status or to obtain a new one when he is displaced. But some union contracts go beyond simple seniority protection. Morever, some informal, noncontractual practices are condoned by unions. Since the opinions of employers in manufacturing industries differ regarding the over-all effect of seniority systems as such, more objective evaluation of hiring practices should be obtainable from examination of actual contractual provisions. In order to appreciate the role of unions it is necessary first to elaborate on the nature of seniority systems and the way in which unions may participate in their operation.

Seniority Systems

Formal and informal systems of seniority antedate, in many instances, the establishment of collective bargaining, but the scope and variety of seniority arrangements have been greatly influenced by the expansion of unionism. Seniority is not a simple system universally applied, but a somewhat protean rule frequently "tailored" to meet the particular needs of the firm or the work force. It may be simple, in the sense that length or tenure is the only criterion for layoff and recall to employment, or it may take account of several other factors in determining the person to be laid off. Basically all seniority systems give more or less weight to length of employment in the plant or firm as the basis for determining the person to be laid off because of a shortage of work.

While the job rights of long-tenure workers can be protected as long as a particular employer or seniority unit is active, such protection tends to vanish when the operation of a plant or department is suspended or when a job is abolished. In the latter case, the worker may, depending upon the wording of the seniority clause, retain limited rights to employment in other departments. However, the seniority system can only protect against layoffs in a particular plant (or even more narrowly in a seniority unit). If for any reason cutbacks in employment are sufficiently sharp, or if a plant or division of a plant is shut down permanently, the seniority system cannot protect long-tenure workers against layoffs.

Though the correlation is far from perfect, there does exist a correlation between seniority and age. Seniority rights tend to protect the jobs of older workers *within a seniority unit.* A serious problem for the older worker arises when he is laid off because the operation of a plant or a department is significantly cut back or entirely suspended. The greater job-finding difficulty facing older workers may be noted from comparing rates of long-term unemployment of men in different age groups. The rate of unemployment extending fifteen weeks or more for the 25–44 year group unemployed in July 1961 was 39.7 per cent and for those 45 years and older, 49.3. In July 1962, the rates were respectively 27.2 per cent and 43.6 per cent. For unemployment of twenty-seven weeks or more the 25–44 year group had a rate, in July 1961, of 24.2 per cent as compared to 33.7 per cent for the older group. In July, 1962, the differences were even greater; for the lower age group, the percentage of unemployment of twenty-seven weeks or more was 18.1 per cent, for the older group 29.6 per cent.[1] In July 1963, 29 per cent of the unemployed who were 25–44 years of age experienced fifteen weeks or more of unemployment, while the 45-year and over group reported 35 per cent unemployed. Unemployment of twenty-seven weeks was experienced by 18.3 per cent of the lower age group and 25.3 per cent by the older one.[2] Approximately the same differences are evident in 1964.

In a study of long-term unemployment, the United States Department of Labor found,

> There was some greater tendency for older male claimants to exhaust extended benefit rights than for younger claimants in the Temporary Extended Unemployment Compensation program. This finding, generally consistent among all states, reflects the known difficulty of employed older workers in finding new employment. Fifty-two per cent of male exhaustees were 45 or more years older, compared with 44 per cent of those who did not exhaust. The median age for men who exhausted was 45 years; for men who did not exhaust it was 42. The median age for women was 41 for exhaustees and 40 for nonexhaustees.[3]

In view of the effect of union organization upon the labor market, the policies of union organization with regard to the re-employment of older workers are of interest. Providing jobs to those who have no prior employment in a particular plant implies control or at least influence over hiring. Outside of the printing trades the closed shop has never been widespread in manufacturing industry, and it is forbidden today by the Taft-Hartley law. Consequently, in many instances, the union may not have any voice in determining hiring policy. To the extent that the union does influence hiring or controls labor supply, it may be able to place its members in employment.

Ability of the union to place workers is facilitated if the union controls a hiring hall or administers one jointly with an employer. Then a displaced worker, regardless of age, can be directed to a job when his turn is reached. Of course, depending upon the conditions of the arrangement, older workers can still be rejected by the employer. Nevertheless, easier access to employment may be gained by

[1] The *monthly report on the Labor Force,* (August 1962), pp. 13, T-6.
[2] *Ibid.,* (August 1963), p. 28.
[3] *Family Characteristics of the Long-Term Unemployed,* a report on a study of claimants under the Temporary Extended Unemployment Compensation Program, 1961–1962, (Washington: United States Department of Labor, Bureau of Employment Security, 1963), p. 9.

older workers. Rejection of older applicants is likely to meet opposition from the union—even though unions may sometimes "load" a job with older or less productive workers because an employer has aroused the displeasure of the officers.

Attempts on the part of unions to widen the application of seniority so as to protect older workers are likely to face opposition from employers, and from some workers who are members of the union. From the employer's viewpoint, interplant seniority is more costly to administer. Moreover, extension of seniority further restricts an employer's choice in the selection of his work force, compelling him to utilize those already on his payroll.

Reactions of union members to more widespread seniority depend upon employment in the plant to which transfer would be made. In plants where unemployment is prevalent, resistance will be strong. Such a reaction is not dissimilar to the refusal of local craft unions to accept transfers of members from another local when local members are not fully employed. In addition, attempts to protect older workers by means of broadened tenure rules may shrink employment opportunities for the youngest workers, even under conditions of full employment in a plant. Younger workers are simply displaced by older ones. However, there is evidence to indicate that younger workers are more mobile. They adapt more easily to other kinds of work; they can be trained more readily and their training costs can be spread over a longer working horizon. To the extent that younger workers are idle for a shorter span of time, broadened seniority systems would operate to reduce total unemployment.

It is a reasonable surmise, supported by some evidence, that extension of seniority to more than one unit by multi-plant firms is likely to be the result of union demands. This is not to deny that employers have voluntarily extended seniority rights to more than one plant. But, like the system of seniority itself, its wider application is normally the result of requests by the union. Since union-management agreements cover a variety of tenure conditions, an examination of contractual provisions will help to explain the way in which seniority affects the employment status of older workers.

Manufacturing Industries

Some union contracts seek to go beyond simple seniority protection, recognizing that workers may become incapacitated, lose part of their productive power, or become unable to perform the physical labor required by their work assignments. Unions operating in manufacturing industries have evolved, jointly with managements, formulae which allow older workers no longer able to perform assigned work to bid for other jobs. An example of these arrangements is the following clause in the contracts of the local of the International Association of Machinists with the Borden Chemical Company of Bainbridge, New York:

An aged or other employee who gives long and faithful service in the employ of the company, and has become unable to handle his or her assigned work to advantage, shall be given every consideration for such other work as may be available which the employee is able to perform at the rate for such job. If the company is unable to provide other work which they are able to perform, they shall be considered for severance allowance depending upon length of service.

A similar clause in the contract between the International Association of Machinists with the Avien Company of Woodside, Long Island, New York, provides:

Any employee who gives long and faithful service in the employ of the company and who becomes unable to handle heavy or his assigned work efficiently, shall be given every consideration for such other work as is available which the employee is able to perform, at a rate commensurate with the services to be performed, and to be agreed upon by the parties hereto.[4]

Older workers when transferred to jobs they can perform efficiently may in some instances carry their job rate of wages with them; in other instances the wage rate of the new job will be paid.

There are a variety of clauses defining the conditions under which the older worker will be able to bid for a job different from the one he holds. For example, the contract between the Grinnell Corporation and the United Steelworkers of America provides:

An employee who has given long and faithful service in the employ of the Company and who has become unable to handle his regular work to advantage shall be given every consideration for such light work as is available and the employee is able to perform, at a rate of pay com-

[4] Quoted clauses are taken from the contracts on file at the headquarters of the International Association of Machinists and were made available through the courtesy of Albert S. Epstein, an economist of the association.

mensurate with the services to be performed and the length of service of such employee.[5]

Some contracts allow older workers no longer capable of performing the work in their assigned jobs to displace (1) employees with lesser seniority in their department, and (2) if unable to do so, replace employees in other departments with less seniority on jobs the incapacitated empolyees can perform. If the incapacitated employee is unable to bump any employee on the basis of seniority on a plant-wide basis, the incapacitated employee can request that he be placed on a preferential hiring for work he can perform "over and above any new employee."

Under the agreement between the Aluminum Company of America and the International Union of the United Steelworkers of America an "employee with one year or more company seniority who is scheduled to be laid off shall be offered transfer to such other departments of the Works as may be decided upon by the Company" provided work is available which the employee is able to perform for which he is presently qualified or the work is in a classification for which "little or no training or little or no experience is required, or his company seniority is greater than that of the employee working in a classification for which he is presently qualified or in a classification for which little or no training or little or no experience is required, and he can perform the work, in which case he will replace the empolyee with the least company seniority in such classification." [6]

This type of clause allows older workers to bid for semi-skilled and unskilled light work if they lack the skill to obtain employment in a skilled job or are physically incapable of performing heavy work. It provides some protection to older-age workers because they are able to bid for some jobs they might be able to peform. In the event an employee is displaced because of a major change in process, improvement, or permanent elimination of an operating unit or department, he can be "transferred to such suitable department within the Works as may be decided by the Company provided there are employees in such department with less company seniority and provided he is able to do the work." [7]

[5] *Contract of Grinnell Corporation with United Steelworkers of America,* p. 33, Section 11.

[6] *Agreement Between Aluminum Company of America and International Union of United Steelworkers of America,* August 1, 1959, pp. 3–39.

[7] *Ibid.,* p. 38.

Some of the contracts between the Aluminum Company and its unions specify the conditions under which transfers can take place and the department to which they can be made. The following clause in the contract between the company and the Aluminum Workers of America describes the rights of a laid-off employee to transfer to a department other than the one in which he is employed, and the conditions under which these rights can be exercised.

> An employee with one year or more of company seniority who is scheduled to be laid off, shall, upon request, be transferred to such other department of the works as may be decided upon by the Company, provided that in the department to which he is to be transferred:
>
> 1. There is work available which the employee is able to perform in a vacancy in one of the classifications listed in the attached Appendix II [the jobs are given by department and job title] pertaining to the respective plant location, or
> 2. His company seniority is greater than that of an employee working in one of the above listed classifications, and he is able to do the job, in which case he will replace the employee with the least company seniority in such classifications. An employee so transferred shall earn departmental seniority as of the date he starts work in the new department.[8]

The significance of such provisions in the contracts of the Aluminum Company is the listing of jobs that workers with one year's seniority can seek if they are laid off. It is, of course, assumed that the worker has the ability to perform the jobs listed and that his seniority rating is higher than that of others holding such jobs. But the setting up of a "list of jobs" means that workers no longer able to perform their normal tasks will be given an opportunity to bid on the group of jobs set aside. The setting up of special labor classes is in fact a "codification" of the arrangement which should tend to reduce friction. For example, the contract covering the Lafayette Works includes jobs in the Remelting, Tube Plant, Extrusion, Maintenance, Die Manufacturing, Shipping, Box Shop, and Inspection and Accounting. Fifty-six separate jobs are listed in the above eight departments.[9]

The jobs in the Massena Works cover both the Fabricating and the Smelting Divisions: seventeen divisions are listed in the Fab-

[8] *Agreement and Working Rules Between Aluminum Company of America and Aluminum Workers Internationl Union Local Nos. 110, 405, 105, 115, 415, 420,* August 1, 1959, p. 33.

[9] *Ibid.,* Appendix II in contract for Lafayette Works.

ricating Division and six in the Smelting Division. A varied list of jobs are set aside for which higher seniority employees can bid. Among the jobs listed in the General Division are laborer, custodian, helper, skinman; Covered Conductor Division—insulation stripper, production helper; Cable Mill division—floorman, helper (cable), steel winder; Merchant Mill division—chamferer, cleaner, spool conditioner. Among the fifty-five jobs in the Fabricating Division at the Massena Works, nineteen are helpers.[10]

The list of jobs is arranged on a local basis in accordance with the particular needs of the company and the kind of operations carried on in the individual plants. The common characteristic of all contracts is the listing of jobs which workers with one or more years of seniority can obtain if they have been employed longer than others whom they "bump" or displace. In all instances ability to perform the particular job is assumed. As written, the clause can be used by workers of any age if they meet the requirement of one year's seniority and ability to perform the new tasks. But it is likely to be more important for older workers whose opportunities on the general labor market are not too promising. They are more likely than younger workers to accept downgrading.

The Automobile Industry

Unions and firms in the automobile industry have devised a variety of provisions for protecting the job rights of their workers. An agreement between General Motors Corporation and the United Automobile Workers provides that when "changes in methods, products or policies would otherwise require the permanent laying off of employees, the seniority of the displaced employees shall become plant-wide, and they shall be transferred out of the group in line with their seniority to work they are capable of doing, as comparable to the work they have been doing as may be available, at the rate for the job to which they have been transferred."[11] This clause allows workers whose jobs have been abolished to seek work they are capable of doing in other departments within the plant.

The contract between the UAW and the General Motors Corpora-

[10] *Agreement and Working Rules Between Aluminum Company of America and Aluminum Workers Internatioal Union Local Nos. 110, 405, 105, 100, 115, 415, 420, Appendix II Massena, New York, Plant.*

[11] *Agreement Between General Motors Corporation and the UAW-AFL-CIO,* September 20, 1961, 59, page 47.

tion also provides that for eighteen months after production begins in a new plant the company gives preference "to the applications of laid-off employees having seniority in other plants over individuals who have not previously worked for the Corporation, provided their previous experience in the Corporation shows they can qualify for the job." [12] Such employees retain their seniority in the plant "where originally acquired" until they establish seniority in the new plant.[13]

When job transfers between plants lead to a permanent release of employees holding seniority, the union and the corporation seek to negotiate "an equitable solution." Employees transferred under this provision carry their full seniority with them. Moreover, those transferred after January 1, 1962, are entitled to a relocation allowance providing the plant to which the employee is to be relocated is at least fifty miles from the plant from which his seniority was transferred. The allowance ranges from 55 dollars to 580 dollars depending upon distance and marital status.[14] In order to be eligible for such payments, the applicant must change his residence permanently.

In addition, workers with seniority laid-off from General Motors plants in a given community and who make application will be given preference over other applicants, provided previous experience in General Motors shows they are qualified for the job. This clause regulates area hiring, so that workers who are being laid-off at the same time other plants are hiring will be given first choice. Such jobs can be refused without any impairment of the employee's seniority rights. Area market hiring is conducted from a central list, and in the three-year period, 1959 through 1961, 14,910 workers were re-employed through the area hiring lists.

On the same order, the UAW and the Ford Motor Company negotiated, in 1951, an Area Availability Agreement providing that employees on laid-off status from any Detroit area activities shall have employment preference at any other Ford Detroit area plant requiring additional personnel. Transfer is administered from an interplant referral system. Between 1951 and 1959, "the agreement has resulted in over 34,000 job referrals and in excess of 25,000 job placements in the Detroit area." [15]

[12] *Ibid.*, 95, p. 72–73.
[13] *Ibid.*
[14] *Ibid.*, 96(a), p. 73–74.
[15] *Statement of Ford Motor Company by Malcolm L. Denise, Vice President Labor Relations, Submitted to the Special Committee on Unemployment*

Contracts between the United Automobile Workers Union and the Chrysler Corporation as well as the Ford Motor Company also include a variety of methods for protecting workers with long tenure in their employment. Under 80(a) of the Chrysler contract, "When operations or departments are transferred from one plant to another plant of the Corporation, employees engaged on such operations or employed in such departments up to the number needed in the receiving plant to perform the transferred operations, may if they so desire, be transferred to the other plant with their full seniority." [16] This clause has, at times, been a source of difficulty. A well-known example of the problems of enforcement arose when the company merged its stamping operations at the Nine Mile plant in Detroit. This was a new plant, and the workers that were directly employed held "date of entry" seniority. Those who followed the work were likely to hold higher seniority, and the new Chrysler employees were concerned with the effect that the transferred employees might have on their tenure. Sensitivity to layoffs was acute because of the reduction in hourly employment by the Chrysler Corporation amounting to almost 60,000 workers in several preceding years.

The local union at the Nine Mile plant opposed the transfers, but both the company and the international union insisted that the provisions of the contract be obeyed. An unsuccessful attempt to decertify the International as bargaining agent was initiated, but it was thrown out by the National Labor Relations Board on the ground that the bargaining unit was nationwide in scope.

Considerable protection is given to workers with high seniority in the automobile industry, and employees

> laid off from a division or from a department if it is not part of a division, who desire to displace employees in the plant with less seniority, shall within two (2) weeks of such layoff apply in writing to do so at their plant Employment Office. Within seventy-five (75) days of such layoff, such applicants shall be recalled to displace employees in the plant with less seniority, provided, however, that an applicant must have at least one (1) year more seniority than employee having seniority he displaces.[17]

Problems, United States Senate, Detroit, Michigan, (November 12, 1959) (mimeographed) p. 7.

[16] *Agreement between Chrysler Corporation and the UAW,* November 2, 1961, p. 72.

[17] *Ibid.*, 75(d) p. 65–66.

The contract goes further. Currently, the Chrysler-UAW agreement provides that in employing new people in any department, the company will give work opportunity to qualified laid-off employees in the following order:

(a) To employees of other departments, and then
(b) To employees of other plants of the Corporation covered by the Agreement and the Parts Plants Agreement . . . in the same labor market area.

Employees accepting work under this rule start work as new employees in the plant, and have no right to return to former plants unless and until they are permanently laid off from the new plant. They can decide then whether to retain their seniority in the new or former plant. If they decide on the latter, they can return to their former plant with full accumulated seniority, and in "such case their seniority at all other plants shall terminate." Under this clause thousands of workers have been transferred between plants in the same labor area, and many older employees have been given work opportunities.

One of the more important clauses designed to protect those employed in the contracts of the automobile manufacturing industry is the one governing transfer of employees between plants. An employee who is transferred by the corporation or at his own request retains his seniority for twelve months in the plant from which he has shifted and starts as a new employee in the other plant except in instances when operations are transferred.[18] The clause offers the worker who transfers an opportunity through direct experience to decide if he wishes to transfer his job or return to his former job (if it is still available) or accept a layoff at the former job and take his chances on being recalled for work.

Workers' response to the opportunity for transference and movement has varied. In the early 1950's between 400 and 500 out of 1,200 workers voluntarily moved from San Francisco to a Chrysler plant in Los Angeles. In 1959 more than 600 out of 900 transferred when the Dodge Dart operation was moved from Detroit to Saint Louis. The Ford Motor Company shut down its operations at Iron Mountain, Michigan, in 1951. Employment elsewhere was offered to the 1,323 workers. Twenty-five per cent refused to move; 18 per

[18] *Ibid.*, 80, p. 71.

cent who had agreed to move later refused to work in other plants of the company; and another 6 per cent retired.[19] On the other hand, in April 1954, the operations of the Richmond, California, plant were transferred to Millpitts, sixty miles from the older plant. Between 1,300 and 1,400 employees, about 98 per cent of the total, shifted to the new plant. The evidence suggests that workers' willingness to transfer depends not only upon distance but also upon efforts made by the employer and the union to induce movement.

The Building Trades

A different arrangement for providing employment for the older worker is used in many sections of the building and construction trades. In the building and construction industry, the unions are an important source for supplying labor, and jobs are retained for relatively short periods. The worker is seldom employed for an entire season or year; at least only a small percentage of those in the industry remain on a job on a permanent basis. The constant labor turnover and the influence of the union added to the skill of the great majority of the work force means that a union policy on the employment of the older worker would have some influence.

The building trades unions have for years been aware of the need to protect their older members against discrimination. As many building tradesmen are more than 45 years of age, and many are over 50 or even 60 years, the question of their ability to find jobs is very important to their organizations. In his report to the 1950 convention, President Harry Bates of the Bricklayers, Masons, and Plasterers' International Union of America called attention to the

> thousands of members sixty years of age or older who will not be employed by the contractors as long as younger men are available for the jobs. Therefore, it is the duty of the arbitration boards of our subordinate unions to have sections inserted in their collective bargaining agreements with their employers providing that on jobs where five men or less are employed one of these men shall be at least sixty years of age or over, and that for each additional five men employed on the

[19] Statement of Ford Motor Company by Malcolm Denise, *op. cit.* See also the study by Margaret S. Gordon and Ann H. McCorry, "Plant Relocation and Job Security A Case Study," *Industrial and Labor Relations Review,* (October 1957), pp. 13–36, which deals with the same issues.

operations at least one man to five shall be sixty years of age or over, as long as the older men are available and willing to work.[20]

In fact, clauses requiring the hiring of workers over a given age are found in some, but not all, of the locals of the Bricklayers' Union. The same is true of the locals representing plumbers, steamfitters, and lathers. Nevertheless, where clauses do not appear in local contracts, often "gentlemen's agreements" exist which require the contractors to accept workers above a certain age if they are available and if the contractor has hired a number of younger journeymen. Interviews with officials of the locals indicate that some feel worker clauses in contracts are unenforceable, while others rely upon greater experience to insure employment for older workers. In the Carpenter's Union, for example, contracts do not as a rule provide for older worker hiring. But the belief persists that older journeymen are generally competent mechanics and can hold their jobs by means of greater skill.

Similar to other building trades unions, the painters have a large number of members over 40 years of age. The International Union has recognized the need for making employment easier for the older or partially disabled worker by agreeing that members "whose age or physical condition debars them from earning the current rate of wages, shall be permitted to work for less but must first obtain permission of their local union before doing so." [21] Nevertheless, several locals take the view that older workers are better trained and more skilled than many younger workers. There does not appear to be much difficulty in placing older journeymen with contractors at going wage rates. If there were objections from an employer, however, the union would insist that older workers be hired.

The International Brotherhood of Electrical Workers operates in a number of industries. Originally organized as a union of workers in the building construction and utility industries, the organization has recruited workers in communication, railroad, and electrical manufacturing. In "building construction, the erection and maintenance of electric power and telephone lines, and to a lesser extent,

[20] *Sixteenth Biennial and Sixty-eighth Report of the President and Secretary of the Bricklayers, Masons, and Plasterers' International of America,* 1950, pp. 54Pr–55P. R.–55 P.R.

[21] *Constitution of the Brotherhood of Painters, Decorators and Paperhangers of America,* 1960, Section 107, p. 51.

in electric sign shops, electric motor and appliance repair shops, and similar establishments" the Electrical Workers' Union has established "a ratio between older and younger qualified and fully-trained, (i.e., 'journeymen') electricians employed in any shop or working crew." [22] These are called "50 and over" clauses, and require that in the employment of a given number of electricians, a given ratio must be over a specified age (if such workers are available). The contract between the National Electrical Association and the Martinez and Contra Costa County Local Union 302 specified that "on all jobs at any shop employing five or more journeymen, exclusive of foremen, if available, every fifth journeyman shall be fifty years of age or older." [23] The agreement between the New York Electrical Contractors Association and Local 3 specifies that one journeyman out of ten must be 55 years of age or older. The higher ratio of younger journeymen to those over 55 in Local 3 agreements is explained by the favorable retirement plan sponsored by the local.[24]

Utilities

The International Brotherhood of Electrical Workers has carried its concern for the older worker beyond its original jurisdiction. It is not able outside of building construction to compel the hiring of a ratio of workers above a given age to younger ones because the union does not control hiring. Nor would the pattern of employment enable the union to place its older members. Nevertheless, the Electrical Workers' Union has tried to devise arrangements to offer some employment protection to older workers. One of the reasons which in part accounts for the spread of concern for the older worker to other industries is the importance of the international office of the brotherhood, which must finally approve all agreements. In the contract between the Central Hudson Gas and Electric Company and IBEW Local Union #320, "Where an employee with ten years or more of continuous service is demoted because of physical disability rendering him unable to perform the work required of his job classification and is transferred to a job carrying a lower rate of pay than the existing rate of pay of the employee, the rate of pay

[22] James E. Noe (Research Director for International Brotherhood of Electrical Workers) in a letter October 20, 1960.

[23] Agreement effective June 1, 1959, to May 31, 1962.

[24] Interview with Mr. John Macay, Business Agent of Local 3, New York.

of such employee until retirement, death, resignation, or discharge for cause shall not be reduced below the following percentage of his existing pay at the time of such demotion"; [25]

Continuous Years of Service	*Adjustment in Pay*
10 years or more and up to 15	To not less than 80 per cent of existing pay
15 years or more and up to 20	To not less than 90 per cent of existing pay
20 years or more and up to 25	To not more than 95 per cent of existing pay
25 years or more	No reduction

There are a number of variations of these provisions. For example, the contract between the IBEW and the Concord Electric Company prescribes that a full-time employee partially incapacitated because of age or noncompensable disability will be placed in the highest classification in which he is able to perform the work assigned and in which there is an available opening. "The employee will be given a reasonable opportunity for training to fill an available opening." Employees who have completed between twenty and twenty-four years will receive 90 per cent of their former rates; twenty-five to twenty-nine calls for 95 per cent and thirty years or over, a full 100 per cent.[26]

A somewhat similar agreement is in force at the Detroit Edison Company except that the maximum rate on the new job, if it pays a lower rate than the one from which the employee has been transferred, is 90 per cent of the old rate for employees of thirty years or more of service.[27]

Similar provisions appear in other contracts, such as that with the Delaware Power and Light Company and the Portland General Electric Company. In each instance the contract specifies some minimum pay scale following upon job transfer due to factors related to age.

Conclusion

A variety of contractual provisions and a variety of informal practices are revealed by the evidence cited. Other evidence would disclose even greater variety. For example, the International Brother-

[25] Contract between Central Hudson Gas and Electric Company and IBEW Local Union #320 (Poughkeepsie, N. Y.)

[26] *Agreement between Concord Electric Company* [Concord, N.H.] *and Local Union #1034, IBEW.*

[27] *Contract between Detroit Edison Company and Local Union 17-IBEW,* covering employees in Overhead Lines Department, and Crane and Elevator Division, Detroit, Mich.

hood of Bookbinders does not have explicit rules, but locals are authorized to make concessions to protect older workers' jobs. Special rates for workers whose productivity has diminished have been negotiated in some cases. In other cases the locals are unable to effect such arrangements, or they are unwilling to do so because of reluctance among other members to accept a wage differential by age.

In addition, informal efforts on the part of other workers may protect the older worker. In interviews union officers were quite certain that under some circumstances other workers cooperate to take up the "slack" resulting from a loss of capacity by some older workers, thus concealing their decline in productivity. Of course, the extent of this and similar practices are extremely difficult if not impossible to document.

From the evidence examined here the greatest job protection is given in the building construction industry and the utilities industries in which employment conditions are basically different. The building trades require employees for short spans of time, and the unions, including the IBEW, are an important source of journeymen in their trades. Seniority systems are not workable, and no worker has the right (as one might under a seniority system) to bid for a particular job. Because of fluctuations in employment and the relatively short duration of jobs, the unions have been able, in cooperation with employers in the industry, to provide some employment for the older worker. The utilities, in contrast, provide steady employment for their work force, and they have been able to devise in many instances, in cooperation with their unions, provisions for protecting the older worker who is no longer able to perform satisfactorily. The IBEW appears to place more stress on protecting the older worker than most unions, including those in the building trades or its rivals in communications and electrical manufacturing. But it should be noted that utilities do not employ large numbers of workers; their capital to labor ratio is comparatively high and their returns are regulated.

The type of clause found in utility and building trades' contracts is not common in manufacturing contracts made by the IBEW. A typical example is the following: "Employees who have rendered faithful and honest service and who have become unable to handle heavy work to advantage will be given consideration for such light work as may be available from time to time where they shall be physically and mentally capable of performing such work, in which case such employee shall be paid the rate then being paid in the classification to which he is assigned." [28]

The agreement covering the position of the older worker made by the IBEW is close to those found in the contracts of other unions operating in the same areas. Because of the requirement that contracts be approved by the international union, it is likely that more emphasis will be placed upon the incorporation of such clauses than is found in other unions. It would appear that the greater consciousness of the building trades unions of the problems of the older worker induced in part by the age distribution of their memberships, and in part by the form of demand for labor, has influenced the stress placed upon this aspect of labor-management relations. Acceptance of such provisions by utility companies is easier than in many other kinds of enterprises because of the relatively small amount of labor employed and the regulation of prices charged for service. It may also be more difficult for utilities, because of the exigencies of public relations, to lay off older workers.

Examination of the provisions of contracts and the formal and informal arrangements found in union-management relations leads one to conclude that the nature of the demand for labor, the difficulty in developing interplant let alone intercompany transfers, and the resistance of younger workers to the introduction of exceptions which dilute their right to employment make it extremely difficult for many unions and firms to insist upon liberal transfer rules for older and partially incapacitated workers. The reluctance of workers to move is also an impediment. While the contributions of many unions and managements to more humane policies should not be minimized, it is necessary to recognize that much remains to be done to make the re-employment of the older worker easier.

In relation to the statistical analysis of Chapter 4, it is not surprising that a systematic pattern of union influence fails to emerge from the aggregated statistics on manufacturing employment. Satisfactory statistical data are available only for manufacturing industries, whereas union-negotiated employment contracts provide most job protection in building construction and utilities. There is considerably less protection in manufacturing. The contract clauses regarding job tenure vary from one manufacturing industry to another. Even within a given industry there is variation

[28] *Killark Manufacturing Company* [St. Louis, Miss.] *and Local Union 1-IBEW*, effective May 1, 1959 to April 30, 1961.

among firms.

As a summary of the industry-oriented study, three main conclusions are suggested by the statistical data and union-employer practices and attitudes. First, the demand for older workers is weak as compared to the demand for workers in the intermediate or younger age groups. Underlying this weak demand are an inverse relationship between productivity and age beyond the age of 45 or 50, relatively high supplementary employment costs of hiring older workers (both indirect costs such as damage to the morale of the younger workers and direct monetary costs such as pensions and workmen's compensation), and substitution of female labor to a greater extent for older males. There are individual exceptions to this behavior of course. But as a general rule business firms, in seeking to maximize profits, will strive to avoid policies that contribute to inefficiency. Unless restricted by contract provisions by unions, they hire the most productive labor obtainable at the price that has to be paid. As a consequence, whenever relatively young males are available in the job market, or females in cases where the type of work is appropriate, they are preferred by employers.

Second, on the supply side of the labor market older workers are significantly less mobile than their younger contemporaries. Movement from farms to higher paying nonfarm jobs within a state is dominated by the younger members of the labor force. The quantitatively more important labor movements in response to higher income—from one manufacturing industry to another and between manufacturing and service employments within a state—are also inversely related to age. Given that industry demand for older workers is weaker than the demand for younger workers, growth of the entire economy and the expansion of industrial production should increase the total demand for labor at all age levels. Although relatively less hiring of older workers occurs, expanded employment and income opportunities are created. However, the older a worker is the less responsive he is to making the changes necessary to take advantage of these opportunities. As a consequence, the more slowly growing and lower income industrial sectors tend to retain the oldest members of their work force, thus contributing to a widening of the income gap between the oldest workers in the labor force and those in the intermediate age category.

Third, labor unions act in a variety of ways to affect both the demand for and the supply of labor of different ages. Through collective bargaining unions do influence labor demand on the part of employers. Negotiated employment contracts contain clauses regarding job tenure, seniority privileges, relocation in the event of displacement, etc. To the extent that they organize and provide work crews in the skilled trades, supervise hiring halls, or by other means control job applicants, labor unions also affect the supply of labor to industries. Several means have been utilized to protect the jobs of older workers and to attempt to force their re-employment. However, the types of protection are so diverse and vary in effectiveness to such extent that unions have not been able to ameliorate on a broad scale the economic problems faced by the oldest members of the active labor force.

PART III

Age and Geographic Mobility

CHAPTER SEVEN

Factors Affecting Mobility by Age

DECISIONS to migrate geographically are long-run investment decisions. There are many ways in which a person can invest in himself, thus treating his embodied labor services as a stock of human capital. Education is one obvious example. By an expenditure in the present, a person's productivity and lifetime earnings are raised. Geographic migration is likewise an investment, especially long-distance moves, entailing a cost in the present and presumably an expanded return over the remainder of the worker's lifetime. The ability and willingness to migrate in response to higher earnings in other regions of the economy is one determinant of income distribution. If ability and willingness differ among age groups, then the distribution of income according to age is also partly determined by geographic mobility.

The analysis of Chapter 4 assumes that interstate migration is zero. Because a cross-section sample was utilized, the supply of labor to an industry within a state at a given point in time was taken as dependent upon the available quantity of labor within the state. This quantity is, of course, affected by any interstate migration that has occurred prior to that point in time. Although the supply equations showed differential labor mobility by age among manufacturing industries within a state and between manufacturing and nonmanufacturing within a state, these equations give no indication of whether interstate migration also differs among age groups.

The present section is devoted to interregional labor migration in order to determine the effect of age upon the willingness to move geographically in response to better employment opportunities in other regions of the economy. Given that migration does occur, and given the age structure of the migration flows, the impact of these flows upon the age composition of the labor force in each region is also investigated.

Until quite recently multiregional migration data have been sparse, especially data that cross classify migrants by age, sex, color, etc. Data recorded in the 1950 Census of Population and, in much more detail, in the 1960 Census of Population reveal that migrants move simultaneously in both directions between any pair of regions. That is, gross migration in both directions greatly exceeds the net figure, regardless of whether the net flow is positive or negative. Moreover, these migrants display great variety with respect to economic and demographic characteristics. But aside from data availability there are many theoretical problems that have contributed to a scarcity of multiregional migration analyses:

(1) For any given region, outmigration to several other regions is possible. And in each of these other regions employment in several industries is possible.

(2) Migration from several industries in a given region is possible, and intraregional movement to any of a number of other industries within the region is possible.

(3) Labor inputs, even if regarded as homogeneous in their capacity as factors of production, are not homogeneous with respect to other determinants of migration.

(4) Decisions to migrate are influenced by nonpecuniary factors that are not subject to direct measurement.

A theoretical discussion of labor migration that takes account of these difficulties [1] is followed by an empirical test of the hypotheses inferred from the theory and an exploration of the migration statistics. The focus throughout is upon age as a determinant of migration.

Expected Gross Returns from Migration

Nonpecuniary forces affecting migration are treated as costs of migrating out of a given region. Net pecuniary returns are defined

[1] A more systematic theoretical structure that takes account of occupational differences, varying industry mixes among regions, and interrelated capital and labor movements is presented in M. J. Brennan, "A More General Theory of Resource Migration," pp. 45–64, in M. J. Brennan (ed.), *Patterns of Market Behavior* (Providence, R.I.: Brown University Press, 1965).

as gross returns minus pecuniary costs. Since migration decisions are long-run investment decisions, gross returns are construed as comparative regional expected income streams. In general, let region i ($i = 1, 2, \ldots, I$) be a region in which expectations are formed, and let region j ($j = 1, 2, \ldots, I$) be a region about which expectations are formed. Thus migration from i to j is being considered.

The complexity of simultaneous multiregional and multiindustrial migration can be reduced to manageable proportions by focusing upon a single measure of returns from migration between any two regions i and j. Gross returns are defined as the value of a future income stretching from the present to the working horizon from employment in j as compared to such a future income in i. Let $y_j(t)$ denote real income in year t expected from employment in region j, common to all workers regardless of the region of present location. The present value for a worker of age a is

$$(1) \qquad y_j(a) = \sum_{t=1}^{A-a} \frac{y_j(t)}{(1+d)^t}$$

where 1 represents the current year, A the terminal age of life expectancy, and $(1/1+d)$ the appropriate discount rate. The discount rate and life expectancy are assumed identical for all individuals. If in addition the expected income at (hypothetical) age a is the same for all workers, regardless of actual age, then the present value will differ among workers only with respect to age differences. Thus age is an important determinant of returns from migration. For the shorter is a worker's time horizon, the smaller is the interval over which he can enjoy greater income (i.e., the smaller is the present value).

The discounting of future income allows for differences among regions in the time patterns of earnings which are not reflected in an alternative definition of expected returns such as average lifetime earnings. It will be shown in the empirical application that this present value can be estimated in such a way that unemployment by age in region j is also taken into consideration.

The second component of gross returns from migration—the present value of the expected income stream from employment in i, $y_i(a)$—is similarly defined. Finally, the expected gross return for migration of an individual of age a from i to j is the difference

$$(2) \qquad g_{ij}(a) = y_j(a) - y_i(a).$$

It follows that there will be a separate expected gross return for each age group, where together these age groups comprise the labor force in region i. On the basis of the relation between income expectations and age, it was seen that $y_j(a)$ varies inversely with age. Likewise, $y_i(a)$ will vary inversely with a. But $g_{ij}(a)$ need not. For with a given difference in the average expected lifetime earnings between two regions, a radical difference between the time patterns of earnings could operate to produce a positive correlation between $g_{ij}(a)$ and a. For example, income streams in j and i, such that expected income at higher ages is sufficiently greater in j, while expected income at lower ages is sufficiently greater in i, tend to generate this result. As a consequence, $g_{ij}(a)$ can vary directly with a in principle. However, this outcome is virtually impossible, so we may be assured that $g_{ij}(a)$ will be negatively, though imperfectly, correlated with a. The greater is age, the smaller are expected returns to migration.

Pecuniary Costs and Net Returns

The pecuniary costs of labor migration include:

(1) personal transportation cost of the worker,
(2) cost of transporting his dependents,
(3) cost of transporting movable personal property plus any loss from sale of nonmovable property,
(4) income forgone during the period of migration.

Needless to say, precise measurement of cost is difficult, and any estimate used must be arbitrary to more or less degree. Most of the components of cost depend upon geographic relocation of the household, whereas employment either within region i or within region j may occur at any one of several geographic points. In addition, intraregional migration may entail zero or nonzero cost, depending upon whether or not the household must relocate. This difficulty is less formidable than it appears, however. For only between regions for which $g_{ij}(a)$ is of very small positive magnitude are costs likely to play an important role as a pecuniary determinant of migration. And in these instances an "average" cost will likely suffice to predict the direction of migration. In all other cases expected gross returns will be of much greater magnitude than cost, and so will constitute the principal component of net pecuniary return.

There are three cost comparisons that a potential migrant will consider: (1) the cost of migrating interregionally, (2) the cost of migrating intraregionally, and (3) the zero cost of not migrating. For simplicity we shall assume the cost of intraregional migration is zero, and let $c_{ij}(a)$ denote the cost of migration from i to j by a potential migrant of age a. Between any two regions this cost will be a constant for a worker of age a. While personal transportation cost may be taken at the same for all workers regardless of age, the other components of cost are likely to be correlated (though, again, not perfectly correlated) with age. To the extent that number of dependents, property holdings, and present income are related to age, so will cost between any two regions be related to age.

The *net* expected pecuniary return from migration, r_{ij}, is gross return minus total cost. Thus, for a worker of age a in region i, contemplating migration to region j, the net expected return is

$$r_{ij}(a) = g_{ij}(a) - c_{ij}(a) \tag{3}$$

The entire labor force in region i can be classified into a set of age groups, for each of which there exists an $r_{ij}(a)$. Because $g_{ij}(a)$ tends to vary inversely with a, and $c_{ij}(a)$ is likely to vary directly with a, it is to be expected that one would find a negative correlation between $r_{ij}(a)$ and a.

Nonpecuniary Determinants of Migration

Nonpecuniary factors affecting migration have presented a stumbling block to economic analysis. The usual approach is unsatisfactory, namely to take account only of pecuniary returns and costs, and then to assume the unexplained residuals in migration patterns are *somehow* determined by nonpecuniary factors. Though not subject to direct measurement, nonpecuniary factors can be treated more systematically.

Aside from monetary returns expected in region j, the willingness to migrate is affected by climate, urban versus rural living, differences in community culture, etc. On the cost side there are nonpecuniary costs connected with migration: the divorce of established social and family ties, the educational displacement of children—in general, a type of inertia factor. For this reason one cannot assume that those who do migrate will migrate to the region of highest expected net pecuniary return, or that all those with positive expected net returns will even migrate.

Certain plausible assumptions about the effects of these forces can be made, however. On the returns side, $r_{ij}(a)$ tends to vary inversely with age for all j, and age is a restraining factor in the willingness to migrate. For greater age normally implies more firmly established community ties with relatives and friends. In addition, greater age often implies seniority rights in present employment, and the greater security provided by these rights operates to discourage migration. On the cost side, personal and real property holdings are usually associated with community status; they also entail higher pecuniary costs of migration. Likewise, as a rule, the greater the number of dependent children, the more a household is involved in the activities of the community, and the greater is the pecuniary cost of transporting dependents. It follows that more advanced age, a larger number of dependents, and greater property holdings act to lower gross pecuniary returns and/or raise pecuniary costs, thus reducing net pecuniary returns to outmigration. These characteristics may be taken as proxies for the unobservable psychological and cultural factors affecting migration. Such an argument simply reflects the common-sense observation that, given the existence of any positive pecuniary returns to migration, younger persons with more adventurous spirits, fewer dependents, and fewer property holdings tend to migrate most readily. And it is precisely these groups which have the highest expected gross returns and the lowest total cost. This is, nevertheless, no more than a tendency, so allowance must be made for exceptions.

Since our emphasis is upon age, the labor force in region i can be divided into a set of, say, Q expected return classes and ordered from the largest to the smallest median expected return $r_{ij}(a)$. The number of workers in each class is then known. Because of the relationship between $r_{ij}(a)$ and a already noted, this constitutes an (imperfect) ordering by age from the youngest to the oldest, but expressed in terms of expected net pecuniary returns.

Also, the same labor force can be ranked into any number of migration classes. Suppose there are S migration classes, a general class being denoted by s $(s = 1, 2, \ldots, S)$ such that all members of class s migrate before any member of class $s + 1$. Then the return classes can be mapped into the migration classes. If, on the basis of the reasoning presented above, one assumes that the probability of migrating is greater the larger is the expected return, the transformation can be performed [2] such that the first class to migrate is comprised of the largest percentage of the highest return group, a smaller percentage of the next highest, and so on to the smallest percentage of the lowest return group. The pattern swings as the transformation process continues, until the final migration class (the last class to migrate out) consists of the smallest percentage of the highest return group and the largest percentage of the lowest return group.

It follows that the number in each migration class and the age structure of that class are determined. The first workers to migrate (the most probable outmigrants) do not consist entirely of younger workers. But these most probable migrants have the greatest proportion of younger workers, just as the least probable migrants have the greatest proportion of older workers. It also follows that a pecuniary return is computed for each migration class—a weighted average of the $r_{ij}(a)$'s falling into that migration class. Letting $r_{ij}(s)$ denote this return, then $r_{ij}(s) > r_{ij}(s+1)$ for all s.

A function $R_{ij}(M_{ij})$ can be formed, where M_{ij} denotes the total migration *ordered by migration classes* and R_{ij} represents the *cumulative* total expected returns from migration. R_{ij} is seen to be composed of a series of linear segments, one corresponding to each class s. If no migration class has a positive expected return, outmigration shall be defined as zero. With at least one class (the first to migrate) having a positive expected return, as migration proceeds R_{ij} will increase at a decreasing rate, reach a maximum, and then decline.

Equilibrium Migration Flows

For I regions let the expected return from employment in a given region be the same for a worker of age a regardless of whether he is located in that region or in any other region. Then the expected gross pecuniary return from migration differs only with respect to sign for workers of age a in region i as compared to workers of age a in region j:

$$g_{ij}(a) = -g_{ji}(a), \qquad i, j = 1, 2, \ldots, I.$$

[2] Transformation of return classes into migration classes can be based upon probability theory. See *Ibid.*, pp. 52–57.

But it does not follow that $r_{ij}(a) = -r_{ji}(a)$. In particular, it is possible that

$$r_{ij}(a_1) > 0 \text{ and } r_{ji}(a_2) > 0$$

even if $a_1 = a_2$, so that

$$r_{ij}(s) > 0 \text{ and } r_{ji}(s) > 0$$

for $s = 1$. This possibility of positive expected returns for at least one migration class in both regions may be due to unequal costs of migration. For only if workers have the same foregone income during migration, the same number of dependents, and the same property holdings will their costs of migration between two regions be identical. Or if the costs are identical for each a, the time patterns of expected returns could be such that for some age group in each region (not the same age group in the two regions) a positive return is obtained.

Where returns are positive, it is assumed outmigration from i to j proceeds up to the point at which the expected net return *per worker* is zero. In terms of the cumulative function, R_{ij}, this is the horizontal linear segment, or the maximum of R_{ij}. For I regions let R_{ij} be approximated by a smooth unimodal function, and let the equilibrium flow of gross outmigration be represented by $\overline{M}_{ij}$. Then the general equilibrium conditions may be written

$$(4) \qquad \frac{dR_{ij}}{dM_{ij}} \leq 0; \frac{dR_{ji}}{dM_{ji}} \leq 0, \qquad i, j = 1, 2, \ldots, I, \quad i \neq j.$$

These equations can be solved to obtain $\overline{M}_{ij}$ and $\overline{M}_{ji}$ for all i and j, $i \neq j$; thus net migration flows are given as $\overline{M}_{ij} - \overline{M}_{ji}$. For $\overline{M}_{ij} = 0$ the inequality on the left holds, while for $\overline{M}_{ij} > 0$ the equality on the left holds. Likewise, for $\overline{M}_{ji} = 0$ the inequality on the right holds, and for $\overline{M}_{ji} > 0$ the equality on the right holds.

It should be noted that the model permits $\overline{M}_{ij} > 0$ and $M_{ji} > 0$ simultaneously. Gross migration can move in both directions between any pair of regions. Their magnitudes depend mostly upon regional industrial composition, distances among regions, and the age distributions of regional labor forces. The mapping of return classes into migration classes also yields predictions of the age structure of migrants (in terms of percentages of migrants in each age category) for each pair of regions.

Age: Cause and Effect

The theoretical migration model predicts the magnitudes of labor migration flows among regions and the age structure of these flows. Age is an important causal factor explaining the amount of migration and the composition of the labor transfers among regions of the economy. This composition, in particular the age distribution of migrants, in turn has an effect upon the characteristics of the labor force in the regions of net inmigration and the regions of net outmigration. In the theory of migration three factors explain how age affects the willingness or ability to migrate.

First, the migration decision is regarded as a long-run investment decision based in part upon the financial rewards (gross returns) to be gained by undertaking relocation. These rewards stretch over the remaining employment life of a worker. As a consequence, greater age, i.e., a shorter working horizon, acts to reduce the gross return to migration. For example, suppose two workers are identical in every respect but age. The younger worker has thirty years of future working life, whereas the older worker has only ten years. Both are located in Region A, where (for simplicity) assume each can expect to earn 5,000 dollars per year for the remainder of his working life. However, from employment in Region B each can expect to earn 6,000 dollars per year. The younger worker, with thirty remaining years of employment, has an undiscounted present value of future earnings amounting to 150,000 dollars in Region A and 180,000 dollars in Region B. His gross pecuniary return to migration from A to B is the difference of 30,000 dollars. The older worker, with only ten working years remaining, expects to earn 50,000 dollars in Region A and 60,000 dollars in Region B. His gross return to migration is only 10,000 dollars.

Thus, even if two workers are identical in productivity, educational attainment, etc., the pure effect of greater age operates to reduce the gross monetary returns to regional migration. This assumes the two workers have an equal probability of finding employment in the region to which they might migrate. But the results in Part II indicate that older workers face a difficult re-employment situation that would be applicable to the search for employment in the regions to which they migrate. When the gross returns are weighted by these differential probabilities of finding employment in Region B, the gap between their gross returns to migration is enlarged.

Second, the monetary costs of migration are likely to be larger for older than for younger members of the labor force. In the theoretical formulation, costs depend upon number of dependents and holdings of personal property. For the transportation of each entails a cost. Although the relationship between age and number of dependents and/or amount of personal property to be transported is not perfect, it has been argued that there is an imperfect positive correlation between these cost items and age of the worker. Therefore, the cost of migration tends to increase with more advanced age. Net monetary returns to migration are defined as gross returns minus the cost of movement. If this cost is higher for an older than for a younger worker, the differential between their net returns to migration becomes even greater.

Third, the nonpecuniary constraints upon migration increase with age. Unlike economic or pecuniary returns, the many psychological and cultural factors that affect the willingness to migrate cannot be measured directly. However, the migration theory postulates the hypothesis that these diverse factors operate to weaken mobility as age increases. Attachments to the community and to a fixed way of life are stronger in the case of older, married workers with children in the intermediate school age than in the case of younger, married or unmarried workers whose children (if any) are less likely to have established school ties.

Of course such an assertion is probabilistic rather than certain. There are exceptions; it cannot be said that each older individual is rendered less mobile than any one young person. In the formal language of the model it is said that the probability of migrating, given pecuniary returns, declines as age increases. In this sense, the postulate of a probability at each age is a device for taking into account the unobservable nonpecuniary forces affecting migration. Statement of the hypothesis in this form is similar to probabilistic statements in the physical sciences. For example, the behavior of each single particle cannot be expressed without some random component, even though the over-all pattern of the entire set of particles can be predicted. When these probabilities for each age group are used to define migration classes and to weight the pecuniary returns to each class, the effect is to predict declining willingness to migrate as age increases due to a complex of nonpecuniary variables.

For these three reasons, the model predicts that migrants will move in the direction of greater expected lifetime earnings. But among those who do migrate to take advantage of higher earnings, the age composition will be such that fewer older workers move. The percentage of total migrants falling in each age class decreases as the age level of the class increases.

Age is not only a causal factor in the willingness or ability to migrate. The age structure of migration flows also exerts an effect upon the average age of the labor force in each region. If workers move from depressed to prosperous areas, and if it is the young who are most mobile, then these young migrants leave behind a pool of older labor. Migration adds a greater percentage of young workers to the labor force of already prosperous regions, thereby acting to reduce the average age of the work force in those regions. The less mobile older workers operate to raise the average age of the work force in low income or depressed areas.

Age is a proxy for other characteristics. As pointed out in Part I, educational attainment declines with more advanced age. In Part II it was indicated that older workers tend to be less flexible and adaptable to changing technology (less productive). Thus the quality of the labor force in each region is affected by the age structure of migration. Regions of high growth and low unemployment experience an improvement in the quality of their work forces. At the same time, regions of low growth or high unemployment experience a deterioration in the quality of their work forces. The impact of migration is to stimulate greater growth in faster growing regions and retard the relatively slow growth rate in depressed regions of the economy. If these forces are at work, the distribution of income by age for the economy as a whole is attributable in part to the pattern of geographic migration within the economy.

Economic theory has traditionally predicted that labor moves from low-wage to high-wages areas. The effect is to increase the supply of labor in high-wage areas and reduce the supply of labor in low-wage areas. Assuming the demand for labor is held constant in each area, the effect of migration is to equalize wage rates and income per worker among regions. The present analysis comes to a different conclusion, however. With labor demand given, the changes in labor supply do not operate to equalize incomes. The direct application of traditional price theory to the problem of migration implicity assumes that all labor is homogeneous. If, on the other hand, it is the most productive workers who migrate to high-wage areas and the least productive who remain in the low-wage areas, then the average wage rate rises in the high-wage areas and falls in the low-wage areas. Differences in wages and earnings per worker are widened rather than narrowed by migration.

Capital might move into the low-wage areas as firms seek to take advantage of low-wage costs. This would operate to raise employment and income *if* all labor were homogeneous. But since the quality of the labor force is deteriorating, such a labor force is not attractive to employers. Certainly the effect of migration upon the age of the labor force will restrict entry of capital into these areas. We have already seen that firms are reluctant to hire older workers. Unless the effect of migration upon the age structure of the labor force is more than offset by other forces, expanding firms will not be attracted to low-wage regions.

CHAPTER EIGHT

The Migration Evidence

WITH THE AID of some simplifying assumptions, which are necessary for the empirical application, it is possible to test the hypotheses of Chapter 7. The primary source of statistics on returns to migration and of the migration figures themselves is the 1960 Census of Population. In the 1950 census migrants were classified by residence in 1949 and residence in 1950. By cross-classifying former and present residence according to the nine census divisions, a measure of the number of migrants having moved in each direction between each pair of divisions was recorded. This type of tabulation had not been undertaken prior to the 1950 census. However, no breakdown by age was given. The 1960 Census of Population went a step further. Residence in 1955 and residence in 1960 is recorded according to census division, and the number of migrants is broken down by age groups. Therefore, for the first time it is possible to obtain data on the direction and magnitude of migration for different ages.

The statistical evidence from the Census of Population is used to compare the predicted migration magnitudes against actual migration. More important for our purposes, the predicted age structure of migration flows is testable against the facts. Direct application of the theory uses the census division as a definition of a region, but additional evidence utilizing a narrower definition of a region is also presented.

Predicted and Actual Migration

The theory predicts that labor will migrate predominantly from regions of relatively low expected returns to regions of high expected returns. By inserting quantitative gross returns and costs, the theoretical mechanism estimates the magnitude of migration flows and the age composition of each flow.

Expected gross income by age, assumed common to all workers, was approximated for each of nine census divisions by means of age-income profiles for males adjusted by a trend factor. The expected income at each age was computed for the 1960 Census of Population as the following weighted average:

$$\text{Income at age } a = \left\{\frac{\text{Number of males age } a \text{ employed}}{\text{Male labor force age } a} \text{X median Income for males age } a\right\} + \left\{\frac{\text{Number of males age } a \text{ unemployed}}{\text{male labor force age } a} \text{X zero}\right\}$$

Thus unemployment in each age group as well as earnings of those employed is allowed to affect expected gross returns in each division. The resulting age-income profile at a point in time was adjusted by a 40-year linear trend of median income in each division in order to reflect more closely the expected future movements over time. Using the long-term government bond rate as d in equation (1), setting $A = 75$, and setting a as the median age in each age group, a present value for each age group was computed. The six age groups are 20–24, 25–34, 35–44, 45–54, and 65–74.

Estimated cost of transportation per person was related to the distance from the approximate geographic center of one division to another, using bus fare schedules. Transportation cost for a worker varies with the number of his dependents. For each division the Census of Population gives the relation between age and marital status (including dependents), thus permitting the computation of transportation cost per worker in each age group if such a worker were to migrate to any other division. It was assumed that all property is moved by moving companies, the cost being derived from the average cost per mile reported by a government publication [1] with no distinction by age. To these cost items was added one day's income foregone for each 400 miles of movement. This foregone income for each age group is, of course, the median income in the

[1] *The Cost of Geographic Mobility*, Area Redevelopment Administration, U.S. Department of Commerce (Washington, D. C., 1964).

division of potential outmigration.

Finally, for the six age groups, the net return (present value minus cost per worker) was computed. The transformation adopted to map the net return classes into six migration classes is the following:

Migration	*Net Return Class*					
Class	*1*	*2*	*3*	*4*	*5*	*6*
1	0.40	0.25	0.15	0.08	0.04	0.02
2	0.30	0.35	0.20	0.12	0.06	0.05
3	0.15	0.20	0.30	0.15	0.12	0.08
4	0.08	0.10	0.20	0.30	0.20	0.15
5	0.05	0.07	0.10	0.20	0.35	0.30
6	0.02	0.03	0.05	0.15	0.23	0.40
Total	1.00	1.00	1.00	1.00	1.00	1.00

Return class 1 has a larger net pecuniary return than 2, 2 greater than 3, etc. Likewise, migration class 1 migrates out before 2, 2 before 3, etc. Reading the first column, this means 40 per cent of the *number* in return class 1 were assigned to migration class 1, 30 per cent to migration class 2, 15 per cent to 3, and so on. The same interpretation is given to each other column, the total of each column adding to 100 per cent to exhaust the number in each return class and thus the labor force. The expected net return to a *migration class* (not a return class) is obtained by horizontal interpretation. The return per worker in migration class 1 equals 40 per cent of the return for return class 1, plus 25 per cent of the return for return class 2, etc. That is, the return to each migration class is a weighted average of the returns per worker assigned to that class. Because of this simplified transformation, the weights do not sum to unity, but it does follow that the return per worker in migration class 1 exceeds that in 2, 2 exceeds 3, etc.

Ordering the returns to migration classes in descending order, and picking the midpoint of the greatest *cumulative* return to determine predicted total migration, is an approximation to the solution of equations (4). Actual migration among census divisions and predicted migration (shown in parentheses) are presented in Table 8–1.

The migration figures include both males and females 20–74 years of age, but only those born outside the division of inmigration in order to omit returnees whose prior migration was temporary. Uti-

Table 8–1. ACTUAL AND PREDICTED MIGRATION AMONG CENSUS DIVISIONS, 1955–1960
(THOUSANDS OF MIGRANTS BORN OUTSIDE THE DIVISION OF 1960 RESIDENCE, AGED 20–74)

From	*To (1960 residence)*								
(1955 residence)	*New England*	*Middle Atlantic*	*East North Central*	*West North Central*	*South Atlantic*	*East South Central*	*West South Central*	*Mountain*	*Pacific*
New England		72.8 (68.4)	28.5 (36.6)	9.0 (21.8)	95.7 (13.1)	6.6 (0.0)	14.0 (21.4)	13.6 (18.7)	68.6 (78.8)
Middle Atlantic	109.2 (60.0)		133.5 (166.9)	24.9 (32.6)	359.7 (60.1)	24.6 (16.6)	40.1 (50.8)	43.4 (54.7)	177.0 (238.3)
East-North Central	33.5 (21.2)	90.6 (71.0)		111.7 (87.3)	282.7 (47.6)	51.6 (38.5)	70.9 (88.1)	102.8 (100.4)	293.0 (209.3)
West-North Central	11.7 (7.1)	23.1 (30.4)	120.4 (136.5)		64.7 (8.4)	17.0 (11.7)	67.7 (88.1)	119.8 (131.9)	222.8 (186.9)
South Atlantic	45.3 (34.4)	156.6 (106.1)	127.8 (146.0)	37.2 (53.3)		73.2 (60.0)	66.2 (84.5)	38.4 (53.9)	138.3 (179.6)
East-South Central	8.9 (14.8)	25.1 (36.4)	175.7 (214.2)	24.7 (24.0)	152.2 (22.0)		64.2 (77.6)	17.1 (29.6)	57.1 (111.8)
West-South Central	11.4 (8.3)	23.3 (18.3)	61.6 (67.9)	63.9 (72.4)	73.4 (23.1)	39.6 (6.1)		98.8 (80.3)	195.0 (135.5)
Mountain	6.9 (0.0)	10.3 (17.1)	20.9 (34.0)	25.5 (28.7)	25.6 (0.0)	6.7 (0.0)	33.8 (32.0)		197.5 (261.7)
Pacific	18.2 (13.0)	32.3 (21.1)	44.1 (49.7)	31.3 (28.3)	74.6 (14.7)	14.7 (0.0)	46.7 (49.0)	124.4 (86.2)	

Source: Table 2, *Lifetime and Recent Migration*, Subject Report PC (2), 2D, U.S. Census of Population, 1960.

Table 8–2. AGE COMPOSITION OF MIGRANTS, 1955–1960
(PERCENTAGE OF ALL MIGRANTS 25–74 YEARS OF AGE)

From	*To*								
	New England	*Middle Atlantic*	*East North Central*	*West North Central*	*South Atlantic*	*East South Central*	*West South Central*	*Mountain*	*Pacific*
New England									
25–44		74.9	79.5	82.2	55.4	81.0	84.5	73.0	74.1
45–64		20.1	18.1	14.5	28.8	14.3	11.9	21.0	20.3
Mid. Atlantic									
25–44	70.3		75.7	79.0	50.8	76.5	75.7	67.9	68.5
45–64	23.2		19.9	16.8	32.1	18.8	19.0	24.9	24.4
East-North Central									
25–44	79.1	75.5		73.4	48.8	72.4	71.2	64.7	68.0
45–64	17.1	20.6		21.7	32.3	22.5	20.8	26.7	23.9
West-North Central									
25–44	84.3	79.6	75.8		63.9	75.5	70.5	68.2	68.3
45–64	14.3	16.8	20.2		25.2	21.2	22.4	25.4	24.0
South Atlantic									
25–44	82.1	75.7	77.6	83.5		78.3	82.1	77.9	80.7
45–64	14.8	21.1	18.9	14.1		18.0	15.0	18.7	16.2
East-South Central									
25–44	84.3	79.3	74.9	77.4	72.8		75.9	75.0	77.8
45–64	13.7	17.7	21.8	19.3	22.7		20.4	21.8	18.8
West-South Central									
25–44	88.5	82.5	78.8	77.0	79.2	78.9		73.3	74.9
45–64	10.3	15.2	18.4	19.6	17.6	18.1		23.6	21.8
Mountain									
25–44	87.5	81.6	78.3	77.0	77.0	81.6	74.7		69.0
45–64	10.4	15.8	17.9	19.3	18.1	16.3	20.5		25.5
Pacific									
25–44	86.2	77.4	78.3	78.0	78.5	83.4	76.3	66.5	
45–64	11.7	18.9	17.4	17.3	17.0	13.9	18.6	27.4	

Source: Table 2, *Lifetime and Recent Migration*, Subject Report PC (2), 2D, U.S. Census of Population, 1960.

lizing the available data, the model is not as sensitive as one might hope. However, considering (1) that pecuniary returns were computed from male income while the labor force in a division and migration had to be defined to include both males and females, (2) that no breakdown by occupation is available in multiregional migration data, and (3) that industry mix varies among divisions, the theory does predict migration reasonably well. The poor results for inmigration to the South Atlantic, especially Florida, probably should be ignored. Ignoring the South Atlantic immigrants, the standard error of prediction (square root of the ratio of squared errors to the number of predictions) is 29.4 thousands of migrants. More revealing, the average percentage error (difference between predicted and actual as a per cent of actual migration) is 35.85 per cent. This can be interpreted to mean that the theory explains about 64 per cent of observed migration—not at all a disreputable showing for the limited form of empirical returns and costs, and the simplified transformation method adopted.

The age structure of each migration flow is shown in Table 8-2. The data were combined into two age groups (25–44 and 45–64) for clarity of presentation, and the figures are percentages of the total number of migrants 25–74 years of age. Once more ignoring immigrants to the South Atlantic, the 25–44 age group constitutes from 65 to 87 per cent of all migrants, typically about 78 per cent. The 45–64 age group ranges from 10 to 27 per cent of all migrants, generally about 18 per cent. The extremely small percentage of migrants 65–74 years of age can be seen from the difference between 100 per cent and the sum of the percentages for the other two groups.

To avoid cluttering the table, the predicted age percentages have not been entered. It should be pointed out, however, that the theory does a better job of predicting age structure than it does of predicting the magnitudes of total migration. The 25–44 age group percentage is consistently underestimated, and the 45–64 percentage is overestimated—traceable, no doubt, to the somewhat arbitrary transformation method used. But the standard error of prediction is only about 7 per cent for each age group; the predicted percentages are typically 71 and 25 for the 25–44 age group and the 45–64 age group respectively.

Greater age appears as a severe constraint on geographic mobility regardless of the direction or distance of movement among census divisions. The correlation between median age for the five (rather than two) age groups and the percentage of all migrants falling in the age group is —0.8595 for those born outside the division of 1960 residence and —0.8736 for all migrants 25 years of age or more (those born within plus those born outside the division of 1960 residence). Since the theory infers that migrants move predominantly from relatively low to relatively high net return areas, the older a worker is the less likely he is to move in response to better employment opportunities elsewhere.

Some Further Evidence

It might be thought that the degree of aggregation in the data gives a distorted picture of the effect of age upon migration. Census divisions are large and hardly homogeneous with respect to subregions within them. Average returns and costs may well miss the true pecuniary incentives that vary widely within a division. In addition, migration data included both males and females with no distinction other than age. Other characteristics, such as color and sex, may be correlated with age and operate to produce the observed patterns.

To account for these factors Table 8-3 presents two sets of correlation coefficients. The first set refers to persons who migrated to a different state over the five-year interval. Using yearly ages from 25–84 inclusive (not grouping the ages), the number of migrants of each age was correlated with years of age. Separate correlations were run for males and females by color. All of the coefficients are negative, very large, and statistically significant at the 1 per cent level.

Table 8–3. CORRELATIONS BETWEEN AGE AND MIGRATION

1. Persons Who Moved to a Different State	
White Males	—0.9767
Nonwhite Males	—0.8319
White Females	—0.9001
Nonwhite Females	—0.8849
2. Heads of Households Who Moved to a Noncontiguous State	
Total Males	—0.7810
Nonwhite Males	—0.6285
Total Females	—0.8352
Nonwhite Females	—0.6711

Source: Tables 3 and 8, *Mobility for States and State Economic Areas,* Subject Report PC (2), 2 B, U.S. Census of Population, 1960.

The second set of correlations refers to heads of households who migrated to noncontiguous states. The age groups are 25–29, 30–34, 35–44, 45–64, and 65 and over. Median age was defined as 70 for the last open-ended category, and median age was correlated with migration for total and nonwhite males and females. Because of the unequal age spreads and unequal numbers in each age group, migration was measured as the ratio of migrants to the total population of that age group. The somewhat poorer correlations as compared to the first set are due in part at least to the age groupings. Although nonwhite heads of households appear to be less affected by age than whites (other factors play a more important role than they do for whites) all correlations are negative and statistically significant at the 5 per cent level.

To narrow the geographic definition of a region even further and to shed light upon the effect of migration on per capita income differentials among regions, correlations were also run for state economic areas. Fifteen metropolitan standard economic areas with the highest unemployment rates in 1960 and fifteen with the lowest unemployment rates were chosen. The high unemployment areas included seven that have been classified as depressed areas on the basis of chronic high unemployment. Also, fifteen standard economic areas with the lowest per capita incomes and fifteen with the highest per capita incomes were chosen. The age groups are 20–24, 25–29, 30–34, 35–39, 40–44, 45–54, and 55–64. Number of *out-migrants* as a percentage of the population in that age group was correlated with median age for low income areas and high unemployment areas. As expected, the coefficients were negative and large: —0.82 and —0.88 for low income and high unemployment respectively. Of course, the number of *inmigrants* in low unemployment and high income areas likewise showed negative coefficients, but somewhat smaller: —0.76 and —0.69 respectively.

Younger workers are the first to move from depressed to prosperous areas, leaving behind a pool of older workers. If, as Chapter 7 has suggested, older workers are less productive as a rule, then divergence in productivity of the labor force between depressed and prosperous areas will increase as a result of migration. From the evidence discussed in Chapter 1, it is already known that per capita income varies with age. Different geographic mobility by age acts to widen per capita income differentials among regions as well as among age groups, at least in the short run.

Conclusions

Appeal to the theory designed to explain migration, and appeal to the various forms of evidence presented in the two previous sections, leaves little doubt that greater age is a major constraint upon migration. It is not just age in itself as a pure physical phenomenon that operates as a causal factor. Associated with greater age is not only smaller net pecuniary returns from migration, but also a host of nonpecuniary deterrents to movement. Greater age is normally associated with a marital and dependency status, property holdings, and certain psychological and cultural views of one's place in the community. Underlying the migration patterns by age are these factors that find expression in the age statistics.

Nevertheless, the economic effects of these migration patterns are likely to be serious. The relatively low economic status of the older worker is not totally a matter of individual productivity, discrimination in hiring practices, or female substitution. Geographic immobility, as well as job immobility within a geographic region, is a prime contributor.

The picture that begins to emerge at this point is certainly not favorable to the older worker. First, the demand on the part of employers for workers over 45 years of age is weak as compared to their demand for younger age groups. It is not just in a few industries that firms are reluctant to hire older workers. The age effect extends across manufacturing industries with different product demands and production techniques. Except for extensive job protection in some trades, especially building construction and skilled workers in the utilities industry, the older worker is not guaranteed employment or re-employment in the clauses of union-employer contracts regarding job tenure and seniority rights. Decreasing productivity with advancing age, greater supplementary employment costs such as pension costs and workmen's compensation, and substitution of female labor underlie this relatively weak demand.

Absorption of displaced workers should be possible when the economy is growing and additions to the work force are needed in expanding industries. However, the economy does not grow evenly. Some industries and regions grow more rapidly than others. Indeed some may show little or no growth. Reallocation of resources from the declining to the expanding, higher paying sectors of the economy feeds and stimulates the over-all growth of the entire economy. The analysis in Part II indicated that reallocation of labor among industries within a state occurs at the younger ages. Older workers are less mobile in movements from farm to nonfarm jobs, from one manufacturing industry to another, and between service and manufacturing employments.

Now geographic immobility on the part of older workers appears as another force affecting their economic status. The dynamic process of economic growth includes a relocation of firms among regions of the economy. The availability of jobs and the earnings associated with those jobs shift geographically as national production expands. Younger workers are more willing and able to make the adjustments necessary to take advantage of potential higher earnings in other regions of the economy. As a result the older worker retains financially less attractive employment or accepts unemployment and perhaps departure from the labor force.

The fact that the lowest incomes are found among older workers who are not in the labor force (see Chapter 2) suggests that it is departure from the labor force that is accepted with a sense of resignation in many instances. What is important is that departure from the labor force is motivated by a set of poor alternatives. An older worker finds that local demand for his services is weak. He may not be able to hold on to his customary job because he does not have the physical skills, or he does not have the skills required for advancing technology. Once he is displaced, re-employment is difficult. If jobs for which he might qualify are opening in other industries or other regions, he is reluctant to make the transfer for both economic and personal psychological reasons. Acceptance of downgrading in job status and income may be possible. But early departure from the labor force, even with a less than adequate retirement income, may present a more attractive course of action than undertaking the effort and psychic cost of relocation.

Downgrading of job status, rather than departure from the labor force, can be conceived of most meaningfully in terms of changing occupations. If a worker cannot survive in one occupation, he may be able to obtain employment in another. Thus, two questions are relevant and important. In which occupations is survival for the older worker most likely? If older workers are less mobile than their younger contemporaries industry-wise and regionally, are they also less mobile occupationally?

PART IV

The Age Structure of Occupations

CHAPTER NINE

Age and Occupational Choice

A THIRD facet of the economic phenomena affecting the labor force status of different age groups is occupations. The present chapter is devoted to a theoretical analysis of occupational choice and change with special reference to age. Since the empirical investigation necessary to pursue the inferences drawn from the theory is lengthy, analysis of the statistical data is presented in Chapters 10 through 12.

Forces Affecting the Structure of Occupations

Economics alone cannot explain the distribution of a population among various occupations. Naturally, factors determining occupational choice are myriad and complex. The occupational structure of the labor force is dependent upon the economy's stage of economic and social development, which sets boundaries to the number and kind of occupations that can exist. No doubt prospective earnings play an important part in the decisions of individuals when they choose or change an occupation, but the distribution of physical and mental abilities in the population, and personality characteristics such as aggressiveness, play a significant role as well. The attributes necessary for entry or survival differ among occupations. In addition, the distribution of subjective interests and tastes, the prevalence of custom or family tradition in the choice of an occupation, and the concentration of wealth are all contributing factors.

Even when one restricts the analysis of occupational structure to the pecuniary variables influencing decisions, the operation of economic forces is complex. It is possible to formulate a model of choice based upon utility and uncertainty theory. Since two or more occupations can be practiced simultaneously or in sequence, some occupations forming career ladders to others, it is not an occupation but an occupational sequence that is chosen. For a given individual, not all these sequences are regarded as feasible objects of choice, however. What is feasible is determined environmentally by the nonpecuniary factors already mentioned.

To each defined feasible sequence a pecuniary return can be attached. This return over time, and even in any one time period, is uncertain. Most occupations display a wide dispersion of earnings in any given time period. Some individuals may prefer risky occupations—those with a small chance of very large earnings and a large chance of small earnings—while others prefer a large chance of average earnings. To simplify matters a limited number of the parameters of the earnings distribution might be used to define returns, e.g., a measure of central tendency and a measure of dispersion. Then the pecuniary returns, thus defined, can be ranked by means of a utility function, expressing the preferences of the individual for each occupational sequence-return combination. However, this ranking is affected by the relative nonpecuniary attractiveness of each occupation to the individual. There is no assurance that the sequences are ranked from largest to smallest return. In the final outcome, a general economic theory appears to be nonoperational.

As a consequence, the theoretical discussion will be restricted to pecuniary returns and costs of occupation choice and change. Moreover, the definition of returns (prospective earnings), which are in fact highly uncertain, will be simplified to permit the derivation of testable hypotheses. The resulting model does not, of course, determine the size and composition of each occupation. It does, however, help to specify the relevant economic variables to be included in the empirical investigation. The model also establishes the directional relationship between changes in these economic variables and changes in employment within an occupation, given all nonpecuniary factors. More important for our purposes, the effect of age upon occupational choice and change is hypothesized in the context of an explanatory mechanism.

Occupational Choice

Although earnings vary within and among occupations, the normal time pattern of earnings is one of relatively low income and high costs (education and job training) during the early years with relatively high income and low cost during the following years. Little in the way of explanatory power is lost if we assume for simplicity that the time periods are collapsed to two: the period of training or education and the period of pure earnings (no cost). Returns associated with the earnings period can be construed as the present value of an expected future income stream stretching over the employment life of the individual, and all costs are assumed to be incurred in the period of training or education.

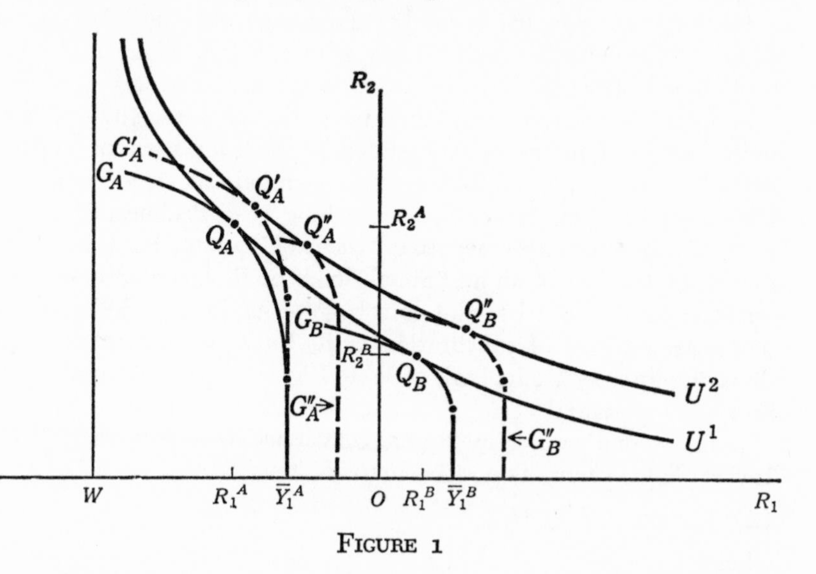

FIGURE 1

In general, for any time period t a person's income in that period is divided among spending on consumer goods, spending and investment on himself to increase future productivity and earnings, and saving:

(1) $Y_t = C_t + S_t + I_t = R_t + I_t$

where Y_t denotes disposable income, C_t denotes consumption, S_t represents saving, I_t signifies investment, and $R_t = C_t + S_t$. The usual formulation of the income-disposal equation ignores I_t, lumping all household spending under the heading of consumption. Rather than the usual concept of disposable income, Y_t, it is R_t that determines the present economic well-being of an individual or family, i.e., that amount available for consumption or saving. Furthermore, it is this variable that forms the criterion on which decisions are based.

Given two periods, a utility function in R_1 and R_2, $U(R_1, R_2)$, is postulated for each individual, where R_2 is a discounted present value. This preference function is assumed to possess the usual properties assigned to the utility functions of consumers in postulating their preferences for different commodities. More of R_1 is preferred to less for a given R_2, and vice versa; the rate at which R_2 will be substituted for R_1 diminishes as R_2 increases relative to R_1 (the indifference curves are drawn in Figure 1).

Since R_2 is discounted, it might be assumed as a special case that R_1 and R_2 are perfect substitutes, with the individual willing to trade off a dollar of one for the other with no change in utility. The assumption is not necessary, however. Rather than the straight lines with a slope of minus unity entailed by such an assumption, it is more likely that the indifference curves appear as they are drawn in Figure 1: varying in slope and bunching as R_1 declines. Before R_1 falls to zero S becomes negative because C cannot be zero. As R_1 decreases, the loss of an additional dollar of R_1 becomes more burdensome as compared to the gain from an additional dollar of R_2. The marginal rate of substitution of R_2 for R_1 diminishes because dissaving approaches its limit of W in Figure 1, present wealth plus borrowing potential.

In the second period, investment is assumed to be zero, so $Y_2 = R_2$. Investment is generally positive in the first period:

$$(2)\quad I_1 = E_1 + J_1 + H_1$$

where

$E_1 =$ expenditure on formal education,

$J_1 =$ expenditure on job training (including reduced or foregone income associated with on-the-job training),[1]

$H_1 =$ expenditure on health intended to maintain or increase productivity.

Any one or more of these components may, of course, be zero. In particular, H_1 will become relevant only at the upper age levels to be discussed in the succeeding section.

Earnings in the second period are a function of expenditures on investment in the first period, and income in the first period is taken as given, $\bar{Y}_1$, generating the following relationships:

[1] See G. Becker, "Investement in Human Capital: A Theoretical Analysis," *Journal of Political Economy,* Vol. 70, No. 5, Part 2 (Supplement: October 1962) pp. 9–49.

$$(3)\ \overline{Y}_1 = R_1 + I_1 \qquad \frac{dR_1}{dI_1} = -1$$

$$(4)\ Y_2 = R_2 = Y_1 + f(I_1) \qquad \frac{df}{dI_1} \geqq 0, \frac{d^2f}{dI_1^2} \leqq 0.$$

In (3) each dollar spent on investment entails a 1 dollar decrease in consumption plus saving. In (4) if $I_1 = 0$, $Y_2 = \overline{Y}_1$; no investment brings no additional income in the second period. For $I_1 > 0$, income in the second period increases with respect to increases of investment expenditures, but income increases at a decreasing rate. It is assumed there are diminishing returns to human investment.

Now Y_1, Y_2 and the function f will vary among occupations. The pecuniary attractiveness affecting occupational choice can be construed as maximization of the utility function subject to the constraints implied by (3) and (4). Since R_1 is a function of I_1 and R_2 is a function of I_1, substitution of (3) into (4) yields a transformation of R_1 into R_2, $G(R_1, R_2)$. It is seen that this function is such that $dR_2/dR_1 < 0$. More formally, for n occupations the problem is

$$\text{Maximize } U(R_1, R_2)$$
$$\text{Subject to } G_i(R_1, R_2)\ i = 1, 2, \ldots, n.$$

For two occupations, a solution is portrayed in Figure 1. Occupation A has high educational requirements, such as the professional groups. Occupation B has intermediate educational requirements and costs associated with on-the-job training, such as in the case of semiskilled groups. The constraints are shown as the unbroken curves G_A and G_B; the broken curves are to be disregarded for the moment. Thus $\overline{Y}_1^A$ is substantially less than $\overline{Y}_1^B$ because of greater investment cost. Were the individual to choose A, the returns in A, R_2, will be zero unless the individual invests an amount that leaves his R_1 at $\overline{Y}_1^A$. But R_2 is substantially higher for A than for B once this investment is made. Added investment causes R_2 to rise at a decreasing rate up to the limit that exhausts the individual's "wealth", W. A similar relationship would hold if the individual were to choose B. With zero investment, his consumption plus saving equals $\overline{Y}_1^B$. If he allows R_1 to fall below $\overline{Y}_1^B$ (if he invests), then R_2 will rise at a decreasing rate.[2]

[2] Actually, the constraints will eventually turn downward if the individual must borrow in period one to finance the investment and then repay the

The constraints have been deliberately drawn so that they are tangent to the same utility indifference curve. If the individual were to choose A, then he would settle at point Q_A, i.e., he would choose the combination (R_1^A, R_2^A). If he were to choose B, then he would select point Q_B yielding (R_1^B, R_2^B). But this individual is indifferent between points Q_A and Q_B. If all persons had utility functions in R_1 and R_2 identical to those in Figure 1, if they all had identical abilities (the same constraints), if they all had the same "wealth," and if they all had the same tastes with respect to nonpecuniary aspects of the two occupations, then they would choose so as to give a random distribution of persons between the two occupations.

Little can be said in economics about nonpecuniary tastes. But this much can be said. If such tastes are identical, individuals will still differ with respect to their utility functions and their constraints. For some the tangency point Q_A will be on a higher utility indifference curve, while for others Q_B will lie on a higher curve. Then individuals will choose A or B, depending upon which yields the greater pecuniary satisfaction.

Unlike most previous economic models,[3] this theoretical formulation does not imply that individuals act so as to maximize their income, even when the analysis is restricted to pecuniary determinants of choice. Occupations are chosen on the basis of utility maximization. It is entirely possible, given his preferences with respect to R_1 and R_2 and given his abilities, that Q_B can yield more satisfaction to a person (be on a higher utility curve) than Q_A. At the same time $R_1^B + R_2^B$ can be significantly less than $R_1^A + R_2^A$ because period two is of much longer duration.

The Inferences

Once the preference function and the constraints for an individual are given, utility maximization yields a solution. Since preferences

borrowed funds out of R_2. This does not affect the main conclusions, however, so it has been ignored.

[3] See, e.g., G. Becker, *op. cit.*, where nonpecuniary factors are mentioned but the formal analysis is restricted to pecuniary factors. His analysis is based upon the implicit assumption that income (not utility) is maximized. Though his analysis refers only to on-the-job training, by converting it to the language of the theory presented here, his equilibrium condition implies $\triangle R_2 = \triangle I_1$, where $\triangle I_1 = - \triangle R_1$. That is, investment is carried to the point at which marginal revenue from increased productivity equals marginal cost. This condition would prevail in our presentation only if R_1 and R_2 are everywhere perfect substitutes.

are subjective, this analysis, like any utility analysis, is operational only in the sense that it permits us to trace the effects of changes in the observable variables that determine the constraints. Starting with any initial equilibrium position, reactions to these changes can be inferred for *given* tastes and preferences, both pecuniary and nonpecuniary.

First, an increase in the demand for the services of an occupational type of labor will shift the constraint for that occupation upward in Figure 1. The greater demand operates to raise expected income, R_2, by reducing unemployment and/or increasing earnings of those employed in the occupation. For example, an increase in demand for occupation A, with no change in demand for B and no change in investment costs, will shift the constraint G_A to a position like G'_A. Utility maximization implies the individual would then choose A because Q'_A yields greater utility than Q_B. A decrease in the demand for labor in occupation A would have the opposite effect, and the same inferences apply to occupation B.

Because of differences among individuals in their abilities and their tastes, not all would revise their decisions and choose A over B for the kind of change described above. Those on the margin, with points Q_A and Q_B giving equal or very nearly the same utility, would be first affected. How many would revise their decisions is an empirical question that hinges on abilities and tastes. Nevertheless, one can infer that greater demand and expected future income will increase employment in an occupation without resorting to an assumption that individuals choose simply on the basis of maximizing income.

Secondly, a decrease in the "price" of education or training, *ceteris paribus,* will shift the constraint to the right for all occupations requiring that education or training. For instance, a reduction in the cost per unit of higher education required for occupation A will shift the constraint from G_A to G''_A. The individual then selects A over B because Q''_A gives greater utility than Q_B. Similarly, a decrease in the worker's cost per unit of intermediate education and/or on-the-job training will shift G_B to G''_B. With no change in G_A or his tastes and preferences, the person chooses *B* over *A* (Q''_B is on a higher indifference curve than Q_A). A rise in the price of education or training has opposite effects, shifting the constraints to the left.

Although we are not directly concerned with the economics of education, the demand for education or training "falls out" of the theory. Like the demand curve for any other good or service, the demand curve for education is negatively sloped: quantity demanded is inversely related to price. Also, from the preceding analysis of labor demand and income, it follows that education is a superior good. An increase in labor demand and expected income in an occupation will raise the demand for the type and quantity of education required for that occupation as more people choose it over others.

Thirdly, a change in the educational requirements associated with an occupation will affect occupational choice. A decrease in the time period of training needed to practice occupation A shifts G_A to G''_A, just like a decrease in the cost per time unit of education, and leading to the same results. An increase in requirements raises the investment expenditure necessary to obtain a given future income, so the constraint shifts to the left, discouraging choice of that occupation. The same analysis applies to occupation B. Therefore, one can infer an inverse relationship between quantitative educational requirements and employment in an occupation, other things being the same.

Occupational Change and Survival

Up to this point the theoretical analysis has been limited to the youngest ages when the initial occupational choice occurs. Attention has been centered upon one time point and a variety of occupations. But the theory extends readily to changes over time by an application of the same fundamental model to different age groups.

Each worker presently established in an occupation can be viewed as contemplating the possibility of a change. At each age in his lifetime, period one is still relevant because he could transfer to another occupation, and such a transfer normally entails some investment cost. Whether or not a change of occupation does in fact happen, the alternatives are constantly present. In turn, the alternatives can be described by an investment period and a return period associated with each *other* occupation (and possibly his own) with current earnings, Y_1, in his present occupation greater than the Y_1 he earned in the past when he made the initial choice.

Assuming no change in the individual's utility function, the effect of advancing age is to alter the constraints faced by any one individual. First, in contrast to his constraint at an earlier age, Y_1 and R_1 are larger for his chosen occupation. The constraint for his present occupation lies farther to the right in a diagram like Figure 1. This operates to put him on a higher utility indifference curve for that occupation vis-à-vis others. Secondly, at greater age R_2 becomes smaller for any other occupation as well as his own, because R_2 is now computed over a smaller future life expectancy (see Chapter 6). At the same time investment expenditures are still necessary in order to practice other occupations, thus acting to shift the constraint for other occupations downward. The effect of these two forces is to reduce the (maximum) utility that can be derived from other occupations relative to his own. As a consequence, occupational mobility declines as age increases.

Suppose the individual for which Figure 1 was drawn had chosen occupation A. As he approaches intermediate age his earnings expand. Therefore his current income, Y_1^A, moves to the right, well beyond the zero point and very likely to the right of Y_1^B. The constraint for occupation B is stationary. By remaining in A the difference between the (most) utility derived from A and that to be derived from B becomes larger. Similarly, if he had chosen B, Y_1^B and the constraint G_B move to the right while G_A remains stationary. The constraint G_A may even move downward and to the left because of reduced productivity in occupation A when entering at a higher age. As a consequence, the worker's demand for higher education declines, educational requirements become more of a barrier to entry, and the incentive to move diminishes.

The model does not imply that occupational mobility is reduced to zero. A distinction should be drawn between types of occupations. The model does imply that when occupational change occurs, it will occur between occupations for which the "solution" yields the closest utility levels. In turn, since the solution depends upon the constraints, transfer will most often occur between occupations for which the constraints are similar. With similar education, training, and ability requirements, a prior investment expenditure for entry into one will permit later entry into the other without a significant increase of investment expenditure at the later date. Therefore, the constraints for the adopted occupation and a similar one will closely resemble each other. On the other hand, where a vast difference in training and ability requirements exists, the investment cost of occupational change is very large. Then the constraints will differ greatly, and occupational change is discouraged.

As a worker ages beyond the intermediate stage and approaches advanced age, these forces continue to operate. Even though earnings in his present occupation decline, those expected in other occupations do likewise while the investment cost of change persists. Indeed, this cost is very likely to increase because of a shrinkage of learning capacity, thus restricting mobility further.

In those occupations having strenuous physical or skill requirements, the expenditure necessary to maintain health, element H_1 in the investment cost, tends to rise. In addition, element J_1 may be positive because of retraining needed to keep pace with changing technology. Even to *survive* in an occupation there are investment costs. The proposition that older workers cannot meet physical or skill requirements can be expressed in the language of this theory by saying the investment expenditure needed to maintain productivity and earnings becomes progressively larger. If enough investment expenditures are incurred, the older worker might maintain his earnings. However, the expenditure may well be exorbitant relative to earnings.

Interpreted by a diagram like Figure 1, the constraint shifts to the left for a worker's own occupation as well as for others. If the older worker is in occupation B, a larger share of Y_1^B must be devoted to I_1, so R_1 is smaller for any given R_2. Consequently, G_B shifts to the left at the same time that G_A shifts downward due to greater age and constant investment cost for entry into A. In the context of many alternative occupations, the outcome (the tangency solutions) depends upon the extent of the shift for his present occupation as compared to others. If there is another occupation for which the older worker can qualify without large investment expenditure, that constraint will tend to lie outside the constraint for his own occupation and be tangent to a higher utility indifference curve. Occupations of low skill and low physical requirements are of this kind, and he will choose one of these over his present occupation. However, the demand for labor may be declining in these occupations, depressing the constraints there as indicated in the previous section. Then the outcome may be departure from the labor force as the best available alternative.

Empirical Hypotheses

Utility theory in any area of economics is based upon given subjective preferences and therefore is not directly testable against empirical evidence. Utility theory does, however, yield inferences about the relationships among observable and measurable economic variables. No statistical data presently available permit a direct measurement of occupational choice or occupational change. Employment in an occupation is the closest approximation to this theoretical variable. But, of course, employment within an occupation can vary from causes other than transfer into or out of the occupation.

If one accepts employment as an indicator of occupational change, then the model predicts a directional relationship between employment and the following economic variables:

(1) Income is directly related to employment. Income affects expected earnings, and therefore greater income shifts an occupation's constraint upward for given investment cost.

(2) The unemployment rate is inversely related to total employment. Aside from earnings of those employed, the unemployment rate acts to reduce prospective future earnings in an occupation. Given investment cost, greater unemployment shifts the constraint downward.

(3) Educational requirements are inversely related to employment. Given expected earnings, greater educational requirements increase investment cost and shift the constraint to the left.

These directional relationships are hypothesized for each age group and each occupation. In addition, the theory implies differences among age groups in the strength of their reactions to these variables. The youngest groups, having the most flexibility in occupational choice, should show the greatest reaction to the earnings variables (income and unemployment rate). For greater ages the importance of income should diminish because of occupational immobility. Also, educational requirements should provide the greatest barrier to entry for the intermediate age group. The youngest are less committed to a given occupation, while the oldest have exorbitant investment costs for formal education (so education is not a relevant object of choice). With reference to the older worker's problem, differences among occupations are of special importance. Since occupations of low skill and low physical requirements are a predicted source of occupational transfer, the availability of employment for older workers in these occupations deserves special attention.

The empirical investigation to follow takes account of several explanatory variables in addition to those indicated here. Race, sex, and self-employment have to do with specific differences among individuals with respect to their constraints, even though their constraints are of the same general form. Labor unionization, a productivity index, and the concentration ratio in the industry of employment affect the earnings, R_2, and thus the constraints in certain occupations. These individual and occupational differences have been ignored here for the sake of unity and simplicity of presentation.

CHAPTER TEN

Occupational Change: The Data

THIS AND the following two chapters are focused upon observed differences that workers of various ages exhibit in their ability to retain employment with the passage of time. Stress is laid upon occupational change over time, taking account of the fact that employment patterns of a particular age group can be judged only in relation to the patterns of all age groups comprising the work force. In the present chapter the empirical data are discussed. Chapter 11 is an interpretation of the results of the regression analysis, and Chapter 12 deals with the problems of predicting changes that will occur in the future.

Measurement of Employment

Theoretical analysis has shown that a great number of causal factors operate on both the demand and the supply side of the labor market to determine changes in employment over time.[1] Direct empirical estimation of the effects exerted by these factors is clearly impossible for the degree of disaggregation needed to generate meaningful interpretations of the time trends. Rather than measure the number of workers employed at a moment of time, the variable adopted is the very useful concept of a *survival rate:* the fraction of

[1] In addition to Chapters 4 through 9, see also M. B. Schupack, "Changes in Occupational Structure," pp. 109–132, in M. J. Brennan (ed.), *Patterns of Market Behavior* (Providence, R.I.: Brown University Press, 1965).

workers in an occupation who survive in that occupation from one point in time to another.[2] One well-documented phenomenon is that too many older workers cannot retain employment, i.e., the survival rate for older age groups is too low. Thus, the survival rate is specified as the dependent variable, and the various factors operating on supply and demand are invoked as explanatory variables.[3]

Data required must include information about the number of workers in each age group and occupation at two different points of time, for the two points of time are inherent in the notion of a survival rate. The definition of an occupation must be the same at both points of time, as must the age categories used. Explanatory (or independent) variables must also be available for the same occupational and age breakdown. The occupational divisions should be as fine as possible so that explanatory effects are not hidden by heterogeneity of the group of workers studied. Although there is no way of telling just how fine this division should be, dividing the labor force into just the twelve major occupational groups used by the Census of Population is too aggregate. More detailed occupations must be utilized. Finally, all of this information must be available in comparable form for several time periods if one wishes to trace the movement of survival rates over time.

One set of data which partially fulfills these requirements is the set of questions about occupation and age asked in each decennial population census. The 1960 census divides the labor force into more than 400 detailed occupations and many age groups, both of which are comparable for each time period from 1940 on. For the 1930 census and before, some adjustments must be made in the definitions of occupations and age groups. Information contained in a census working paper [4] and unpublished work sheets underlying this working paper [5] were used to develop age-occupation categories from 1900 to 1930 which are comparable with the 1940 to 1960

[2] See Chapter 3.

[3] Consequently, the regression equations must be interpreted as reduced-form equations, and the estimated coefficients represents neither supply nor demand reactions alone. Such is the state of the world dictated by data availability.

[4] U.S. Bureau of the Census, *Occupational Trends in the United States: 1900 to 1950, Bureau of the Census Working Paper #5* (Washington: GPO, 1958).

[5] Thanks are due to Mr. William Milligan of the Population Division of the Bureau of the Census for providing these work sheets.

classifications. Further adjustments were made to allow for differences in the age categories for 1910 and 1920.[6]

Adjustment of the census data in this way yields comparable age-occupation distributions for each decade from 1900 to 1960. The survival rate—the fraction of those in a particular occupation and age group who survive to appear in the next decennial census in that same occupation but in an age group ten years older—can then be computed for each of the six decades. A survival rate can be above unity if there was net entry into the occupation during the decade at the particular age level considered, or less than unity if there was net withdrawal from the occupation.

The age groupings used throughout the analysis are listed in Table 10-1. Some double counting is involved because of the open-end categories for the very youngest and very oldest workers, but few workers are involved at either end.

Table 10–1. AGE GROUPS USED IN THE ANALYSIS

Age Group Number	*Age at Beginning of Decade*	*Age at End of Decade*
1	Under 24	25–34
2	25–34	35–44
3	35–44	45–54
4	45–54	55–64
5 *	55–64	65 and over
5 †	55–64	65–74
6 †	65–74	75 and over

* 1900–1950 data.
† 1950–1960 decade only.

Set out in Table 10-2 is the number of occupations into which the work force is divided. These groupings follow the major occupations found in the Census of Population with two exceptions. Household workers are combined with service workers, and the two major farming categories (farmers and farm managers, and farm laborers and foremen) are merged into one group.

Unionized occupations are those for which at least some workers

[6] A procedure suggested by A. Edwards was used: A. Edwards, *Population: Comparative Occupation Statistics for the U.S., 1870–1940, 16th Census of the United States* (Washington: GPO, 1943), p. 154. This work is somewhat arbitrary, especially for 1910 when age data were particularly deficient, but nothing better is available.

belong to a labor union. These occupations have been separated from others to facilitate comparison with the rest of the work force.

Observed Patterns of Survival Rates

Net survival rates do not reveal the number of workers entering or leaving an occupation (or dying while in the occupation). They give only the final balance of transfers in and out. Lack of information about the sources and origins of occupational transfers is an important deficiency in the data, and necessarily makes the attempted explanations incomplete. There are interrelationships between occupations which may be important for explaining the observed survival rates. For example, some occupations form career ladders with others and act as feeders for them. Such might be the case with some sales occupations acting as feeders for management occupations. In the other direction, the availability of easy

Table 10–2. NUMBER OF OCCUPATIONS USED IN THE ANALYSIS

Major Group Detailed Occupations	*1900–1950*	*1950–1960*
Professionals	27	56
Farmers	5	6
Managers	21	59
Clerks	11	21
Sales	9	12
Craftsmen	45	72
Operatives	65	114
Service	19	28
Laborers	42	64
Total	244	432
Unionized Occupations		
Professionals	6	9
Managers	4	5
Clerks	5	7
Sales	0	2
Craftsmen	26	34
Operatives	42	63
Service	8	11
Laborers	30	42
Total	121	173

unskilled work might affect the survival of older workers in other highly skilled or strenuous occupations. None of these factors can enter an analysis of occupational change until such time as information is collected about interoccupational transfers. Nevertheless, survival rates are undoubtedly the best available indicators of movement in and out of occupations. Evidence presented in Chapter 12 suggests that accurate prediction of survival rates lays a strong foundation for prediction of the actual number of workers in each occupation.

Average survival rates per decade for major occupation groups are presented in Table 10-3. The 1950–1960 rate and the average of the five decade rates 1900–1950 are recorded for each major occupation and age group. Although the later analysis is concerned with explanations of rates for detailed occupations within each major occupational group, discussion of the intergroup differences serves as a background for the intragroup comparisons. Obviously the data are too voluminous to be presented in tabular form for detailed occupations.

Survival rates do indeed decline with greater age, but the decline is by no means uniform across occupations. Neither does the early time period show the same pattern as the most recent decade. The wide differences among occupations shown for age group 1 are due in some part to different education requirements, especially for the professionals and managers. In the earlier period few people under 24 entered these occupations compared to the influx during the 1950–1960 decade when education was more widespread. Age group 6 for the 1950–1960 decade is subject to more volatile and random fluctuations than the others because of the very small number of workers involved.

The so-called older workers' problem can be seen by comparing age groups 5 and 6 of the 1950–1960 decade with younger age groups and with age group 5 of the earlier time period. The rapid drop between age groups 4 and 5 for the early period demonstrates the relative ability of workers to stay in an occupation towards the age of 65, but the relative inability to survive in it through the next decade. Some of the drop is due to deaths, but no death rate information classified by detailed occupations is available. Age group 5 for the early period is not strictly comparable with 5 or 6 for the later period; it combines both 5 and 6 and is somewhat too high for a decade survival rate. However, age group 6 for the later

Table 10–3. AVERAGE SURVIVAL RATES FOR MAJOR OCCUPATION GROUPS

	1950–1960, Age Group						*1900–1950,* Age Group*				
Occupation	*1*	*2*	*3*	*4*	*5*	*6*	*1*	*2*	*3*	*4*	*5*
Professionals	7.03	1.33	0.97	0.85	0.45	0.25	4.74	1.23	1.07	0.98	1.08
Farmers	1.60	0.80	0.70	0.70	0.30	0.10	1.30	1.30	1.00	1.00	0.80
Managers	6.71	1.75	1.16	0.83	0.40	0.20	6.46	1.85	1.17	1.03	0.62
Clerks	1.75	0.93	0.98	0.88	0.40	0.26	1.84	1.05	1.20	1.01	0.67
Sales	3.01	1.44	1.17	0.94	0.54	0.32	2.21	1.16	1.13	0.93	0.66
Craftsmen	3.91	1.32	1.02	0.79	0.28	0.12	3.01	1.28	0.93	0.79	0.53
Operatives	1.53	0.90	0.91	1.07	0.25	0.10	1.80	1.10	1.00	0.87	0.60
Service	3.13	1.10	1.08	0.93	0.51	0.21	2.88	1.29	1.11	0.97	0.86
Laborers	0.97	0.78	0.87	0.80	0.22	0.09	1.52	1.06	1.01	0.95	0.71
All Occupations	3.40	1.15	0.98	0.90	0.34	0.16	2.83	1.23	1.03	0.91	0.66
All Unionized Occupations	2.35	1.02	0.96	0.83	0.27	0.11	2.18	1.13	0.98	0.82	0.61

* Rates given are averages per decade.

period is quite small, and even combining[7] the age group 6 survivals with those for age group 5 still leaves the survival rates for the earlier decades larger than for 1950–1960. The implication is that there is a problem of employment survival for the older workers and that it has become worse in recent years.

Changes in occupational patterns between the two time periods reflect the continuing trend of employment away from agricultural and blue-collar jobs towards professional, service, and white-collar jobs.[8] The latter groups have maintained higher survival rates as compared to the former groups. This difference is also apparent when looking at the older age groups for the recent decade, especially age group 5. The blue-collar group (craftsmen, operatives, and laborers) and farmers have rates distinctly below the other occupation groups. How much of the difference is due to shifts in the occupational structure of the labor force alone and how much to other factors will be discussed in the following chapter. Although the blue-collar group is at a disadvantage for both time periods, the disadvantage has become more pronounced for the most recent decade.

There is nothing very surprising about the generally lower survival rates experienced for all age groups of the unionized occupations. The lower rates reflect the primarily blue-collar composition of the union group of occupations. Looking within the individual groups which comprise the blue-collar workers (the data are not presented here), unionized occupations have slightly lower survival rates than all occupations in the craftsmen subgroup, slightly higher rates in the operatives subgroup, and virtually the same rates in the laborers subgroup. Whether or not an occupation has *some* union members appears to make little difference in the average level of survival rate. Another question, to be discussed in the next chapter, is

[7] If it can be assumed that, for the later-period definitions of age groups, the survival rate for age group 5 was the same for the 1940–1950 decade as for the 1950–1960 one, the combined age group 5 and 6 survival rate (comparable to the age group 5 survival rate for the early period) is given by:

$$SR_{5+6} = SR_5 + (SR_5)(SR_6)$$

Where SR stands for the survival rate and the subscript indicates the age group. If SR_6 is small, as it is, the second term is small, and SR_{5+6} for the 1950–1960 decade does not nearly equal SR_5 for the early period.

[8] See, e.g., Max Rutzick and Sol Swerdloff, "The Occupational structure of U.S. Employment, 1940–1960,"*Monthly Labor Review,* Vol. 85, No. 11 (November 1962), pp. 1209–1213.

whether, among those occupations which have at least some union members, the degree of unionization affects the size of the survival rate.

The Explanatory Variables

Survival rates have been noted by other investigators, but no attempt has been made to explain the observed patterns by means of economic variables reflecting forces at work in the labor market. The chosen economic variables are those which can be measured for approximately the same categories as the computed survival rates. Three aspects of each explanatory variable will be discussed. First, sources of the data are given. Second, the probable effect of the variable upon the survival rate is outlined. This cannot be done in a rigorous manner for the model used here, but an appeal to a more complete model, at least implicitly, can give some idea of the variable's effect. One can infer the expected sign the coefficient of the variable will take in the multiple regression equation with the survival rate as the dependent variable. Third, major occupation group averages, similar in form to the survival rate averages in Table 10-3, are presented for each variable.

1. Occupational growth rates. The growth rate is the number of workers of all age groups in an occupation at the end of the decade divided by the number of workers in this occupation at the beginning of the decade. Growth rates over unity indicate a growing occupation, below unity a declining one. The growth rate averages for major occupation groups are listed in Table 10-4. As with the survival rates, the growth of the white-collar occupations relative to the blue-collar and farmer groups can clearly be observed. One major difference, and a discouraging difference for the older worker, is the low growth rate of the service occupations. The service group displays one of the highest survival rates at the older age levels. Combining this with the relatively low skill required for most jobs within the group, the service group appears to be a major source of employment for workers who are forced to leave more strenuous jobs before retirement age. However, not many such jobs will be available if the group maintains a low growth rate.

It is assumed that if the entire occupation is growing, the demand for each individual age group has increased. The effect will be, *ceteris paribus,* to increase the number of workers hired from each age group. High growth rates should be associated with high survival rates in the regression equations, so occupational growth rates should have a positive sign.

There is not complete independence between the growth rate of an occupation and the survival rate of one of the occupation's age groups. All the survival rates together combine to determine the occupation's growth rate. Therefore, some positive correlation would be expected between the survival rates and the growth rates even without the behavioristic implication of a changing demand for labor. However, there are sufficient age groups used in the analysis so that the use of growth rates in the regression equation still retains some validity for testing the demand side of the market.

Table 10–4. AVERAGE GROWTH RATE FOR MAJOR OCCUPATION GROUPS

Occupation	*1950–1960*	*1900–1950* *
Professionals	1.63	1.54
Farmers	0.70	1.20
Managers	1.21	1.40
Clerks	1.26	1.35
Sales	1.32	1.33
Craftsmen	1.11	1.28
Operatives	1.09	1.45
Service	1.03	1.36
Laborers	0.93	1.41
All Occupations	1.14	1.40
All Unionized Occupations	1.08	1.37

* Rates given are averages per decade.

2. FRACTION OF WORKERS UNEMPLOYED. The 1950 census and 1960 census give the number of workers employed by occupation and age as well as the number in the experienced civilian labor force. The difference between the two figures was taken to be the number unemployed in each occupation and age group. No earlier unemployment figures by detailed occupations appear to be available. The 1960 census also gives the number of unemployed workers who last worked during various periods of time back to 1950. From this information, it is possible to estimate the median time of unemployment for those workers who were unemployed in 1960. This is a median in the sense that half of the unemployed workers had been unemployed for a shorter period of time and half for a longer period.

This information is available only in 1960 and only for all age groups combined.

The expected effect of unemployment would be to reduce the survival rate, i.e., to have a negative coefficient in the regression equation. If there is a large amount of unemployment in any labor market, supply would tend to decrease as workers left one market and entered another labor market. A worker cannot change his age group, but he can certainly shift occupations. The longer has unemployment been present, the more likely the worker is to perform this transfer.

When matching the independent variables with appropriate survival rates, a question arises as to which value of the independent variables to use. Survival rates are computed by utilizing information about age and occupation from the beginning and the end of a decade. The independent variables are also measured at the beginning and the end of the decade, and the resulting values are generally different. The survival rate refers to events which take place during the decade, and so should the independent variables. Values at either end of the decade are not exactly appropriate. Some measure, like the expected value of the variable throughout the whole decade, would be most suitable. In the absence of information from which this could be computed, the simple average of the beginning and ending values is used.

One further possibility is present. If the survival rates react strongly to differences in the values of the independent variables, the most meaningful measure for the independent variables may be the change in value between the beginning and the end of the decade, rather than an average value. If, however, a relatively long lag is involved in the process of change, then averages may be most appropriate. The crucial factor seems to be the rapidity with which changes in the independent variable will force a change in the survival rates. In the absence of any concrete information, both measures of independent variables were used whenever possible. These two measures are designated in the tables as averages and changes. The same distinction will also be maintained in the next chapter where two sets of regressions are computed, one for average values of the independent variables and one for changes.

The unemployment data for major occupation groups are given in Table 10-5. There is no apparent pattern to the time unemployed. Perhaps more meaning would be obtained if it were possible to derive this figure for individual age groups instead of the entire occupation. The unemployment fractions follow the expected pattern with relatively high rates for the very youngest and oldest age groups, and for the blue-collar and service occupations at all age levels. Changes were mostly positive during the decade; 1960 was a year of higher employment than 1950. As compared to the other groups professionals, sales, service, and laborers seemed to resist this trend, reflecting perhaps either continuing high demand for labor (professionals and sales) or discouragement and departure from the occupation (laborers and service). The negative signs occur mostly in the youngest age group, probably indicating the higher educational levels achieved by young people in 1960 before they considered themselves part of the labor force. With a smaller number trying to enter the labor force at this level, fewer are likely to be considered unemployed.

The last two points raise a conceptual problem when considering occupational unemployment rates. If a person is not now at work, who can say with certainty what his occupation should be? He may report his occupation as the last one at which he worked, but especially among older workers this may be entirely unrealistic as an indication of the occupation within which he will find his next job. The longer a person remains unemployed the more nebulous the notion of his occupation becomes. The line between being unemployed and leaving the work force altogether is also vague and uncertain. It is impossible to know just how biased the occupational unemployment figures are as a measure of the true labor reserve in each occupation. The true occupational reserve should exert direct influence upon the survival rate, not the phantom labor reserve statistically created by persons reporting themselves to be in a position which will never be sustained by the labor market. Since it is impossible to determine how the unemployment figures should be adjusted, they must be used as reported.

3. Fraction of workers who are nonwhite. Both the 1950 census and 1960 census give the number of nonwhite workers in each age-occupation category. It is simple to compute the fraction of all workers representing nonwhites. No such detailed data are available before 1950.

Nonwhite workers may have less mobility between jobs and less durability on the job. Less durability implies that occupations with a high fraction of nonwhite workers will have lower survival

Table 10–5. UNEMPLOYMENT DATA FOR MAJOR OCCUPATION GROUPS, 1950–1960

Occupation Group	*Average Median Time Unemployed (Years)*	*Average Fraction Unemployed, Age Group*						*Change in Fraction Unemployed, Age Group*					
		1	*2*	*3*	*4*	*5*	*6*	*1*	*2*	*3*	*4*	*5*	*6*
Professionals	1.31	0.0032	0.0287	0.0297	0.0206	0.0476	0.0527	0.0411	−0.0159	−0.0170	−0.0551	0.0117	0.0158
Farmers	1.35	0.0290	0.0207	0.0212	0.0388	0.0325	0.0360	−0.0169	0.0189	−0.0021	0.0097	0.0137	0.0083
Managers	2.38	0.0165	0.0142	0.0118	0.0176	0.0231	0.0210	−0.0070	−0.0080	0.0035	0.0069	0.0129	0.0122
Clerks	1.57	0.0550	0.0245	0.0290	0.0220	0.0307	0.0487	0.0157	0.0053	−0.0179	0.0117	0.0172	0.0395
Sales	1.52	0.0392	0.0237	0.0195	0.0272	0.0268	0.0365	−0.0313	−0.0163	−0.0017	−0.0045	−0.0085	0.0155
Craftsmen	2.50	0.0458	0.0368	0.0205	0.0336	0.0626	0.0671	−0.0137	−0.0024	0.0101	0.0118	0.0259	0.0400
Operatives	2.03	0.0688	0.0482	0.0492	0.0511	0.0794	0.1032	−0.0054	0.0150	0.0146	0.0213	0.0246	0.0463
Service	1.63	0.0645	0.0517	0.0440	0.0450	0.0668	0.0499	−0.0007	−0.0130	0.0011	0.0073	−0.0140	−0.0127
Laborers	1.41	0.1088	0.0806	0.0748	0.0846	0.0992	0.0825	−0.0031	0.0083	0.0099	0.0189	0.0450	0.0060
All Occupations	1.90	0.0505	0.0418	0.0228	0.0332	0.0591	0.0684	−0.0009	0.0007	0.0412	0.0277	0.0195	0.0316
All Unionized Occupations	2.03	0.0726	0.0478	0.0450	0.0540	0.0801	0.0972	−0.0050	0.0034	0.0246	0.0242	0.0415	0.0781

rates, *ceteris paribus.* This is particularly true of the older age groups. A negative sign would be expected in the regression equation. Less mobility means they do not enter growing occupations as fast as white workers, nor do they leave declining occupations as rapidly. Since the expected regression coefficient is thus negative for the growing occupations and positive for the declining ones, the sign of the coefficient which is actually observed may depend in large part upon the distribution of nonwhite workers among growing and declining occupations.

Nonwhite data for major occupation groups are presented in Table 10-6. The nonwhites are far more prevalent in the laborer and service groups, the bottom of the economic scale. Most groups have a smaller fraction of nonwhites as the age level goes up—reflecting some falling off due to the durability effect and also, probably, a less satisfactory situation for the nonwhites in comparison to employment requirements before World War II when these older age groups first entered the work force. Increases in the fraction of nonwhites for the first two age groups may be a result of improvements in nonwhite training and acceptance in the last two decades. Much of the increase is in the laborer group (perhaps traceable to the withdrawal of whites), but an encouraging amount is in the more promising operative and clerical groups. The low manager figures reflect to some degree the relative dearth of business capital for nonwhites, since most of the manager occupations are associated with small retail and service businesses. The sales figures may reflect pure discrimination, the professional ones a lack of advanced education.

4. Fraction of workers who are self-employed. The number of wage and salary workers in each age-occupation category is available for 1950 and 1960. The difference between the total number of workers in each category and those who work for wages and salaries was taken to be the number of self-employed in that category. Actually, this residual of workers includes both self-employed and unpaid family workers, but virtually all of the residual are, indeed, the self-employed. In processing the data for this study, however, the subtraction was not done, so the data remain in the form of the fraction of wage and salary workers, i.e., the fraction of nonself-employed. For changes in the fraction, a negative sign indicates increase in the fraction of self-employed, and vice versa.

Table 10–6 NONWHITE DATA FOR MAJOR OCCUPATION GROUPS, 1950–1960

Occupation	*Average Fraction Nonwhite, Age Group* 1	2	3	4	5	6	*Change in Fraction Nonwhite, Age Group* 1	2	3	4	5	6
Professionals	0.0473	0.0374	0.0325	0.0293	0.0362	0.0246	0.0078	0.0120	0.0010	0.0053	0.0273	—0.0070
Farmers	0.1050	0.1120	0.1010	0.1070	0.0890	0.0860	—0.0234	0.0374	0.0142	0.0180	0.0191	0.0042
Managers	0.0253	0.0230	0.0208	0.0187	0.0168	0.0251	0.0006	0.0032	—0.0006	0.0013	—0.0011	0.0072
Clerks	0.0648	0.0929	0.0693	0.0545	0.0347	0.0171	0.0481	0.0254	—0.0008	0.0145	—0.0211	—0.0054
Sales	0.0267	0.0260	0.0201	0.0310	0.0141	0.0173	—0.0104	—0.0161	—0.0043	—0.0126	—0.0034	—0.0033
Craftsmen	0.0474	0.0469	0.0441	0.0385	0.0311	0.0269	0.0101	0.0101	0.0027	—0.0019	0.0025	0.0086
Operatives	0.0897	0.1027	0.0982	0.0885	0.0541	0.0475	0.0383	0.0293	—0.0003	—0.0009	0.0166	0.0143
Service	0.2175	0.2304	0.2212	0.1894	0.1266	0.1283	0.0067	0.0225	—0.0081	—0.0181	0.0278	0.0076
Laborers	0.1873	0.2424	0.2477	0.2196	0.1606	0.1173	0.0896	0.0249	—0.0175	—0.0130	0.0362	—0.0083
All Occupations	0.0883	0.1010	0.0970	0.0860	0.0619	0.0517	0.0326	0.0172	—0.0023	—0.0027	0.0138	0.0042
All Unionized Occupations	0.1054	0.1280	0.1260	0.1110	0.0790	0.0657	0.0424	0.0146	—0.0066	—0.0033	0.0150	0.0114

It has been hypothesized that workers who are self-employed will have a much greater chance to survive at the older age levels. They will not be subject to arbitrary forced retirement rules and can more easily regulate and adjust their work to changing physical conditions. The decline of self-employment in the labor force over the last few decades has been cited by some as a possible major cause of the decline in older workers' labor force participation.

For the younger age groups, the chief determinant of the relationship between the survival rate and the amount of self-employment may be the general economic conditions. Under near full employment (as in 1950 and 1960) self-employed people are encouraged to stay in their occupations and new one are drawn in—except perhaps in some professional occupations where long specific training is involved so that entry can take place only at the youngest age levels. Even if the pattern of final product demand is moving away from them, the self-employed may still hang on hoping that generally good economic conditions will improve their situation eventually. Thus, for all age groups a negative sign would be expected for the regression coefficient (the data being in the form of the fraction of nonself-employed).

Major occupation group averages and changes are presented in Table 10-7. The peculiar appearance of the farmers averages springs from the fact that there are only six occupations in this group, half of which are defined as self-employed people and half as wage earners. The general increase in the fraction of self-employed for older ages in all occupations may reflect two tendencies: (1) self-employment takes place more easily at older ages as capital and experience are collected; (2) nonself-employed are concentrated in the white-collar and farm groups. There seems to be a general movement towards more self-employment, particularly in the sales group. This is a little misleading, however, and seems to represent one case where our unit of measure, the occupation rather than the worker, has distorted the averages. In fact, self-employment in the nonagricultural sector has been virtually constant over the decade at about 10 per cent of the nonagricultural work force.[9] The slight change which took place has been a decline in self-employment. However, the variable computed in this form retains its value for use in estimating the regression equations.

[9] John E. Bregger, "Self-Employment in the United States, 1948–1962," *Monthly Labor Review*, Vol. 86, No. 1 (January 1863), pp. 37–43.

Table 10–7. SELF-EMPLOYMENT DATA FOR MAJOR OCCUPATION GROUPS, 1950–1960

Occupation Group	*Average Fraction of Wage Earners, Age Group*						*Change in Fraction of Wage Earners, Age Group*					
	1	2	3	4	5	6	*1*	2	3	4	5	6
Professionals	0.8800	0.8030	0.7590	0.7500	0.7040	0.5777	–0.0110	–0.0240	–0.0040	–0.0710	–0.0260	–0.0160
Farmers	0.5000	0.5000	0.5000	0.5000	0.5000	0.5000	0	0	0	0	0	0
Managers	0.6300	0.6280	0.6200	0.6210	0.6180	0.5940	0.0020	–0.0010	0.0070	–0.0010	–0.0050	–0.0190
Clerks	0.9900	0.9800	0.9750	0.9745	0.9780	0.9100	–0.0090	–0.0170	–0.0200	0.0510	0.0220	–0.1320
Sales	0.8690	0.7820	0.7200	0.7080	0.6890	0.6720	–0.1010	–0.1050	–0.0760	–0.0930	–0.1000	–0.0630
Craftsmen	0.9430	0.9200	0.8990	0.8960	0.8680	0.7880	–0.0160	–0.0320	–0.0290	–0.0430	–0.0540	–0.1300
Operatives	0.9870	0.9710	0.9650	0.9730	0.9320	0.8380	–0.0020	–0.0100	0.0200	–0.0090	–0.1320	–0.1210
Service	0.9300	0.9120	0.8770	0.8810	0.8760	0.8850	–0.0059	–0.0560	–0.0460	–0.0420	–0.0520	–0.0470
Laborers	0.9670	0.9750	0.9680	0.9630	0.9530	0.8830	0.0230	–0.0040	0.0060	0.0080	–0.0150	–0.0870
All Occupations	0.9020	0.8800	0.8630	0.8640	0.8400	0.7670	–0.0090	–0.0200	–0.0120	0	–0.0520	–0.0880
All Unionized Occupations	0.9610	0.9460	0.9320	0.9290	0.9140	0.8750	–0.0030	–0.0160	–0.0090	–0.0140	–0.0340	–0.0540

5. EDUCATION. Data representing educational achievements, presumably related to occupational requirements, come from the 1950 and 1960 census information giving the median number of school years completed by workers in each of the detailed occupations. No age breakdown is available at all for 1950, and in 1960 such a cross-classification is given only for an intermediate list of occupations. It is therefore impossible to deal adequately with changing educational requirements over time.

Table 10–8. EDUCATION DATA FOR MAJOR OCCUPATION GROUPS, 1950–1960

Occupation	*Average Median Number of Years of School Completed*	*Change in Median Number of Years of School Completed*
Professionals	14.955	0.195
Farmers	9.167	0.483
Managers	12.183	0.405
Clerks	12.071	0.238
Sales	11.883	0.658
Craftsmen	10.165	0.650
Operatives	9.575	0.375
Service	9.589	0.632
Laborers	8.559	0.498
All Occupations	10.788	0.437
All Unionized Occupations	9.704	0.497

The amount of formal schooling required by an occupation is expected to be negatively related to the survival rate. A high required level would make entry difficult at any age level. It would also give the highly educated workers now in the occupation a valuable qualification to use in transferring to another occupation should their present one lose its relative attractiveness. In sum, high educational requirements make an occupation harder to enter then to leave; hence, the expected negative coefficient in the regression equation. The data refer only to formal schooling, leaving out all training acquired outside the academic framework, particularly training provided on the job. Yet for many of the blue-collar jobs and perhaps for some of the lower-income white-collar jobs the varying amount of nonschool training may be the most important factor affecting the education-survival rate relationship.[10] Unfor-

[10] See Gary Becker, "Investment in Human Capital: A Theoretical Analysis," *Journal of Political Economy*, Vol. 70, No. 5, Part 2 (Supplement: October 1962), pp. 9–49.

tunately, suitable measurements of nonschool education are not available.

Table 10-8 shows the major occupation averages for the median number of years of school completed. All groups showed increases over the decade. The professional groups probably had such a small increase because of the very high base from which the change is measured and because of the census practice of lumping all education beyond a bachelor's degree in one open-ended category. It is in the latter category where most of the educational advancements for the professional occupations probably occur. The averages in Table 10-8 exhibit the familiar pattern of low achievement among the blue-collar and farm occupations and higher levels for the white-collar and professional workers.[11] If true education could be measured, including on-the-job training, the gap might be closed somewhat since it is in the blue-collar occupations where most of the nonschool training is given. However, it is not likely that the relative rankings of the occupation groups would be changed.

6. Female labor force participation. The censuses of 1950 and 1960 provide age-occupation breakdowns for females identical to those provided for male workers. From these, it is easy to compute the fraction of females in the total work force in each age-occupation category and the survival rates for females. For the decades before 1950, the number of female workers in many age-occupation groups was so small that the inherent errors in the past data preclude the computation of any reliable survival rates. The only past information used is the fraction of females based on occupational totals. The figures presented in the final column of Table 10-9 represent averages for the five decades between 1900 and 1950.

A large number of females in an occupation-age category will probably make it somewhat more difficult for the males in the same category to survive, especially if the women are willing to accept a lower wage. As indicated in Chapters 2 and 5, it has been hypothesized that this trade off between men and women is one of the main causes of the older worker problem. A negative coefficient is expected in the regression equation.

A high female survival rate may work either way. It may be

[11] Further details are given by Denis F. Johnston, "Educational Attainment of Workers, March, 1962," *Monthly Labor Review*, Vol. 86, No. 5 (May 1963) pp. 504–515. The data deficiencies noted above are not corrected in this article

achieved at the expense of male survival, implying a negative regression coefficient. On the other hand, the presence of conditions which are favorable to female survival may also be favorable to male survival. This may be quite independent of the fraction of the work force that is female; the fraction of females and the female survival rate must be considered as two separate effects.

The data in Table 10-9 show that the fraction of females declines with age, but a general increase in the fraction of female workers took place over the last decade. Decline in the first age group may be due to a number of factors which kept young females out of the labor market: decrease in the marriage age; increase in formal schooling relative to male schooling; and greater general unemployment in 1960 with the young females being most susceptible to the shrinking job opportunities. Every occupation group shows a slight increase in the fraction of females in the latest decade compared with the earlier decades.

Female survival rates show the same general pattern as male survival rates, except on a higher level, largely due to a much larger growth in female workers in the last decade relative to male workers. The percentage of females in the work force increased from 35.02 per cent in 1950 to only 38.91 per cent in 1960. However, this represented a 63.25 per cent growth in the number of female workers during the decade compared with only a 14.01 per cent growth in male workers. The older worker problem for females seems concentrated in the service and clerk groups, which have the highest fractions of females but the lowest survival rates for age group 5.

7. Fraction of full-time workers. Both the 1950 census and the 1960 census provide various measures of the proportion of workers in each occupation who worked full time. The measure used here is the fraction who worked fifty to fifty-two weeks during the year previous to the taking of the census. As with the education variable, there is no breakdown available by age group, nor are there any useful data prior to 1950.

Availability of part-time work in any occupation will probably make it easier for workers to survive, particularly at the older age levels. The amount of energy and durability required to survive is less if one can work only part time. The variable used to represent such availability is expected to have a positive sign in the regression equation; or to put it the other way around, the variable "frac-

Table 10–9. FEMALE DATA FOR MAJOR OCCUPATION GROUPS

	1950–1960											
	Average Fraction of Females, Age Group						*Change in Fraction of Females, Age Group*					
Occupation	*1*	*2*	*3*	*4*	*5*	*6*	*1*	*2*	*3*	*4*	*5*	*6*
Professionals	0.2623	0.2282	0.2379	0.2511	0.2353	0.2056	—0.1191	—0.0082	0.0227	0.0191	0.0038	0.0288
Farmers	0.1329	0.1558	0.1785	0.1818	0.1575	0.0803	0.0066	0.0453	0.0117	—0.0115	—0.0613	—0.0125
Managers	0.1458	0.1305	0.1539	0.1491	0.1343	0.1135	—0.0658	0.0211	0.0276	0.0103	0.0252	0.0139
Clerks	0.4514	0.4572	0.4603	0.4358	0.3685	0.3075	—0.0340	0.0540	0.0323	0.0032	0.0150	0.0164
Sales	0.2588	0.2549	0.2538	0.2301	0.2125	0.1731	—0.0285	0.0694	0.0854	0.0439	0.0405	0.0097
Craftsmen	0.0645	0.0569	0.0556	0.0500	0.0434	0.0431	—0.0317	0.0012	0.0034	0.0032	0.0025	0.0178
Operatives	0.2241	0.2549	0.2620	0.2349	0.1012	0.1534	—0.0095	0.0294	0.0042	—0.0187	—0.0077	0.0247
Service	0.4500	0.4686	0.4639	0.4240	0.3881	0.3480	0.0057	0.0963	0.0616	0.0334	0.0267	0.0075
Laborers	0.0719	0.0913	0.0885	0.0727	0.0532	0.0217	0.0138	0.0103	0.0040	—0.0119	0.0023	—0.0160
All Occupations	0.1962	0.2006	0.2063	0.1922	0.1658	0.1368	—0.0292	0.0227	0.0169	0.0007	0.0050	0.0136
All Unionized Occupations	0.1791	0.1965	0.1970	0.1756	0.1449	0.1199	—0.0143	0.0248	0.0113	—0.0042	0.0068	0.0152

	1950–1960						1900–1950
	Female Survival Rate, Age Group						*Average Fraction of Females*
	1	*2*	*3*	*4*	*5*	*6*	
Professionals	2.91	1.19	1.67	2.04	1.03	4.11	0.2260
Farmers	0.55	0.96	1.07	0.41	0.22	0.09	0.0690
Managers	6.78	2.47	2.30	1.62	2.11	0.87	0.0935
Clerks	1.07	1.39	1.36	0.94	0.43	0.26	0.4197
Sales	1.91	2.83	2.33	2.01	1.62	0.40	0.2278
Craftsmen	4.44	2.61	1.79	2.85	1.50	1.35	0.0406
Operatives	1.80	1.64	1.15	1.13	1.05	1.46	0.2409
Service	5.04	2.96	2.51	1.86	0.61	1.25	0.3832
Laborers	3.35	1.33	1.74	1.06	0.71	0.50	0.0812
All Occupations	3.45	1.91	1.70	1.64	1.16	1.35	0.1709
All Unionized Occupations	2.72	1.54	1.55	1.08	1.14	1.16	0.1823

tion of full-time workers" is expected to show a negative sign.

Data for the major occupation groups are shown in Table 10-10. The occupational pattern of the fraction of full-time workers seems to follow that observed for several of the other variables: high for the professional and white-collar groups; low for the blue-collar and farmer groups. In particular, the relatively similar pattern observed for unemployment rates, Table 10-5, suggests that this variable may indeed reflect unemployment conditions more than willingness to accept part-time workers. The situation is a little more encouraging when one looks within each major occupation group, however. The

Table 10–10. DATA ON FULL-TIME WORKERS FOR MAJOR OCCUPATION GROUPS, 1950–1960

Occupation	*Average Fraction of Full-Time Workers*	*Change in Fraction of Full-Time Workers*
Professionals	0.730	0.027
Farmers	0.669	−0.022
Managers	0.861	0.008
Clerks	0.748	−0.037
Sales	0.716	−0.007
Craftsmen	0.695	0.012
Operatives	0.620	0.006
Service	0.638	−0.042
Laborers	0.532	−0.014
All Occupations	0.680	0.001
All Unionized Occupations	0.632	−0.004

simple correlation between fraction of workers unemployed and fraction of full-time workers is usually negative but quite small. The results will not force rejection of the full-time employment variable before at least trying it in the regression analysis.

8. FRACTION OF WORKERS WHO MIGRATED. The 1950 census presented some information about changes in residence location for workers in the detailed occupations. No age breakdown was given, nor are such data available for 1960 or before 1950. The particular move which caused a person to be classified as a migrant for our present purposes was his living in a different county in 1950 than he did in 1949. This measure will capture most of the people who moved and changed jobs at the same time without counting too many of the people who moved to a different neighborhood in the same general area without changing jobs. There is no way of telling whether this measure really corresponds very closely to the

number of job-inspired moves, and thus to an employment situation which can affect survival rates.

If an occupation requires a great deal of mobility on the part of the worker, it is likely that the survival rate will be lower. This is especially true at the older age levels where the subjective inconvenience of moving increases along with an increasing social attachment to one's friends and present community. A negative sign would be expected for this variable in the regression equation.

Table 10–11. MIGRATION DATA FOR MAJOR OCCUPATION GROUPS, 1950

Occupation	*Fraction of Workers Who Lived in a Different County in 1950 Than They Did in 1949*
Professionals	0.1397
Farmers	0.0770
Managers	0.0692
Clerks	0.0765
Sales	0.0811
Craftsmen	0.0600
Operatives	0.0414
Service	0.0660
Laborers	0.0743
All Occupations	0.0709
All Unionized Occupations	0.0567

The migration data in Table 10-11 show a slight tendency for the white-collar and professional groups to move more than the blue-collar and farm groups, but the differences are not pronounced.

9. MEDIAN INCOME. Median income for each detailed occupation is given in the 1950 census and the 1960 census. No age breakdown is available, although the 1960 census does provide the breakdown for an intermediate list of occupations. Income data were not collected at all before the 1940 census, and the 1940 figures are not useful since they are broken down only into an intermediate list of occupations. Also, the 1940 self-employed income is lumped into the under-100 dollars-per-year classification, a serious distortion for occupations which have a fair proportion of self-employed workers.

Incomes may be related to survival rates by providing some measure of the relative attractiveness of the different occupations. Occupations which pay high incomes are more likely to deter transfer to other occupations than are those which offer lower incomes. The high-income occupations are also more likely to attract workers. Of course the mere existence of higher income does not mean that workers will actually be able to make the transfer; lack of ability or training may preclude the shift. If, however, the shift is possible, then higher income should provide the attraction. A positive sign is expected in the regression equation.

For the older age groups, there may be another force that works in the opposite direction. Voluntary retirement might occur in occupations where workers have earned enough to provide a reasonable income during retirement. If this factor is strong enough to overcome the occupational transfer effect (and it may be, since occupational transfers become increasingly difficult for many reasons at older ages), the income variable may have a negative coefficient in the regression equation at the upper age levels. A situation having the same ultimate effect is the possibility that higher-income occupations, especially among the blue-collar group, are associated with pension plans and other rigid retirement schemes. Here retirement is forced rather than voluntary, but still results in a negative association between income and survival rates.

Table 10–12. INCOME DATA FOR MAJOR OCCUPATION GROUPS, 1950–1960

Occupation	*Average Median Income (dollars)*	*Change in Median Income (dollars)*
Professionals	5,300	2,990
Farmers	2,100	913
Managers	5,320	2,630
Clerks	3,580	1,490
Sales	4,140	2,180
Craftsmen	4,330	2,150
Operatives	3,430	1,620
Service	2,500	1,000
Laborers	2,770	1,220
All Occupations	3,940	1,930
All Unionized Occupations	3,690	1,790

The average median incomes for the major occupation groups are presented in Table 10-12 where the rankings are those expected. Note that the occupation groups increased their median incomes over the decade in proportion to their average income; the income gap becomes wider, not narrower.

10. TOTAL NUMBER OF WORKERS IN AN OCCUPATION. This variable consists of the average number of workers in an occupation during the decade. It is included in the analysis to account for differences in survival rates which may be due to the size of the occupation

alone.

Occupations with large numbers of workers may have a better developed market place than occupations which have a small number of workers. The well-developed market place can provide a larger variety of working conditions such as location, skill, ability, durability, strength, income levels, etc. The larger variety of conditions, in turn, should make it possible for workers to survive longer in an occupation, because they are more likely to find a particular job suitable to their circumstances and desires.

On the other hand, largeness may imply rigid organization which enforces compulsory retirement rules. This would reduce the survival rate of large occupations. However, when considering the size of occupations in a multiple regression analysis, the effects of rigid organizations can be partially removed, making it probable that the flexibility associated with large occupations would become dominant. Consequently, a positive coefficient is expected in the regression equation.

Table 10–13. AVERAGE SIZE OF OCCUPATIONS IN MAJOR OCCUPATION GROUPS, 1950–1960

Occupation	*Number of Workers (thousands)*
Professionals	76
Farmers	827
Managers	79
Clerks	149
Sales	238
Craftsmen	117
Operatives	78
Service	96
Laborers	55
All Occupations	105
All Unionized Occupations	125

Table 10-13 presents average size of occupation for the major occupation groups. The averages are useful only as an indication of the relative degree of fineness which the census was able to achieve in splitting up the major occupation groups. For our purposes, the fewer people in each detailed occupation the more likely it is that the members are homogeneous in their economic reactions. But this generalization must be modified by the realization that occupations differ considerably among major groups; e.g., a large group of farmers may be more homogeneous than a much smaller group of laborers.

11. PRODUCTIVITY. It is possible to assign an index of productivity to each occupation in the craftsmen, operatives, and laborers groups for each decade from 1900 to a very recent year.[12] The measure of productivity is output per labor hour, and the base year of the productivity index is 1929. With any degree of detail it is available only for manufacturing industries. Moreover, only in the blue-collar occupations, in large part classified according to industry anyway, can occupations be accurately matched with an industrial index.

The purpose for including this index in the analysis is to provide a rough measure of the amount of technological change. There are, of course, many aspects of technical change which cannot be

Table 10–14. PRODUCTIVITY DATA FOR SELECTED OCCUPATION GROUPS

Occupation	*Average Index Level, 1950–1960 (1929 = 100)*	*Change in Index, 1950–1960 (1929 = 100)*	*Average Rate of Change in Index Per Decade, 1900–1950 (1929 = 100)*
Craftsmen	148.8	4.9	16.2
Operatives	165.0	4.9	20.8
Laborers	170.9	5.6	20.9

represented by such a simple notion of labor productivity, but to go further would require a much fuller knowledge of the demand side of the labor market for detailed occupations than is now available. Rapid technological change should tend to reduce survival rates. The most obvious and pervasive effect is that of substituting machines for labor. However, even if the total number of workers hired remains the same, older workers may have their survival rate lowered. It has been suggested that older workers have a great deal of difficulty in adapting to new methods of work, especially to automated methods which call for less strength but more skill and coordination. Thus the productivity index, and particularly changes in the index, should have a negative coefficient in the regression equation.

Table 10-14 shows the limited productivity data available. Compared to the most recent decade, the index changed much more rapidly per decade during the early period. Part of this can be

[12] John Kendrick, *Productivity Trends in the United States* (Princeton, N.J.: Princeton University Press for the National Bureau of Economic Research, 1961).

attributed to the very low levels forming the base on which the index was computed in the earlier decades relative to the great amount of expansion in capital plant. Part is also due to the fact that, for most occupations, the year used for the beginning of the 1950 decade had fuller employment than the year used for the end of the decade. The figure obtained for the latest decade was therefore not representative of the true long-run trend value of the increase in productivity. This need not trouble us, however, since it is only the index for one period or the other which will enter the regressions. It is assumed that within each period the relative values of the index are unaffected.

12. Degree of employer concentration. The Department of Commerce has compiled a set of concentration ratios for detailed (four-digit) industries from data collected in the 1947 and 1958 Census of Manufacturers.[13] The measure used in this study is the fraction of industry sales made by the eight largest firms in the industry. Like any measure of concentration, this one is arbitrary. But it is no less suitable than other available measures. Because of the strict industrial classification used for the concentration ratios, they could be matched to survival rates only when the occupation classes reverted to an essentially industrial list. This is true only for part of the operatives and laborers. The concentration ratio was used to help explain the observed survival rates only for this group of occupations.

A high degree of concentration is used to represent a situation which has large firms and a less-than-perfectly competitive market place, at least for the final products. It has been suggested that large firms adopt an impersonal personnel policy. With thousands of workers, it is expensive to treat all workers as individual cases. Firms are forced to use a set of rigid rules to govern hiring, firing, retirement, and job shifting. Under such conditions, a great deal of the flexibility present in a small firm is lost. Workers must adapt to the rigid plan or leave. The survival rate should be lower for large firms, especially at the older age levels when change and adaptation become more difficult.

If there is less than perfect competition in the labor market for a particular occupation, it is expected that fewer workers would be hired than under a competitive market. Unfortunately, it is difficult

[13] U.S. Department of Commerce, *Concentration Ratios in Manufacturing Industry, 1958* (Washington: GPO, 1962).

to say much about the degree of competition in resource markets on the basis of concentration of the final product markets. Insofar as the two are related, the negative relationship between the concentration ratio and the survival rates will be reinforced. A negative coefficient is expected in the regression equation.

Table 10–15. CONCENTRATION RATIO DATA FOR SELECTED OCCUPATION GROUPS, 1950–1960

Occupation	*Number of Detailed Occupations*	*Average Fraction of Sales Made By Eight Largest Firms In Industry*	*Change in Fraction of Sales Made By Eight Largest Firms In Industry*
Operatives	57	0.5038	–0.0035
Laborers	49	0.5167	0.0009

The empirical data are presented in Table 10-15. Actual values of the concentration ratios themselves can have little meaning since the particular ratio chosen is arbitrary. It is the relative size of the ratio for the several occupations which may help to explain the observed survival rate differences.

13. FRACTION OF WORKERS WHO ARE UNION MEMBERS. Data pertaining to the degree of unionization was one of the few variables, along with productivity and the concentration ratios, which came from a source outside of the population census. The measure of unionization is the number of members in each union. These data for 1930 were derived by L. Wolman,[14] and for 1960 by L. Troy in an updating of Wolman's work.[15] A judgment was then made as to which occupation the union members belonged and how many were males and females. The result of this judgment was the allocation of all union members to some occupation-sex category. It was then easy to compute the fraction of male workers in each occupation who were union members. No age breakdown was possible.

Of course the effects of unions upon survival rates are complex, with several conflicting forces at work. Unions may insist that more be done to help the workers, especially older ones, adapt to changing conditions of work. This should increase the survival rate. On the other hand, the presence of unions and pension plans adopted

[14] Leo Wolman, *Ebb and Flow in Trade Unionism* (New York: National Bureau of Economic Research, 1936).

[15] Leo Troy, *Trade Union Membership, 1897–1962* (New York: National Bureau of Economic Research, 1965).

jointly with employers may force a worker to retire when he might have been willing and able to remain at work. As discussed in Chapter 2, seniority rules may or may not protect older workers when shifts between plants must be made due to changing geographical or technological patterns of production. The complexity of forces associated with unions precludes any clear-cut statement about the expected sign of this variable in the regression equation. Opposing forces may cancel each other leaving no significant relationship between the degree of unionization and survival rates, or either may dominate to generate either sign for the coefficient.

Table 10–16. FRACTION OF WORKERS UNIONIZED FOR UNIONIZED OCCUPATIONS IN SELECTED OCCUPATION GROUPS

Occupation	*1960*	*1930*
Professionals	0.3970	0.1170
Craftsmen	0.6767	0.2227
Operatives	0.6543	0.1889
Service	0.2320	0.0784
Laborers	0.7860	0.1112
All Unionized Occupations	0.6294	0.1658

The data for unionization are shown in Table 10–16. As expected, there has been a large growth since 1930, with most of the union members now in the blue-collar occupations.

14. TRENDS IN THE 1900–1950 SURVIVAL RATES. It is possible to compute a survival rate for each age-occupation category for each of the five decades from 1900–1950. These individual decade rates are not used in the regression analysis. Instead, a least-squares trend line is fitted to the five rates, and the per decade slope of the trend line is computed. A positive slope indicates a tendency for the survival rate to increase over time; a negative slope indicates a tendency to decrease.

The trend is not an economic variable but merely a statistic describing movements of the dependent variable over time. Therefore, trends are not used in the main regression equations (for the 1950–1960 decade) developed to *explain* survival rates. They are used only in the secondary set of equations constructed primarily for *predicting* future survival rates. The justification for using trends in these equations is quite different from the justification for including all the other independent variables described above. Useful prediction rather than causal explanation is the goal.

Two aspects of the trends can be considered. The first is merely the presence or absence of trends. Except for the youngest age group, the trend means are generally negative. This would imply an older-worker type problem at all age levels. However, the mean trend is a poor indicator of the general movement of survival rates since there is a very wide variation in the trends of the individual detailed occupations within each age-occupation group category. In almost every case (clerks being the major exception, and there is no explanation for this) the standard deviation of the trend coefficients is several times larger than the absolute value of the means. While there is a general tendency for the survival rate to decline over time, which can be corroborated from Table 10-3, the decline has not taken place uniformly in all the detailed occupations (at least for the 1900–1950 time period). Survival rate movements for major occupation groups cannot be described solely by the trends of the individual occupations comprising the group.

The second aspect of trends providing descriptive information about the data is the correlation between the trends and the other variables used. Most of the variables are not closely related to the trends. The two major exceptions are the survival and growth rates where most of the correlation coefficients are significantly negative, implying a movement toward a more uniform survival rate structure among the occupations within each age group. Those age-occupation categories with the highest average survival rates between 1900 and 1950 show the least tendency to increase the rate during this time period. The result will be a smaller variation between survival rates at the end of the period than at the beginning. Greater equality of rates can be the product of increased communication and mobility between geographic and industrial sectors of the work force, and the spread of standardization of working conditions due to union activity and federal labor laws. This movement towards equality is stronger among major occupation groups than within the groups except for laborers.

CHAPTER ELEVEN

Occupational Regression Analysis

PATTERNS in the observed data, such as those reported in the previous chapter, provide only casual and hazardous inferences about the causes of differential survival rates by age. The expectation of directional relationships between survival rates and the explanatory variables does, however, constitute a set of hypotheses about the forces determining survival rates. These hypotheses are codified in the form of a regression equation which yields the net amount and degree of association between the dependent variable and each of the independent or explanatory variables. Given that several such variables operate to determine a survival rate, the empirically estimated coefficient of each independent variable shows the relationship between that variable and the survival rate after the effects of all other independent variables are taken into account.

The Regression Equation

The regression equation assumes the general form:

$$S = k + gG + uU + rR + nN + tT + eE + sS_F + pP_F + fF + mM + iI + oO + lL + dD + cC.$$

Definitions of the variables and expected signs of the constant coefficients, as explained in the previous chapter, are:

S = survival rate.
k = constant term.

G = growth rate, $g > o$.
U = unemployment (fraction of workers), $u < o$.
R = race (fraction of nonwhite workers), $r < o$.
N = nonself-employed (fraction of wage earners), $n < o$.
T = time unemployed (median in years), $t < o$.
E = education (median years of school), $e < o$.
S_F = female survival rate, $s > o$ or $s < o$.
P_F = percentage of workers who are female, $p < o$.
F = full-time workers (fraction of all workers), $f < o$.
M = migration (fraction of workers who migrated), $m < o$.
I = income (median), $i > o$.
O = occupation size, $o > o$.
L = labor unionization (fraction unionized), $l > o$ or $l < o$.
D = productivity index, $d < o$.
C = concentration ratio, $c < o$.

The variables *L, D,* and *C* were included only where appropriate to the occupation.

To estimate the coefficients there are several ways of combining the data on the variables into groups of observations. The grouping should strive to obtain observations on homogeneous workers, as indicated in Chapter 8. One appealing way to combine observations is to use the survival rates of different decades for a single age-occupation category. Two major contributors to heterogeneity will have been eliminated, and the resulting equations will reveal something about the movement of survival rates over time. Unfortunately, available data do not permit the estimation of such equations. First, we have observations for only six decades, and six observations are not satisfactory for the computation of multiple regression equations. Second, the individual decade survival rates for the early decades are probably not very reliable. Third, there are almost no observations for the independent variables except for the recent decades. Therefore, no attempt was made to estimate time series regressions.

Not all past data were eliminated however. The major set of explanatory equations consist of a cross-section study of the 1950–1960 decade. The survival rates of the previous decades for a single age-occupation category were averaged; the average rates were used to compute a second set of explantory equations. The result is two cross-section studies, one for the latest decade and one for average values of the 1900–1950 time period. While neither set of equations is a study over time, comparison of the two sets of equations does suggest some of the changes that occur over time.

Within each of the two time periods, further grouping is necessary. It is possible to compute one regression equation for each occupation using the several age groups as observations. While this eliminates the heterogeneity due to differences in occupation, it does yield a very small number of observations and goes against the basic idea motivating this study: that the survival rate structure changes with advancing age to the disadvantage of the older worker. The only choice left, then, is to fit regression equations for a single age group but across several occupations. For each time period and age group, two basic sets of equations are computed. One uses every occupation in the work force as observations. The other utilizes only the occupations within one major occupation group as observations. There is, of course, one such equation for each major occupation group. As the empirical results work out, both the overall equation and the individual group equations prove useful.

The independent variables are used both in the form of averages for the 1950–1960 decade and changes in the values between 1950 and 1960, representing long-run and short-run effects respectively. Thus, for the later time period, two complete sets of regressions are computed. For the earlier time period, only a form of the average value was available.

A total of 354 regressions were computed. Obviously, comprehension of all regression results presented in a single set of tables is asking too much of any reader. Here we shall summarize and interpret the patterns that emerge.

Empirical Results by Age Groups

Let us begin by seeing how the variables combine to yield an empirical picture of the determination of survival rates for each age group in 1950–1960. The behavior of each group of workers is judged by the sign and magnitude of the regression coefficients of the significant variables. When many variables are significant in the same regression equation, complete interpretation of all of the coefficients simultaneously becomes very difficult: little notice can be taken of the isolated significant coefficient. Concern here is with the broad pattern of coefficients and changes in this pattern at progressively higher age levels. The farmer group will be discussed separately later in the chapter. The equations using the long-run variables are covered first, followed by comparison with short-run variables.

AGE GROUP 1. Survival rates are clearly related to the demand factors represented by the growth rate, although not as strongly as for succeeding age groups. Those who do enter an occupation at a young age will tend to stay with the occupation when the demand is high. Only the service occupations do not show a significant positive relationship between the growth rate and the survival rate. The service group simply does not follow the usual market forces at this age level, for none of the long-run variables is significant except the fraction of workers employed full time. High survival or large entry in the service occupations is not determined by such long-range factors as growth of the occupation or income opportunities; entry can only be associated with whether or not steady employment is available.

The income coefficients are positive and significant in every case but the service group, representing in part the normal market effect of an increasing demand in certain occupations. However, these coefficients may also be associated with occupations where entry delay is necessary due to higher educational requirements, with the increased training leading to higher incomes. Only non-formal training should contribute anything to this effect, since the coefficient for years of school completed is positive and significant for but one group, the professionals (and is significantly minus for managers and laborers). Only in the professional group is formal education a significant delay factor beyond what is incorporated in the income variable.

High survival rate occupations, besides being occupations with higher income and faster growth, have, for the work force as a whole, a higher fraction of nonwhite workers. The causal relationship in this case seems to be that nonwhites will be most numerous in occupations where entry is easiest for other reasons; there is no apparent way in which the presence of nonwhites alone will cause higher survival rates.

Besides the presence of nonwhites as a side effect of favorable survival conditions, females also find these conditions suitable for survival. Lack of any relationship for the professionals, sales, and service groups, and a questionable one for the operatives, is probably due in some degree to the fact that males and females tend to enter different occupations within each of the groups. When either sex is a very small proportion of the workers in a particular occupation, it is unlikely that these few workers will follow very closely what the majority do. Small groups of workers are subject to many random and exogenous fluctuations.

The only other relationship that appears across all occupational groups is a small positive association between the fraction of self-employed workers and the survival rate. Managers and professionals as a class (high survival rates, high fraction of self-employed) contrasted with the blue-collar and clerks groups (low survival rates, low fraction of self-employed) contribute to the observed relationship. Although self-employment may provide an inducement for the entering worker, it is unlikely at this age level that the positive coefficient represents a haven for workers who cannot survive as employees (as has been hypothesized for older workers). It is more nearly the case that the occupations with the most growth and entry delay (managers and professionals) also happen to have the greatest number of self-employed people.

The other variables affect this age group only for some occupations. Besides migration only the variables relating to unemployment appear for more than two occupational groups. The professional, sales, and operative groups display positive coefficients for the fraction-of-workers-unemployed variable and the length-of-time-unemployed variable. This might be termed "unemployment loyalty"—workers who are unemployed do not leave the occupation. The clerks group has a mixed pattern: large numbers of recently unemployed are still loyal enough to help raise the survival rate, but they will not stay loyal for long. It must be remembered that the length-of-time-unemployed variable is for the entire occupation, not just this age group. The negative coefficient for the fraction-of-full-time-workers variable in the case of professionals and clerks may reflect some unemployment loyalty, or it may reflect some entry of workers looking for part-time jobs. At this age level, such jobs would be mostly desired by students, but it is difficult to guess which jobs they would take or how likely it is that such student jobs would be recorded by the census takers. The data on part-time employment refer only to the entire occupation.

In summary, the typical occupation which is favorable to survival at the entering age level can be pictured as one with higher than average demand pressure and, probably, training requirements, and is more than usually favorable for nonwhites and females. The self-employed do a little better, as do a few occupation groups where "loyalty of the unemployed" and availability of part-time work add to the numbers surviving.

There is little change in the pattern of coefficients for the short-run form of the variables. The fraction of nonwhites loses all significance, implying that nonwhites changed their position very little over the decade. While a general increase in the fraction of nonwhites occurred for all groups but sales, the increase was more or less spread throughout all the occupations, not just the ones favorable to survival.

Three factors increased in importance for the short-run variables. Some displacement of males by females took place (increases in the fraction of females associated with lower survival rates), although the positive relationship between male and female survival rates remained, except for sales. Two exceptions to the displacement phenomenon, operatives and laborers, are understandable considering the nature of the work and the unimportant place which women have in most of these occupations. A negative survival rate coefficient for the sales group suggests that males and females survive best under different conditions, i.e., in different occupations, which may account for the lack of male displacement among the sales group.

Except for the professional and service groups, the fraction of full-time workers becomes significant. It is unlikely that all of this effect represents students and others looking for part-time work. The greater importance of the length-of-time-unemployed variable suggests that some unemployment loyalty is present. More detailed cross-classification of both the length of time unemployed and the fraction of full-time workers are needed to resolve this question. The normal amount of part-time work available seems to be an inherent characteristic of many occupations, one which changes little over the course of a decade. Those changes observed reflect changes in the general employment situation, not fundamental changes in occupational working conditions.

AGE GROUP 2. The same pattern found in age group 1 is followed for the growth rate and income variables. As before, there is no way of telling how much of the income relationship is due to a shifting demand and how much to shifting supply as a reaction to increased training requirements. It seems unlikely that training would be very important at this age level, except perhaps in the professional occupations.

The coefficients for the number-of-years-of-school-completed variable indicate that training delay has little effect upon survival rates except for the professional group. For the work force as a whole, and for all groups taken separately except clerks and sales, significant negative coefficients show that higher (formal) training requirements are keeping people out of the occupation permanently, not merely delaying entry. At this age level it is not yet survival difficulties as such that are causing differences in survival rates. Most of the movements of workers in this age group, at least the males, is between occupations, a phenomenon for which no data are available. What can be deduced from the educational coefficients is that, for most occupation groups, higher formal training requirements will deter transfer into the occupation, given similar growth and income inducements.

Self-employment is even more attractive than for age group 1, and continues to be so for all the older age classes. At this relatively young age level, the coefficients still represent desire to enter an occupation with a high fraction of self-employed workers rather than an opportunity to survive in an occupation.

The reactions of the nonwhite and female variables are similar to age group 1, but reduced to about one half the strength of the previous age group.

The clerks and service groups present some differences from the usual pattern, and both depend heavily upon large coefficients for the fraction of full-time-workers variable. The clerks are induced to stay in or transfer into occupations with high growth rates and high income where less migration is required. But after this initial entry they survive best in occupations with a smaller fraction of full-time workers. It is difficult to imagine that at this age level, past the time for most formal training and long before much physical deterioration occurs, many male workers voluntarily choose or look for part-time work. While the computed negative coefficient may make some sense for age group 1, it does not here. The explanation seems to be that the negative coefficients for both age groups are mostly a statistical artifact. There is a very high correlation between median income and the fraction of full-time workers (the correlation coefficient is 0.956). For both age groups, the fraction of full-time workers is positively related to the survival rate, but regressing this variable with one so nearly collinear (income) yields the negative coefficient. This instability is evidenced by the relatively high standard deviations (and low t values considering the size of the coefficients) for both the income and the fraction of full-time workers variables.

The service group is still guided more by the short-run opportunity of steady employment (a negative coefficient for length-of-time-unemployed and a large postive coefficient for fraction of full-time workers) than by the longer-run promise of high growth rates. Here, too, nonwhites face difficulty for the first time using the long-run variables.

For the work force as a whole, steady employment is of some importance, but unemployment loyalty is also present. Perhaps some of this is observed because the highest values for the length-of-time-unemployed variable occur for the manager and craftsmen occupations, which have relatively high survival rates and many occupational benefits to lose by moving to another occupation. Workers in these occupations will wait a relatively long time before transferring. However, the same process is observed within the laborer group, where there seems to be little opportunity cost to making a transfer, although it may be that restrictions from the demand side make transfer difficult. Again, until the data on length of time unemployed is more extensively cross-classified (to include age as well as occupation) it is difficult to explain the observed coefficients.

The change to short-run variables brings about some of the same shifts observed for age group 1: the unemployment variable becomes more important; the nonwhite fraction declines in importance; both aspects of the female relationship assume significance, but with less than half the strength shown in age 1; the fraction-of-full-time-workers variable assumes a negative sign, but, again, with less strength than for the previous age group; and the length-of-time-unemployed variable is more significant. Just as the self-employment variable is more negatively significant using the long-run variables for age 2 compared to age 1, it is more positively significant using the short-run variables. Within the professional, service, and managers groups, self-employment evidently does not produce a strong incentive to enter. The security of a salaried position induces higher survival rates. The higher survival rate may indeed reflect a desire on the part of these workers to enter salaried positions, or it could result from market pressures making salaried positions relatively more plentiful and attractive. There is nothing in the data that can be used to differentiate between the two situations.

In summary, as the work force ages from group 1 to group 2, the major forces explaining the observed survival rates undergo only small changes:

(1) High growth rates and high income still provide the major inducements to entry and survival.

(2) The barrier to entry of high formal educational requirements becomes significant at the second age level; it was not significant for age group 1.

(3) The acceptance of nonwhites in occupations with high survival rates, the positive association between male and female survival rates, and the displacement in the short-run formulations of males by females continue in age group 2, but with much smaller coefficients than were observed in age group 1.

(4) The appeal of full-time work increases, as do the rigidities implied by an increase in unemployment loyality.

(5) Occupations with a high fraction of self-employed workers increase in appeal, but this is contradicted by some occupation groups in their short-run behavior.

AGE GROUPS 3 AND 4. These age groups can be conveniently considered together. They are little different from each other and, for most factors, provide a relatively smooth transition between the younger age groups and the critical age group 5. These age levels are somewhat less complicated than either the earlier ones (where entry takes place) or the later ones (where differences in physical capacities and retirement conventions must be accounted for).

The growth rate is the most important factor explaining survival-rate differences, which should be mostly due to transfers. There is some decline in the importance of growth for age group 4, especially in the operative group, traceable mostly to the peculiar behavior of the apprentice occupations which had very few workers this old. The growth rate coefficient is much higher when the regression is run omitting the apprentice occupations.

Income drops out almost entirely as an explanatory variable, which can be interpreted as evidence of increasing occupational rigidity. Workers do not move easily to take advantage of higher incomes in other occupations. Some coefficients, especially for the short-run variables, are even negative, although small. The education variable still provides a barrier to entry for age group 3, but this is no longer important by age group 4. The only exception is the professional occupations with a positive education coefficient for both age groups. The postive coefficient at this age may represent career ladders which continue to operate, or merely the fact that the occupations with the highest educational achievements provide more incentive for a man to stay working in his chosen occupation.

The coefficient for the fraction of nonwhites is positive but very small for age group 3 and negative for age group 4. Since the position of the nonwhites and attitudes towards them have changed so much in the past two decades, it is difficult to say whether this is an effect of the aging process or, instead, is the result of an irreversible secular change. Will future decades show this same change from the early age groups to the middle-age ones, or will the present relationships for younger groups be carried forward to older ages? No data available now can answer this question.

The female-survival-rate association is weak for both age groups in the labor force as a whole, but only the blue-collar jobs show this individually. Female displacement in the short-run continues, but not as strongly as it does for the younger groups. The effect of self-employment has not changed much.

Some unemployment loyalty is evident in the short-run and long-run variables for age group 3. It is gone altogether by age group 4, where there is only some unemployment *dis*loyalty among the clerks. The positive effect of steady employment has been carried over to age group 3. An over-all negative effect appears for the first time in age group 4, possibly an alternative form of unemployment loyalty (the usual kind is not present), or the beneficial effect of having part-time employment available for those who need it.

Migration continues to show a significant negative relationship for a few occupation groups, especially white-collar ones where most of the migration has taken place. A positive coefficient for clerks with the short-run variables appears to be the result of a special set of circumstances. The occupations with high migration rates are those that offer a more casual type of employment, easy physical work combined with the availability of part-time employment. Such occupations have a relatively high survival rate compared with the low-migration occupations. The latter group requires more physical energy; employers are likely to be larger; and more formal employment contracts insist upon regular work habits. The costs of migration are, in this case, outweighed by fundamental differences in the two kinds of jobs. Those who need casual work may be willing to migrate or, in reverse, those who insist on migrating may be forced to accept casual types of employment.

AGE GROUP 5. This age group is the crucial one from the viewpoint of the older-worker problem. It is here where most of the unemployed older people have left the work force. A cure for the problem can start by raising the survival rates of this age group.

There is a great decline in the explanatory power of the growth rate variable. Survival at this age level no longer follows very closely the changing pattern of the rest of the work force. Unlike other occupations, the sales group maintains a high coefficient (and a regression equation which explains a very high proportion of the survival rate variation). Only the sales occupations provide few barriers to flexible survival.

Negative income coefficients appear for most occupations, especially the blue-collar ones, and for the work force as a whole. Workers at this age are restricted in movement toward occupations with higher incomes and/or they are forced to leave them more rapidly. Part of the process is probably explained by workers in higher income occupations being better able to finance a comfortable retirement and therefore desiring to leave the work force. But part may also come from the fact that pension plans may be associated with higher income occupations, and most pension plans involve forced retirement schemes. No data yet collected concerning pension plans and retirement policies has been classified by occupations in the detail needed to match this set of data. There is no way of separating these two effects, which is unfortunate since it has been claimed that forced retirements are one of the major causes of the older workers' problem. The only positive income coefficient is in the managers group, suggesting that the highest paid workers are generally of too great importance to their firms (or are self-employed) to cause forced (or even desired) retirement.

For the labor force as a whole, high educational requirements are a help in surviving at this age. Since little interoccupational transferring appears to take place at this age level, the education possessed by those on the job merely helps them stay there. However, since the education variable is not significant within any one age group, the significant over-all coefficient is a result of intergroup differences, primarily white-collar versus blue-collar groups. While educational differences do distinguish the two groups, one cannot help feeling that there are more fundamental differences than education that account for the survival rate differences. Education seems to have served as a proxy for things not measured, something not true for the younger age groups.

The female influence is less here than for younger age groups. The number of female workers becomes rather small at this age level. The pattern of female survival observed is subject to many small perturbations compared to the relative regularity of the male pattern.

The unionized occupations as a group generally followed the work force as a whole except for the unemployment variables. Some unemployment loyalty is suggested by the positive coefficient for the fraction of workers unemployed. But the coefficient for the fraction of full-time workers is positive and the fraction of workers unemployed for the craftsmen and operative groups (where many of the unionized occupations occur) has a negative coefficient, thus weakening any unemployment loyalty which might be present. As far as being forced into retirement more often than other nonunion occupations is concerned, the evidence suggests that the reverse is true. The growth and income coefficients for the unionized occupations are slightly higher than for the work force as a whole.

The coefficient for the size of occupation is significantly positive, although it is small. This suggests that the large occupations offer a greater variety of working conditions within an individual occupation, thus providing the older worker more flexibility in finding a niche that sustains his survival. However, this variable is the least important of the significant variables.

The service group is of special interest since it provides occupations with relatively high survival rates and low skill requirements. Some of these occupations might provide a place into which an older worker can transfer when he is no longer able to perform his normal job. The observed pattern of survival rates does not follow very well the market forces which determine the occupational structure of younger workers in this occupation group; the coefficients for both the growth rate and income are lower than for any other occupation group. The most important explanatory variable is the fraction of workers unemployed, which has a positive coefficient. Within the service group, high survival rates occur partly because of high levels of unemployment; favorable survival is achieved not by keeping workers on the job but by having a large number of unemployed people claim it as their occupation. This must be modified somewhat considering the negative coefficient for the length-of-time-unemployed variable in the short-run formulation. While the pool of unemployed is large, the workers leave relatively quickly, presumably out of the work force. Female displacement also occurs. This age group is the only one subjected to displacement for the long-run variables. Moreover, displacement operates on the group most strongly for the short-run variables. Also disturbing is the reappearance of the negative education coefficient for the short-run variables. This transfer barrier exists for no other occupational group at this age level. Consequently, the service occupations do not appear to be a promising source of jobs for older workers who are forced to leave more taxing occupations.

AGE GROUP 6. The explanations for most of the occupation groups and for the work force as a whole are much poorer than for any of the previous age groups. Part of the difficulty is that very few workers survive to this advanced age. Shifts (or misreporting) of a few workers can cause large swings in the survival rates. Part is undoubtedly due to many special circumstances, none of which have been measured here, that are associated with a worker staying on the job beyond 75 years of age. For the over-all work force, no very important explanatory variable is found. For the most part, the coefficients are similar to those observed for age group 5, but are usually much smaller.

Although little explanation has come out of the analysis for age group 6, the deficiency is not serious. This is a rather unimportant age group, for few workers survive physically to this age level. It is in age group 5 where the great majority of older workers become unemployed. Policies designed to improve their situation would probably have the side effect of automatically improving survival for workers fortunate enough to reach age group 6. The situation may change in the future, of course, if mortality rates at age level 6 are reduced.

Empirical Results for Occupation Groups

Most of the important results of the regression equations have been noted in the previous section. There are, however, a few comments which might be made about some of the occupation groups.

Farmers were not discussed so far since the very small number of observations did not permit computations of regressions as large as those computed for the other groups. Only two independent variables were tried simultaneously, and even this procedure leaves one with but three degrees of freedom. The limited results obtained are not unlike those found for the other occupation groups. The growth rate is the most important explanatory variable; income is positive for the first two age groups and turns negative for age group 5. Large negative nonwhite coefficients result from the low survival rates among farm laborers, both wage earners and unpaid family workers, where a great number of nonwhites are concentrated. The primary forces affecting survival rates for farmers seem to be associated with growth rates, and with all the basic secular movements away from agriculture underlying this variable.

There are no easy generalizations to be drawn from the regression results in the other occupation groups. The fundamental forces at work were described above; each occupation group needs a somewhat different combination of these forces to explain its own set of observed survival rates. No group is radically different from the others, but none is quite the same. There seems to be a basic similarity in the way in which the various occupation groups react to market forces, despite the obviously great differences among occupations in the nature of the work required and the environment in which it is carried out.

The set of "not elsewhere classified" occupations from the managers group were analyzed separately to judge the effect of the self-employment variable. This group consists of pairs of occupations, each pair being the manager of a particular type of establishment. One occupation in each pair is a self-employed manager and the other is a salaried manager. The self-employed variable does, indeed, appear with a negative coefficient for the older age groups, whereas it is not significant at all for the entire manager group. Therefore, in the case of occupations which are strictly managerial, self-employment does attract workers and/or help survival at the older age levels.

Two groups of occupations were considered primarily children's or very young peoples' occupations. Regressions were computed excluding these occupations to see if they unduly influenced the results of the basic regressions. One is the occupation of newsboys in the sales group. Since the number of observations was quite low (11), all the sales regressions were computed with a limited number of independent variables. This makes direct comparison of the regressions a little difficult. From the results obtained, however, there appears to be a minimal difference in the explanations obtained with and without the newsboys. The other subgroup consists of apprentices within the operatives group. The major difference observed when the apprentice occupations are dropped from the operative group is the greater importance of the growth rate variable, especially for age group 4. The pattern for the other variables was virtually the same, except for reduction in importance of the self-employed variable.

The "not elsewhere classified" portion of the laborer and operative groups were used to test the importance of the concentration ratio variable. No pattern is evident for the laborer group, but the operative group, for the long-run variables, shows a steady progression from positive to negative with increasing age. The coefficients become negative at age group 3. This tends to confirm the suspicion that more concentrated industries are inclined to hire younger workers (and thus contribute to their higher survival rate) rather than retain older workers. Further investigation of industrial data is needed to determine what combinations of demand factors are associated with or cause the particular concentration ratios which are observed. Without such knowledge very strong statements about the effect of concentration cannot be made.

The final group of occupations for which special regressions were computed are the unionized ones. No meaningful results were obtained for the professionals; the number of unionized occupations was small (8) and the unions quite diverse in purpose and character. For the craftsmen group, the pattern of coefficients for the unionized occupations is quite similar to the basic long-run variable regression equation. For the laborer and operative groups, there is a general reduction in the number of coefficients that remain significant; more of the explanation must rest with the growth rate variable. For the service group, the unionized regression adds some significant coefficients and reverses the signs of some others. Because of the small number of observations in the union group (11), strictly comparable regressions could not be computed. There is also very little difference between the regressions computed for the work force as a whole and all unionized occupations.

The real interest in union regressions, however, is not the change in structure from the basic regressions. There is no reason to expect that the unionized occupations should behave in the same ways as the entire work force. The main reason for computing separate regressions is to test the effect of the fraction-of-union-members variable. Every significant coefficient has a minus sign, the higher percentages of unionization being associated with lower survival rates. For the older age groups, extensive pension plans and formal retirement codes may be the result of pervasive union contracts. For the younger age groups, restricted entry may be associated with more complete unionization. Also, the most rapidly growing occupations and those with rising formal educational requirements are not highly unionized. As with the conclusions regarding concentration ratios, more accurate data matching union membership with both occupations and age groups are needed.

Regression Results for 1900–1950

The regressions computed for the average survival rate between 1900 and 1950 do not provide revealing explanations of the observed survival rate pattern. This is not surprising considering the tenuous nature of the survival rate data and the almost complete inability to provide data for the independent variables at any other time point than the very end of the period, 1950. Further, the occupations had to be less finely divided than for the most recent decade so that the distribution of workers among the regression observations differs for the two periods.

Growth rates and trend values provided most of the explanation; other variables were less important. For the professional and managers group, no other variable was consistently significant, except perhaps education for the professionals. Clerks reacted only to the female fraction (showing displacement), and sales only to the fraction of nonwhites. For the blue-collar groups some income effect is observed, positive for the younger ages and negative for age group 5, as was found for the most recent regressions. Education is a barrier for the operatives; the laborers have a number of significant variables. Where direct comparison of coefficients is possible, we find that the two sets of regressions do not differ very much from each other. Some differences are inevitable, of course, but despite rather different conditions under which the two sets were computed, one feels that there has not been a fundamental change in the forces explaining survival rates between the two periods of time.

As might be expected from the discussion in the previous chapter, the trend coefficients are virtually all negative. Survival rates were becoming uniform among occupations during this period of time.

Conclusions and Implications

Some definite patterns emerge from the statistical regressions. For both age groups less than 35 years of age the major forces affecting survival rates are quite similar. High occupational growth and high income provide the strongest inducements to entry and survival, with some displacement by females in the short run. But there are some differences between age groups 1 and 2. Whereas educational requirement is not a significant explanatory variable for those who are less than 25 years of age at the beginning of the decade, it is significant for those 25 to 34 years of age. Educational requirements do pose a barrier to occupational entry at the higher age. In addition, full-time work is more important for the higher age group, and barriers to the transfer of occupations begin to set in.

For those 35–54 years of age at the beginning of the decade (groups 3 and 4) growth of the occupation is the single most important variable determining survival, but less important for group 4 as compared to group 3. Expanding demand still operates to promote high survival. Income drops out as an explanatory variable, indicating great immobility in occupational transfer. But displacement by females in the short run is much less important than it is for those less than 35 years of age. No doubt experience on the job acts to modify or prevent substitution of females for males.

Workers between the ages of 54 and 65 at the beginning of the decade show radical departures from the characteristics of the younger groups. They also show some continuing trends found in the intermediate age group. The occupational growth rate declines markedly as a determinant of survival, and negative income coefficients appear for the first time. Low survival rates and severe nability to transfer jobs are combined with fewer employment pportunities as product and labor demand expand. Education elps survival only in those occupations with high requirements, uch as professionals and managers. With service occupations failng to provide a source of physically easy or low skill jobs and howing great displacement by females, a dismal employment picure emerges.

Despite the shortcomings of available data, one point is clear. Occupational survival is closely related to changes in the occupaional structure of the labor force brought about by changing denand patterns for various types of workers *and* by different reacions to changing demand by different age groups on the supply ide of the labor market. Several factors combine to explain surival rates in any one age-occupation category. Moreover, the umber of factors and the directional influence of each varies omewhat among ages and among occupations. Most past studies ave concentrated upon one or, at most, just a few variables. The mpirical results found here indicate that such studies would find nly weak relationships between proposed causal factors and surival rates (or another employment variable) if other factors were aken into account.

Certain similarities appear between the analysis of occupations nd the analyses of industries and regions. In the case of occupaions, young workers are attracted to expanding occupations with he greatest prospective earnings. These are also the occupations vith the highest education requirements, and survival is greatest or those who are able to enter such occupations at a relatively arly point in their employment careers. Substitution of females or male workers is also evident, as it was in the case of the analysis f industry demand for labor. An exception is the group of occuations with the highest education requirements.

At the intermediate age, substitution of females for males delines in importance. This was also found in the study of labor lemand by industries. The intermediate age group has acquired aluable experience and is still young enough to be successfully ompetitive. The single most important determinant of survival at he intermediate age is the growth of the occupation. If a worker s in an occupation for which labor demand is expanding signifiantly, his chances of survival are strong. However, occupational mmobility begins to set in. If a worker is not in a rapidly expanding occupation, his ability and willingness to transfer to the growing occupations becomes more restrictive as compared to the youngest age group.

Older workers show the lowest survival rates, even when their occupation is expanding, with the exception of the managerial and professional group. Occupational immobility is quite severe. Just as the older worker does not pursue higher earnings among industries and among regions, so too he does not pursue these earnings among occupations. Even the acceptance of occupational downgrading appears restrictive. When an older worker cannot survive in his normal occupation, the available data indicate that he leaves the labor force. One important reason for this departure is the absence of a sufficient number of physically easy or low skill jobs. He might be willing to accept a lower earned income rather than an even lower retirement income, but the changing structure of occupations does not offer enough such jobs for older workers.

CHAPTER TWELVE

Predicting Occupational Employment

REGRESSION analysis is designed partly to explain observed phenomena and to measure the relative impact of the explanatory variables upon survival rates. Ultimately, however, the analysis will prove useful only if it can predict the future with reasonable accuracy. Unless the coefficients are stable over time, the regression equations may be good descriptions of past events but give no guidance in forecasting future events.

A test of the forecasting ability of the model can be made by predicting the 1960 occupational distribution of the labor force using data available only before 1960. Since the 1960 distribution is already known, the predictive accuracy can be determined by comparing the predicted with the observed values. This procedure means that we cannot use the regressions developed to explain the 1950–1960 survival rates; these are the very rates to be predicted using earlier data. We are forced to use the 1900–1950 regression equations which, as explained in the previous chapters, are of much poorer quality than the equations based on more recent data. However, some indication can be obtained from these early equations about the usefulness of this type of model.

While the eventual concern is with the absolute accuracy of the predictions, initially we want to see whether or not this method of prediction does better than simple alternative methods. Unless it can do better than the simple prediction methods, there is little

point in going to the trouble of building models on relativel
sophisticated and complicated economic ideas. Our present regres
sion model will be judged against three naïve alternative predictio
methods. Little attention will be paid to the absolute accuracy o
the predictions made by any of the methods.

Methods of Prediction

When the number of workers in many occupations is being pre
dicted, it is not immediately clear how the closeness of the pre
dictions should be judged. If one method yields predictions tha
are closer to the actual values for all occupations than those devel
oped by a second method, one could say that the first method i
unambiguously better than the second. The usual case, howeve
is that in which one prediction method will be better for som
occupations and worse for others. There is an infinite number o
ways to compute and add up the prediction errors to arrive at
measure of prediction accuracy. The method chosen as best ma
depend entirely upon just which measure of prediction accuracy i
used. In this chapter, we shall use two measures recently suggeste
by H. Theil, the coefficient of inequality and the measure of infor
mation inaccuracy.[1] The relationships between these two measure
will be studied in some detail.

The previous two chapters described how survival rates wer
computed for each age-occupation category and for each decad
from 1900–1910 to 1940–1950. This yielded five survival rates fo
each category which could be used in various ways to predict th
1950–1960 survival rates and, combining this with the actual num
ber of workers in 1950, the number of workers in 1960. The firs
three methods are naïve methods based on no economic considera
tions, and the last two are based on the regression model. Th
prediction methods are:

METHOD 1: naïve extrapolation of the survival rate. This metho
assumes that the survival rate for each age-occupation category fo

[1] They are fully described in his forthcoming book, *Applied Economic Fore casting,* (Amsterdam, Netherlands North-Holland Publishing Company, 1965 The definition of the coefficient of inequality used here differs from that used i his earlier work, *Economic Forecasts and Policy* (Amsterdam Netherland North-Holland Publishing Company), p. 32. The reasons for making the chang are discussed in his new book.

the 1950–1960 decade will be the same as that experienced in the 1940–1950 decade. This does not mean that the occupational distribution of the work force, or of any age group of workers, will remain the same. It is only the *rate* of survival which is assumed to be the same. Thus, this is not the same as assuming that the number of workers in each age-occupation category will be the same in 1960 as it was in 1950, the usual meaning given to a naïve prediction.

METHOD 2: constant first differences of survival rates. This method assumes that the difference observed between the 1930–1940 and 1940–1950 survival rates for each age-occupation category will be repeated between the 1940–1950 and 1950–1960 survival rates. As with method 1, once a predicted survival rate is obtained, it can be applied to the actual numbers of workers in each age-occupation category in 1950 to compute the predicted number of workers in each category in 1960.

METHOD 3: extrapolation of the trend of survival rates over time. A least-squares trend line is fitted to the five survival rates for each age-occupation category. The trend line is extrapolated to the next decade to get the 1950–1960 predicted survival rate.

METHOD 4: applying the regressions for all occupations as one group using the 1900–1950 data. The coefficients computed with the 1900–1950 data are combined with the 1960 values of the independent variables to derive predicted values of the 1950–1960 survival rates. This method is somewhat different than the first three since it utilizes some information from 1960 in deriving the prediction. In practice, we would not know the 1960 employment figures but would have to predict them as well as the survival rate. The regressions could prove to be poor predictors both because of inherent deficiencies in the coefficient estimates and because of poor estimates of the future values of the independent variables. We are eliminating this last source of error by inserting known values of the independent variables. It is difficult to say how much artificial accuracy is added to the regression predictions by doing this.

METHOD 5: A separate cross-section regression for each major occupation group. This method is exactly the same as method 4 except that, instead of using all 244 occupations in one regression, a separate regression is computed for each of the eight major occupation groups. The procedure for using these regressions and the difficulties involved are the same as for method 4.

Judging Predictive Accuracy

Having obtained five sets of predictions for the number of workers in each age-occupation category in 1960, we must now judge which of the methods is "best" for each age group and various occupation groups. Two measures of the degree to which the predicted number of workers match the actual number of workers will be used, the coefficient of inequality and the measure of information inaccuracy of the forecasts. Although both measures basically set out to do the same thing (measure the relative accuracy of different forecasts) there are several reasons for performing computations using both. They measure different aspects of the lack of correspondence between the actual and predicted values. In fact, the whole problem will be formulated somewhat differently for the two measures. Further, both measures can be decomposed into components which give some indication about the sources of inaccuracy of the predictors, but the decompositions are quite different and tell different things about the inaccuracies present.

The coefficient of inequality is defined as:

$$(1) \qquad U = \frac{\sqrt{\frac{1}{n}\sum_{i=1}^{n}(P_i - A_i)^2}}{\sqrt{\frac{1}{n}\sum_{i=1}^{n}A_i^2}}$$

where P_i, A_i stand for a pair of predicted and actual values, and n is the number of observations. If the predicted and actual values exactly match, $U = 0$. If they do not match, as will usually be the case, U is positive and has no upper bound, the larger the U the worse the predictor. The square of the numerator can be decomposed into three additive terms which, when divided by the square numerator itself, become:

$$(2) \quad U^M = \frac{(\bar{P} - \bar{A})^2}{\frac{1}{n}\sum_{i=1}^{n}(P_i - A_i)^2}; \quad U^S = \frac{(s_P - s_A)^2}{\frac{1}{n}\sum_{i=1}^{n}(P_i - A_i)^2};$$

$$U^C = \frac{2(1-r)s_P s_A}{\frac{1}{n}\sum_{i=1}^{n}(P_i - A_i)^2}$$

where $\overline{P}$ and $\bar{A}$ are the averages of the predicted and actual values, s_P and s_A the respective standard deviations, and r the simple correlation coefficient between the series of predicted and actual values. Since the sum of numerators of each of these three expressions equals the square of the numerator of U, the following holds:

$$(3) \qquad U^M + U^S + U^C = 1.$$

Each of the three expressions in (2) can be interpreted as giving the relative importance of three different reasons for the P_i's and A_i's not being equal. The first, U^M, will be above zero to the extent that the predictions are not centered in the same place as the actual values. The second, U^S, measures the amount by which the variations in predicted and actual values differ. The third, U^C, will be positive if the predicted and actual values are not perfectly correlated. As Theil suggests, the first kind of error is probably most serious, the second less so, and the third an almost-residual nonsystematic error. If we must have errors in our predictions, it is preferable to have them all in the U^C.

A second type of decomposition is possible yielding a different set of inequality proportions. U^M remains as before, but the other two terms become:

$$(4) \qquad U^R = \frac{(s_P - rs_A)^2}{\frac{1}{n}\sum_{i=1}^{n}(P_i - A_i)^2}; \qquad U^D = \frac{(1-r^2)\,s_A{}^2}{\frac{1}{n}\sum_{i=1}^{n}(P_i - A_i)^2}.$$

Again, the following relation holds:

$$(5) \qquad U^M + U^R + U^D = 1.$$

The interpretation of these proportions differs from the previous set. Picture a regression of the actual on the predicted values. If the predictions are perfect, this regression line should have zero intercept, a slope of unity, and no disturbances around the fitted regression line. U^M will be zero if the intercept is zero, U^R will be zero if the slope of the line is unity, and U^D will be zero if there is no scatter around the regression line. U^M and U^R represent systematic errors which should be as small as possible in relation to the U^D error.

The information inaccuracy measure is based on more subtle ideas borrowed from the solution of certain stochastic problems in communication theory. Information theory gives us a precise way of measuring the amount of "information" obtained in a "message," giving us the outcome of certain events. These events are thought to occur with a certain probability, which can be stated beforehand.

To make things clearer, suppose there is one event involved which we feel will happen with a certain probability. The message which comes in afterwards tells us whether this event did, in fact, occur. If the "prior" probability assigned to the event's occurrence is very high, the amount of information yielded by a message saying that it did occur will be quite small. If, however, we assign a small prior probability, then a message saying that the event occurred gives us a great deal of information. This way of reasoning suggests that the information measure will have to be a decreasing function of the prior probability. In fact, information theory uses a logarithmic function:

$$I_D = \log \frac{1}{p} \tag{6}$$

where p is the prior probability assigned to the event, the logarithm is to the base 2 and the subscript ^{D} stands for "direct," to distinguish it from the indirect case, considered below.

This measure is zero, when $p = 1$, i.e. when the message contains no new information, and it increases to arbitrarily large values when p becomes close to zero.

The measure is additive for independent events, so that if there are, say, n events, the total information of all messages about these events is:

$$I_D = \sum_{i=1}^{n} \log \frac{1}{p_i}. \tag{7}$$

Suppose now, that there are n mutually exclusive events $E_1, \ldots, E_n$, of which one certainly will be realized. When we assign prior probabilities to each of them, these probabilities $p_1, \ldots, p_n$ will add up to 1. Now a message comes in, which tells us that event E_i took place. The information of the message that E_i occurs is log $(1/p_i)$, and because the probability that this message comes in is p_i, the expected information is:

$$(8) \qquad I_D = \sum_{i=1}^{n} p_i \log (1/p_i).$$

In economics we are not very interested in direct messages. It is not important for our purposes to know that a certain person went to a certain occupation. What we want to know is how many people went to each of the several different occupations.

Consider, therefore, the following way of reasoning: we have n mutually exclusive events which exhaust all possibilities and we assign prior possibilities $p_1, \ldots, p_n$ to them. Then a message comes in which tells us that the probabilities in fact are: $a_1, \ldots, a_n$. This is what we call an indirect message. (A direct message is a special case: then one a_1 is 1 and all others are 0).

Information theory defines the information contained in an indirect message as:

$$(9) \qquad I = \sum_{i=1}^{n} a_i \log \frac{a_i}{p_i} = \sum_{i=1}^{n} a_i \log (1/p_i) - \sum_{i=1}^{n} a_i \log (1/a_i).$$

The first term after the second equality sign measures the amount of expected information before the actual values are known, and the second term the expected information after receiving the actual values. Thus the measure I gives the reduction in expected information caused by receiving the particular message embodied in the a_i's.

To apply these notions to prediction, we must interpret the predictions as being the prior-stated probabilities and the actual values as the message which tells us the true values of the probabilities. A further condition is that both the predictions and the actual values consist of a set of nonnegative numbers, which add up to 1. When these conditions are fulfilled, formula (9) can be applied straightforwardly on these two sets of probabilities. The I which we obtain in this way will be a function of the predicted and the actual values, as is the coefficient of inequality. The reduction of expected information, indicated by I, can be interpreted as measuring the inaccuracy of the prediction. When we have a very poor prediction, the information obtained by receiving the actual values is very large. So I will be large and this in turn indicates that the prediction was very inaccurate. On the other hand, when a prediction is perfect I will be zero (because $a_i = p_i$ for all i's). So the *in*accuracy is zero, which indicates a perfect prediction.

The procedure for our purposes is to predict by some method the number of workers in the different age-occupation categories. We want to make some statement about the "goodness" of these predictions with the help of the information inaccuracy measure. In this situation we have two sets of absolute values, and it is impossible to apply the measure of information inaccuracy on these two sets. We must have two sets of numbers which resemble probabilities. Fortunately there is an easy transformation which can be made. If in both sets the number of workers in all occupations is divided by their sum, we get two sets of numbers that give the (predicted and actual) fractions of workers in each occupation. So we have two sets of numbers, say $(p_1, \ldots, p_n)$ and $(a_1, \ldots, a_n)$ which both consist of nonnegative numbers, adding up to 1.

Two points of interpretation should be mentioned. First, it is not usual to think of the fractions of the labor force in each occupation as a set of probabilities. Mechanically they do satisfy the requirements for a set of probabilities, but the economic interpretation must depend upon our willingness to consider the problem in this way: given an individual worker, what is the probability that he will be in a certain occupation in 1960? This point of view may have a very tenuous connection with supply and demand forces operating in a labor market. Market theory does not describe market behavior as a probability process operating upon individual workers. We shall allow ourselves the privilege of temporarily considering the fractions to represent meaningful probabilities when talking of the information inaccuracy of forecasts and then reverting to usual market theory for discussing the economic meaning of results.

Second, the conversion from numbers of workers to fractions of the work force means that the predictions refer to a different variable than we originally set out to predict. In one sense it is easier to predict fractions of the work force since there is no need to be very accurate about predicting the total number of workers. On the other hand, there may be cases where one is able to predict the number of workers in most occupations very accurately, but miss badly for a few occupations. In these circumstances, the work force-fraction method will indicate that all occupations were poorly predicted, and it may be difficult to discern the true situation without essentially going back to the original formulation by computing the predicted and actual numbers of workers. In this study, the coefficient of inequality will be computed for both the number of workers in each age-occupation category and for the fraction of the labor force in each category. This should provide some empirical indication of the differences inherent in the two methods of stating the prediction problem.

The measure of information inaccuracy can also be split up into meaningful components. The decomposition considers groups of observations and their effect as groups upon the total inaccuracy. (This differs from the decomposition of U where the observations were never considered separately; only different characteristics of the total prediction of all the observations could be considered.) The data are first divided into N subsets of observations. These subsets should have some economic justification for being considered separately, i.e., the observations within the subsets should be more homogeneous than the observations between subsets. The natural subsets consist of the major occupation groups.

It is easily verified that information inaccuracy I can be written:

$$(10)\quad I = \sum_{G=1}^{N} (a_G) \sum_{i \in G} \left(\frac{a_i}{a_G}\right) \log \frac{a_i/a_G}{p_i/p_G} + \sum_{G=1}^{N} a_G \log \frac{a_G}{p_G}$$

where G is the group index running from one to N, and p_G and a_G represent the sums of the p_i's and a_i's within group G. Thus I is composed of $N + 1$ terms, the first expression on the right representing N terms and the second one on the right representing one term. Each of the N terms included in the first right-hand expression consists of the terms summed by the second (inside) summation sign and then weighted by a_G. A special meaning can be attached to each of the second summations. It measures the information inaccuracy which occurs within a group of observations provided we know we are someplace within that group. That is, it gives the information inaccuracy of predicting the occupation in which a worker will be, given that he is known to be within a certain major occupation group. The second term on the right-hand side represents the information inaccuracy between subsets ignoring the prediction inaccuracies within each subset. The only determinant is whether the predicted and actual values for the total of each major occupation group were close together without regard to how well individual occupations within the groups were predicted.

Comparison of the empirical values of the two terms in equation (10) yields information about the homogeneity of the several groups of observation with respect to the prediction methods used. Further, the empirical values of the *N* conditional information inaccuracy terms can form the basis for judging the relative merits of the predictive method among the eight major occupation groups. This will not tell us in what way the predictions went wrong, as the decomposition of the *U*'s will, but it will reveal which group or groups of observations were more difficult to predict than the others. The contrast between types of knowledge revealed by decomposition of *U* and *I* is one of the major justifications for using both measures in the computations.

Empirical Results

Each of the eight major occupation groups was considered separately in addition to using all 244 occupations as one group. The *I* measure is accomplished automatically with the decomposition described above. For the *U* measure, separate computations had to be run for each major group as well as all occupations as one group. This is accomplished by picking out only certain pairs of predicted and actual value (those belonging to one major occupation group) and summing only over this subset of values to compute the *U*. This gives a measure of the prediction error analogous to the within subset components of the *I* measure, but there is no direct way to use the *U* measure to get a between subset component. Five age groups and five methods of prediction were used, and the summary discussion presented here is based on results too detailed to be presented here.

There are four forms of data for which the predictive accuracy of the five methods was judged: uncorrected number of workers (ucn), corrected number of workers (cn), uncorrected fraction of the labor force (ucf), and corrected fraction of the labor force (cf). *I*'s can be computed only for data in the cf form; *U*'s were computed for all forms of the data. The forms utilizing numbers of workers represent the usual formulation of the prediction problem: how many workers will be in each occupation and age group? The fraction forms divide both the predicted and actual number of workers in each occupation by the total number of workers in the labor force. The result is that we are predicting the fraction of the labor force in each occupation and comparing it with the actual fraction observed.

Corrections are necessary because all prediction methods except the naïve method (method 1) may predict negative numbers of workers in some occupations. Computation of the *U*'s is not affected, but *I*'s cannot be computed if any of the predicted numbers are negative. (There is no way to represent the logarithm of a negative number in a form which can be simply summed.) To eliminate these negative predictions the following correction rule was adopted: if any predicted value was less than 30 workers, call the prediction 30. The number 30 was chosen because 1950 census data were based on a three and one-third percent sample of all census returns. Thus, if just one worker was observed in the sample in any age-occupation category, the census indicated that there were 30 workers in that category, i.e., the minimum positive number of workers which could be observed was 30.

In one sense, this correction process might be considered unjustified. However, for the sake of realism, one might consider a lower limit of 30 workers predicted as a legitimate integral part of any prediction method used. Surely individual predictions of negative workers make no economic sense even though they result quite normally from the application of a prediction process which is economically meaningful. The correction process, besides being necessary if *I*'s are to be computed, seems a reasonable way to proceed. Most of the results are little affected by the application of this correction.

Consider first the results when all occupations are taken as one group. Table 12-1 shows the average ranks over the five age groups for each prediction method and inaccuracy measure. Method one, the naïve method of unchanged survival rates, seems best. The failure of method five implies that the quality of the regressions (based on predictive accuracy) run for the individual major occupation groups varies so much among groups that the results obtained by combining the predictions of the eight separate regressions is not good. Enough of the group regressions are poor so as to make the method poor when considering all occupations as one group. The failure of method 2 is not surprising considering the vast differences between the 1930–1940 decade and the two which followed. The economy and the labor force did not change in the same way between the 1940–1950 decade and the 1950–1960 decade as it did between the depression of the 1930's and the prosperity of the 1940's.

The most promising sophisticated method, method four, is not usually best (except for age group 3 and the fraction form of data). However, it is usually near the top of the rankings. While it is certainly not better than the naïve method 1, it is the next best method.

Inaccuracy measures by age group show that the best predictors are least successful in age groups 1 and 5, the youngest and oldest.

Table 12–1. AVERAGE RANKS OF THE FIVE METHODS; ALL OCCUPATIONS CONSIDERED AS ONE GROUP

Inaccuracy Measure	*Prediction Method* 1	2	3	4	5
U ucn	1.2	4.2	3.0	2.4	4.2
U cn	1.4	4.2	2.2	2.6	4.6
U ucf	1.6	3.2	3.6	2.6	4.0
U cf	1.8	3.6	2.4	2.6	4.6
I cf	1.4	5.0	3.4	2.0	3.2

This is not unexpected. Much of the change in occupation structure occurs through changing patterns of the entering group of workers, age group 1. The behavior of this age group may change a great deal from decade to decade. Retirement age, age group 5, brings forth a variety of reactions in the different occupations. Some of these arise through differences in physical requirements of the jobs, past income allowing a comfortable retirement, the presence of unions and formal pension plans, customs, etc. The middle-age groups display more occupational stability, leading to more successful predictions.

The prediction methods appear worse when measured for all the occupations taken as one group than when the labor force is broken down into major occupation groups. Table 12-2 presents the averages over the five age groups of the inaccuracy measures for each major occupation. In almost every case, the total has greater inaccuracy than do any of the individual occupation groups. This is understandable. Breaking the occupations down into relatively small groups, each presumably possessing some characteristics of homogeneity allows prediction methods suitable for this small group alone to be used. The implication is that a policy maker would not choose a single method for predicting the occupational composition of the labor force; each occupation and age group must be considered separately.

Table 12-2 refers to the *best* prediction method. When the occupations are broken down into major groups, naïve method 1 is no longer consistently the best. Out of the two hundred cases involved (five inaccuracy measures, five age groups, and eight occupation groups), method 4 was best sixty-five times; method 5, fifty-nine times; and method 1 only forty-three times. Either re-

Table 12–2. AVERAGES OVER THE FIVE AGE GROUPS OF THE INACCURACY MEASURES (BEST METHODS) FOR ALL OCCUPATION GROUPS

Occupation Group	*Inaccuracy Measure*				
	U ucn	*U cn*	*U ucf*	*U cf*	*I cf*
Total	0.345	0.328	0.302	0.301	0.117
Professionals	0.247	0.246	0.229	0.229	0.069
Farmers	0.287	0.287	0.045	0.045	0.008
Managers	0.200	0.200	0.174	0.174	0.050
Sales and Clerks	0.279	0.279	0.145	0.144	0.079
Craftsmen	0.193	0.191	0.130	0.130	0.056
Operatives	0.351	0.316	0.197	0.197	0.065
Service	0.355	0.279	0.251	0.251	0.086
Laborers	0.343	0.343	0.228	0.228	0.064

gression method was better than the naïve method 1, and the two regression methods together were better more oftn than all three naïve methods. When the average rank criterion is considered in Table 12-3, methods 1, 4, and (for the fraction formulation of the problem) 5 are virtually identical no matter which measure of inaccuracy is used. There is thus some inconsistency between the average rank and best ranking criterion. When good regressions can be computed, they are very good predictors; but when they are not the best predictors, they are very poor. On the other hand, the naïve method 1 cannot consistently do better than good regressions, but is seldom very poor.

Despite the qualifications, these results are encouraging. The regressions used can be considered nothing more than a first approximation to a quantitative description of the labor market. The operation of market forces was reduced to a single equation regression. Also, uncertain data were used for estimating the coefficients of the regression equations. The closeness with which such a model comes to being superior to simple alternative prediction methods suggests that better market models using better data should produce a formulation which has greater predictive accuracy.

Decomposition of the inaccuracy measures shows that none of the prediction methods is very deficient in the areas illuminated by the decomposition procedures. The between-subset component of *I* is designed to show how much of the total amount of information

Table 12–3. RANKS OF THE FIVE METHODS, AVERAGED OVER THE MAJOR OCCUPATION GROUPS AND ALL AGE GROUPS

Inaccuracy Measure	*Prediction Method* 1	2	3	4	5
U ucn	2.41	4.17	2.84	2.45	3.13
U cn	2.55	4.20	2.70	2.40	3.15
U ucf	2.45	4.32	3.30	2.48	2.45
U cf	2.45	4.32	3.22	2.53	2.48
I cf	2.33	4.60	3.57	2.10	2.40

inaccuracy resulted from our inability to predict the correct fraction of workers in each major occupation group, independent of how wrong we were in predicting the individual occupation fraction within each group. Table 12-4 shows the average values of this component for each method (averaged over the age groups) and for each age group (averaged over the methods). There is little difference between the methods, all values being quite small.

Table 12–4. AVERAGE BETWEEN-SUBSET COMPONENTS OF *I*

	Average over the Age Groups		*Average over the Methods*
Method 1	0.033	Age group 1	0.052
Method 2	0.058	Age group 2	0.025
Method 3	0.039	Age group 3	0.017
Method 4	0.046	Age group 4	0.023
Method 5	0.058	Age group 5	0.117

For the age groups, however, there are substantial differences between the middle three groups and the youngest and oldest groups. As noted before, these are the most volatile age groups, and thus the ones most difficult to predict. This difficulty is evidenced by the relatively large amount of intermajor-occupation-group shifting which has not been accounted for by our prediction methods. The previously cited literature about the older worker's problems suggest that relatively complex and unusual occupational shifts are to some degree undertaken in the older worker's effort to retain employment. Better predictors will have to incorporate more completely these aspects of market behavior.

Decomposition of the *U*'s has been done only for all occupations considered as one group. This should be sufficient as an indication of the relative amounts of systematic and unsystematic prediction errors. The proportion U^M, common to both types of decomposition, is small. For the fraction type of data, it will be zero by definition, since both the predicted and actual values consist of 244 fractions which add up to 1. For the number formulation of the problem, however, U^M is a measure of how poorly we predicted the total number of workers in the labor force. In only one case does the U^M proportion account for as much as 10 per cent of the total prediction error; most of the cases have a U^M of under 1 per cent. Only in age group 1 is it fairly consistently above 1 per cent. At this age level, changes in the trade off made between more education and receiving income at earlier ages may cause relatively large changes in the size of the total work force. In particular, increased amounts of education taken by persons in this age group have decreased the numbers who join the work force.

The four older age groups show clearly that most of the prediction error is in the unsystematic proportion U^C rather than in the more systematic U^S. However, age group 1 again breaks the pattern. We have incorrectly estimated the amount of variation in the entry patterns of occupations, due probably to changing educational requirements and labor demand patterns. Neither of these factors will affect the work force very much, and thus affect U^M or U^S, at older age levels.

The systematic-unsystematic dichotomy represented by the U^R–U^D breakdown of the total *U* shows results very similar to the U^S–U^C breakdown. The systematic part is generally small except for age group 1. However, age group 2 shows a number of cases where the systematic part is more important than the nonsystematic part. For this age group, the relative importance of the systematic and nonsystematic components differs between the U^S–U^C and U^R–U^D types of component breakdowns. The picture suggested is that the regression line between the actual and predicted values differs from unity, and this alone causes a difference, but a relatively small one, in the value of the standard deviation between the predicted and actual values.

Another concern is the comparison between answers given by using *U* and *I* as a measure of the prediction inaccuracy. A simple way to look at the comparison is to consider first only those prediction methods that *U* ranked as best. How would *I* have ranked those same methods? A frequency distribution of the ranks is given in the first line of Table 12-5. In thirty-nine out of the forty-four cases, the method ranked best by the *U* measure was ranked first or second by the *I* measure. In the eight cases where it ranked second by the *I* measure, the method ranked second by *U* was ranked first by *I*. Considering the entire table, *U* and *I* give about the same answer for the vast majority of cases.

Table 12–5. FREQUENCY DISTRIBUTION OF THE RANKING BY THE OTHER MEASURE OF THE METHOD RANKED FIRST BY THE BASE MEASURE

	Other Measure Ranks				
Comparison	*1*	*2*	*3*	*4*	*5*
I–Ucf	31	8	5	1	0
I–Uucn	20	15	7	3	0
I–Ucn	19	13	7	4	2
UCF–Uucf	44	0	0	1	0
Ucf–Ucn	24	8	8	4	1
Ucf–Uucn	22	12	7	3	1
Uucf–Uucn	23	11	7	3	1
Uucf–Ucn	22	9	8	5	1
Ucn–Uucn	41	2	0	2	0

A more stringent criterion for judging the closeness of the results between *U* and *I* is by taking into account how well they matched in all positions of the rankings, not just in picking out the best method. This is given by the size of the statistic tau, which is unity for perfect correspondence or correlation of positions. The large number of cases where there was less-than-perfect correspondence between the two measures must be investigated to see why they did not match in their rankings. Two factors seem able to explain most of the cases of tau less than unity: (1) there were small differences in the values of the *U*'s or *I*'s, or both, among the prediction methods which were ranked differently by the two methods; (2) the predicted values for some occupations were very small relative to the actual values, blowing up the value of *I* to an abnormally high level.

The first factor is related to the way in which the inaccuracy measures discriminate between prediction methods which are almost equally good. If two prediction methods have errors which are close to each other according to one particular inaccuracy measure, it may be very easy for another inaccuracy measure to rank them in the reverse order. When two methods really are almost equally good, it makes little difference from a policy point of view which one is finally picked as the best method. Either inaccuracy measure will lead to methods which, while not the same methods, will yield about the same results. The implication is that rank reversals that occur because the range of prediction errors is small can be considered as relatively harmless. A low tau due to this cause will not be considered a serious mismatch between the rankings of the *I*'s and *U*'s.

The second factor is much more serious. Then the measures *U* and *I* do differ in their definition. The *U* deals with the *difference* between the predicted and actual values; *I* is concerned with the *ratio* of actual value to predicted value. Most of the difficulty comes from the fact that some of the prediction methods, when allowed to go free, sometimes predict negative numbers. The correction procedure described above set a floor of thirty workers for any single prediction. But thirty is a very low number relative to some of the corresponding actual values. Where many of these corrections had to be made, and the actual values were relatively high, the value of *I* has been pushed up. This distortion to *I* we shall refer to as the correction distortion. Here the policy maker is faced with a much more difficult choice. It is no longer a matter of choosing among two or more methods which all give about the same results. Now one prediction method gives quite different rankings just because we are using a difference instead of a ratio to measure goodness of the method. In so far as these types of cases occur, we are forced to the conclusion that the two different inaccuracy measures are giving different answers to the same question.

Each of the age-occupation groups which had a tau of under unity was investigated in an attempt to determine the cause of the rank reversals. This determination was based on judgment, but in most cases the cause was quite obvious. The results are presented in Table 12-6. For tau equal to 0.8, only one rank reversal occurred. A high value of *I* (with respect to *U* as the standard) for just one method is enough to cause the less-than-perfect correspondence of ranks. For the lower-correlation cases, more rank reversals are needed. While correction distortions may contribute to the low correlations, the several rank reversals observed are almost always accompanied by small ranges of the inaccuracy measures among the methods for which ranks do not correspond between *I* and *U*. For the less stringent matching criterion represented by Table 12-5, checking has shown that in the fourteen cases where the best methods did not match, small ranges were always present among the top two, three, or four methods where the mismatching occurred.

Table 12–6. CAUSES FOR RANK REVERSALS IN THE *I-Ucf* COMPARISON

	Number of Cases			
τ	*Small Range*	*Correction Distortion*	*Uncertain*	*Total*
0.8	8	5	4	17
0.6	9	0	0	9
0.4	5	2	1	8
0.2	0	1	0	1
0.0	1	0	0	1

It is concluded that the *I* and *U* measures will usually give the same rankings to the prediction methods except when the methods are approximately of equal goodness (in which case it makes little difference which method is chosen) or when the predicted values become very low. This latter difficulty does make a difference in choice of method, and if the difficulty exists, indicates that careful attention must be paid to choice of inaccuracy measure.

The next question discussed is the effect of the correction procedure on the results even when the same measure of prediction inaccuracy is used. The answers obtained with the corrections applied are compared with those obtained when the predictions are allowed to go free. Three pieces of evidence are available, all of which indicate that the mere act of correction does not change things very much when the same measure is used (but, as indicated above, it may force differences between the *U* and *I* measures). First, a comparison was made between corrected and uncorrected prediction totals for all occupations for each method and age group. In only two cases is the difference between the corrected and uncorrected totals as high as 3 per cent (for method 2), and most of the cases are well under 1 per cent. Second, the between-subset component of I for both the corrected and uncorrected form of data show some differences, especially for methods 2 and 3 where most of the corrections took place. But they are small, except for method 4, age group 1. Third, rank correlations applied to the appropriate pairs of U's, similar to that discussed in detail for the I–U_{cf} comparison above, can reveal differences in ranking the five predictive methods caused by shifting the problem from uncorrected to corrected data. The correlations show that there was virtually no disagreement between the corrected and uncorrected computations as to which method was best. Indeed, correction alone has little effect upon the answers obtained using a given measure of inaccuracy.

The final concern is with the difference in answers obtained when shifting from the prediction of numbers of workers to the prediction of fractions of the labor force. There is some indication that this change does make a difference. The U's are generally higher for the number form than for the fraction form of data. This is because the fraction form assumes that we know the total, while the number predictions generally do a relatively poor job of predicting this total, at least for some age groups. But higher U's alone will not necessarily change the answer we obtain about the best prediction method. The implication is that the form in which the problem is presented will determine the rankings of the prediction methods. One cannot directly transfer prediction methods judged best in one context to use for other data with any assurance that a best prediction method is being used.

Conclusions

In summary, the object has been to predict the numbers of workers who will be in each occupation in 1960 using data from 1950 and before. The work force has been divided into 244 detailed occupations and five age groups. Five prediction methods were devised, all based on the behavior of occupational survival rates for individual age groups. Three of the methods were simple naïve extrapolations, the other two were somewhat more sophisticated regression models. Two forms of data were used, the numbers of workers in each occupation and the fraction which each occupation is of the total work force; two measures of prediction errors are the coefficient of inequality and the information inaccuracy of the forecast; and a correction procedure was applied to limit the predictions to positive numbers of workers. Very briefly, the data indicate:

(1) The regression models, despite the crudities of data and lack of sophistication in their construction, show up well against the naïve methods. Better models with better data should prove to be more useful predictors of employment in each occupation.

(2) Decomposition of the measures of inaccuracy reveal few cases of systematic errors in the prediction methods for the middle age groups. The youngest age group displayed systematic difficulties with poor predictions of the variations in the actual values, or the slope of the regression line between the predicted and actual values, and the oldest age group showed all the methods relatively poor in predicting a worker's major occupational group. These two age groups are affected by a more complex set of factors than the middle groups, and will need more accurate data to develop good predictors.

(3) The two different measures of inaccuracy gave approximately the same answers when applied to the same set of data, but some discrepancies appeared. Most of these could be explained by the measures' failure to rank in the same order two prediction methods which were of approximately the same accuracy. This was considered of minor importance. More important, however, were the different answers given when the predicted values were very low and the actual values relatively high. These differences are inherent in the different definitions of the two inaccuracy measures. Only a few cases of this type appeared in the present set of data.

(4) The differences in answers obtained between the sets of data corrected and not corrected was small. A much larger difference was observed when the number-of-workers formulation of the data was compared with the fraction-of-the-work-force formulation.

The ultimate aim of econometric models is to obtain good predictions. The success of a particular econometric model can only be determined when some kind of analysis is made of its predictive properties. Of primary importance for the study of the economics of age are the hopeful signs revealed by the tests of predictive accuracy. If the single regression technique does as well as the data indicate, there are good grounds for pursuing the economic-model approach based upon more accurate aggregate statistical data. In turn, the success of this pursuit hinges upon the collection and proper cross-classification of the data designated as relevant by the theoretical models.

PART V

Toward a Public Policy on Aging

CHAPTER THIRTEEN

The Analysis of Public Policy

IN RECENT years the national antipoverty program has been directed toward improving employment opportunities for the youth of the nation. For children and young people who have been deprived of the background needed for successful competition in a market economy, attempts are made to promote greater productivity through education, job training, and appreciation for work. Public policies bearing upon the income position of older and aged persons have, for the most part, assumed the form of public relief or assistance rather than efforts to raise productivity. Medicare, income-tax exemptions, and public relief at the state and local levels are examples. Only those who have reached the "normal" retirement age of 65 years are eligible. Almost none of the legislative action has applied to workers below this age who fall in the lowest income categories because of problems associated with age.

Several symposia on remedial policies have been held, and recommendations have been proposed. In the literature on aging many policy suggestions appear. However, as the following chapter will indicate, these proposals have not taken full account of the economic considerations bearing upon a problem that is primarily economic. Evaluation of public policies involves examination of both ends and means. Criteria are needed for judging what ends are desirable. It may not be possible to satisfy two or more ends simultaneously. Moreover, the means adopted may be inconsistent with professed ends, or one means among the available alternatives may be superior to others.

As a consequence, it is highly desirable that an analytic framework be clearly demarcated before issues of public policy are discussed. In turn, the relevance of this framework hinges upon what is known about the market forces determining the distribution of income and employment opportunities among different age groups. A variety of evidence has been examined in this study. A summary of the findings provides a basis for discussion of public policy.

Summary of the Principal Conclusions

The American population and the American labor force have been growing progressively older. Both the number and the proportion of older persons have increased, due primarily to a decline in fertility rates over the past century. There are also strong indications that this aging trend will continue in the future, at least with respect to the number of older people. At the same time there has occurred a decline in labor force participation by older persons. Although the most striking decline is observed for those over 65 years of age, a relatively high rate of nonparticipation begins to appear at about 45 years of age. If nonparticipation in the labor force were accompanied by adequate income from other sources, this type of unemployment would not constitute a poverty problem. However, nonwage income is not adequate. For example, among persons over 65 years of age, the median annual income for those not in the labor force in 1951 was only $774.

Much of the departure from the labor force may be regarded as true unemployment, in the sense that it is not completely voluntary. The occupational structure of the labor force has been changing. Prospects for employment have been rising in some areas (especially in professional, clerical, and other skilled categories) while the have been shrinking in others (notably farm and unskilled categories). Advancing technology and increasing educational requirements have imposed the necessity for flexibility, adaptability, mobility, and retraining potential in the labor force. Unless older persons possess these qualifications, their productivity declines relative to the productivity of younger groups. If they cannot keep pace with the demands made upon them by changing methods of production, their chances of survival diminish in the growing occupations and industries. Once displaced for whatever reason, the older person's failure to find re-employment in expanding labor markets leads to withdrawal from the labor force.

This prospect appears as the best among a very poor set of alternatives.

Improving health and diets and the spread of pension systems might be expected to alleviate the problem of early retirement with quite low income. The former could help the older person to retain employment, while the latter would take the financial sting out of early retirement. However, from the available evidence, neither can be identified as exerting a significant impact which acts to raise the income or improve the employment status of older workers. Rising health standards improve the physical abilities of all age groups, and it is comparison between the qualities of older workers *relative to* younger workers that influence hiring by employers. Indeed, better medical care may simply help more people to survive to an older age at which they face the "older worker problem." Also, it is apparently (psychological) adaptability to change rather than physical endurance or dexterity on a fixed job that determines successful survival in employment.

Likewise, retirement income, though more widespread, is simply not large enough relative to earned income to make voluntary retirement with sufficient income feasible. Only in the high-income occupations—such as the professional, managerial, and highly skilled groups—is retirement income great enough for the worker to maintain a standard of living comparable to that attainable with earned income. In the future, if the growth rate of the economy raises national income to a sufficient level, retirement income can be financed at a greater ratio to earned income. At the present time, however, retirement income from private pension plans and social security is not adequate to prevent poverty among the aged.

Underlying the older worker's problem are a host of specific causes that could in principle create difficult employment prospects, worsen those prospects, or improve them. In this book stress has been placed on the importance of a methodology. Past studies on aging have selected for examination one factor, or at most a few factors, that contributes to observed patterns of earnings and employment opportunities among age groups—with special emphasis on the older worker. In reality, an entire complex of individual characteristics and market forces operate simultaneously to produce these observed patterns. By isolating a single causal factor and ignoring the effects of others, an explanation of the effect exerted by that factor is almost certain to be distorted. Although from a practical viewpoint not all of these factors can be handled simultaneously, an attempt has been made here to incorporate in the analysis several of the most important explanatory variables. These explanatory variables were selected and ordered (thus yielding hypotheses) by utilizing economic theory. Quantitative estimates of the relative strength exerted by the several explanatory variables and tests of the theoretically established hypotheses were based upon aggregate statistical data. In order to test further the inferences drawn from the statistical series, and to provide more detailed information on employment conditions, additional evidence was provided by direct interviews with personnel officers and by examination of union-employer contracts.

The first point to be accentuated is not surprising. Workers 60 years of age and over experience severe difficulties in retaining employment or obtaining re-employment—except for some professional workers and skilled artisans. This fact has already been documented. Indeed, it is the motivating force behind past studies on aging. What is less obvious is the fact that these same income and employment problems begin to set in at an earlier age, approximately 45. If the labor force is divided into three age groups—the young (14–24), the intermediate group (25–44), and the older group (45 and over)—the older workers are at a disadvantage as compared to the other two groups. They display more low-income and high-unemployment problems, with the intermediate and the young age groups holding stronger economic positions in that order. As a young worker ages and passes into the intermediate age group he acquires experience, stability, seniority rights, and promotions that cause his income to rise and make his employment status more secure. However, as he passes the 45–50 age mark, that security tends to deteriorate.

Both the demand for labor by age and the supply of labor by age operate to produce the observed patterns of income and employment by age. It is convenient to summarize the results of this study in terms of six factors that emerged as important explanatory demand or supply variables.

PRODUCTIVITY. Evidence of diminishing productivity with increasing age, beyond the intermediate age level, appears in various forms. Interviews with personnel officers (Chapter 5) revealed that many believe seniority systems constrain re-employment of displaced workers. But whether or not employers' representatives attached much importance to seniority systems, practically all of the thirty-eight interviewed expressed the opinion that they, and other employers, are reluctant to hire older workers on the open market. The reasons given, such as inflexibility, less strength, or less adaptability to technological change, simply reflect the belief that older workers are less productive vis-à-vis younger employees. These beliefs were documented in some instances. But whether such beliefs are documented objectively or not, they do influence hiring policies.

On an aggregate statistical level, a relationship between productivity and age is not directly observable. However, the theoretical formulation (Chapter 4) entails certain demand characteristics that follow upon lower productivity. Although variability among industries exists, the statistical evidence strongly suggests a consistent pattern across industries. As compared to younger groups, older workers show a smaller increase in employment with respect to expansions of product demand and industry output. They also show a relatively low-wage elasticity of demand (another consequence of lower productivity).

Across occupations, the occupational growth rate, a demand variable, assumed much less strength in determining survival in an occupation for older workers than it did for younger groups (Chapter 11). Educational attainment is generally lower for older than for younger workers, and what education older workers do possess is of little help in promoting survival. One exception is the high income group of occupations, such as professionals and managers, for which survival is not a serious problem.

Some laboratory-type studies have suggested that young and old are equally productive on a given observed job. Other experiments, covering different jobs, have found the older worker less productive. Such conflicting results are not surprising since the jobs vary. Also, older workers still on the job, unlike others of the same age, may retain employment precisely because they are unusually productive. On a broader scale—covering specific firms and the interpretation of statistical evidence—the factor of decreasing productivity with age seems inescapable. In jobs requiring physical stamina, declining endurance causes a diminution of productivity. Where acquired skills are important the decline in productivity is not significant. But already noted is a relatively great decline in productivity by older workers in white-collar jobs. Weakened memory, reduced speed, and less education than the young operate to retard productivity. However, even if an older worker can maintain his productivity in an absolute sense under given job conditions, a change in these conditions acts to put him at a *relative* disadvantage. By standing still in a moving world, his ability to perform is reduced relative to that of younger persons who enter the labor force with more education and adapt more readily to changing production methods once they are in the labor force. It is a decline in the ability to make rapid adjustments that appears most important in putting the older worker at a productivity disadvantage.

EMPLOYMENT HORIZON. Of somewhat less probable importance, but still highly significant as a demand factor, is the effect of pension costs and workmen's compensation upon employment by age. Both in direct interviews (Chapter 5) and in the aggregate statistics (Chapter 4) the evidence indicates that a higher total wage rate, inclusive of supplementary contributions by the employer, acts as an important restriction upon the hiring of older workers.

This factor affects the older worker's prospects for re-employment once he is displaced from a job, rather than his ability to retain long standing employment in a given firm. Supplementary employment costs are not greater for an older worker who has been on the payroll for many years. Over this period he has "paid his way" toward the pension income he would receive upon retirement. Nevertheless, in a dynamic economy, the demand for particular products is constantly changing and production methods are revised. Thus jobs are abolished in some areas or firms and created in others. All workers are subject to these forces of the market and must accept relocation. It is at this point that the importance of supplementary employment costs is felt. From the employers' perspective, an older worker is more costly to hire on the open market, even if he is as productive as younger job applicants, because of his limited work horizon under the existence of prevailing retirement income systems.

SUBSTITUTION OF FEMALE LABOR. On the demand side of the labor market, both among occupations (Chapter 11) and among industries (Chapter 4), there is evidence of substitution of females for males of all age groups. However, the oldest males are most strongly affected by this substitution. The youngest males experience a substitution second in magnitude to the oldest males, while for intermediate aged males there is relatively little female substitution by employers. The importance of job experience combined with relatively high productivity at the intermediate ages probably accounts for the greater insulation against substitution of females enjoyed by the intermediate age group.

It has been claimed that substitution of female labor for male labor on the part of firms is the single most important factor explaining the decline in employment of older males (Chapter 3). However, when account is taken of other demand and supply variables, substitution of females does not show a causal impact as strong as productivity, supplementary employment costs, or immobility.

Still, female substitution is operative, and it is not independent of productivity. Indeed, the greater degree of substitution at the upper ages is additional evidence pointing to relatively low productivity at advanced ages. If females are willing to work for less than males, they would be hired even though their productivity is less so long as the same ratio of wages to productivity is maintained for each. Otherwise, female labor would be more costly per unit of product. Under collective bargaining and institutional practices, however, females are likely to be paid the same wage as males. The particular job calls for a standard rate regardless of who performs it. If males and females are paid the same wage rate, then substitution of females suggests that they are more productive than older males. The cost per unit of product is lower for females than for older males.

MOBILITY. On the supply side of the labor market severe immobility predominates as a cause of the older-worker income and employment problem. The older age group as a class is unable or unwilling to take advantage of higher earnings in industries other than the industry of present employment within manufacturing, and between manufacturing and nonmanufacturing industries (Chapter 4). There is an inverse relationship between age and interindustry mobility. The same pattern appears in regional or geographic migration (Chapters 7 and 8). Since migrants move partly in response to greater prospective earnings, a negative correlation between age and mobility tends to widen regional per capita income differentials as well as income differentials by age. Younger, more productive, workers migrate out of relatively poor areas, leaving a labor pool of older average age. Thus, more depressed areas undergo an aging of the work force due to geographic migration, worsening the economic status of older age groups for the economy as a whole. Besides industrial and regional immobility, there is also more occupational immobility among older workers (Chapters 9 through 11). Moreover, the scarcity of employment opportunities in low-skill and low-physical-requirement occupations, typical of the service trades, closes an outlet which might otherwise provide employment for older workers.

LABOR UNIONS. Labor unions affect both the demand for and supply of labor. Through collective bargaining they promote seniority systems which, to some extent, protect the older worker against displacement (Chapter 6). However, these same seniority systems also act to restrict employment opportunities for older workers when they are displaced and seeking re-employment in firms where a seniority system prevails. By means of negotiated clauses in employment contracts unions may be able to effect relocation of older workers at another plant whenever one plant in the firm discontinues production. But in such instances unwillingness to move on the part of the older worker is an obstacle.

To the extent that they participate in the administration of hiring halls or regulate apprenticeships, unions can control the supply of labor and "place" workers who are in the upper age brackets. Their success in doing so has been mixed. In the building trades (where labor is mostly skilled and the union provides the work crews) and in utilities (where the total cost of labor is low relative to the cost of capital) unions have been most successful. In manufacturing industries the degree of job protection varies even from firm to firm. It is not surprising, therefore, that no systematic effect of the degree of unionization upon employment by age could be found in the statistical aggregates. In general, unions have not counteracted the effects of other variables that generate the older worker problem.

MISCELLANEOUS FACTORS. There are many other factors that exert some influence upon employment differentials and labor force participation by age. Different racial composition of each age group, degree of competition or monopoly in the industry of employment, self-employment versus employment by another firm, and the effect of hiring older workers upon the morale of the younger members of a firm's work force are some of these factors. All these so-called miscellaneous variables play some part in explaining observed age patterns in employment. But none of them stands out as a major contributor to the older worker problem. Lower productivity, limited work horizons, and severe immobility emerge from the available data as the three most important contributors to the economic difficulties faced by older workers.

Of course, individual exceptions can be found. Not every older person in every situation is subjected to the same pressures operating in the labor market. What the explanatory variables explain are the forces lying behind the lower average rates of labor force participation and low average income of the older age group generally. In order to fit this explanation into the context of public policy, we turn next to a value framework designed for evaluation of alternative remedial actions.

Welfare Economics

Welfare economics is that branch of economics concerned with normative propositions and the evaluation of public policy actions. Welfare analysis has adopted efficiency as a criterion of production, and maximization of consumer satisfaction as a criterion of product distribution. Efficiency in production implies that resources should be allocated among alternative employments in such a way that aggregate output of all goods and services is a maximum. Given this optimum allocation of resources and maximized output, the distribution of that output among households should be such as to maximize the combined utilities or satisfactions of consumers. Thus, there emerge two conditions of optimality: optimal production conditions and optimal exchange conditions.

For our purposes optimal production conditions can be stated formally in the following way. Let

$x_i =$ the amount of the ith product $\quad i = 1, 2, \ldots, I$
$a_{ij} =$ the amount of the jth resource used in the production of the ith product $\quad j = 1, 2, \ldots, J$

In total there are I products (goods or services), and there are J different resources. Then the problem is to maximize

$$X = \sum_{i=1}^{I} x_i \tag{1}$$

subject to the constraints

$$x_i = x_i(a_{i1}, a_{i2}, \ldots, a_{iJ}) \qquad i = 1, 2, \ldots, I \tag{2}$$

$$\sum_{i=1}^{I} a_{ij} = A_j \qquad j = 1, 2, \ldots, J \tag{3}$$

Equation (1) is the sum of all produced goods and services. Equation (2) specifies a production function or input-output relationship for each product, where it is assumed each production function shows diminishing returns. Equation (3) states that the allocation of any resource among various uses or employments much be such as to exhaust the given available amount of that resource, A_j. There is one such equation for each resource, thereby requiring full employment.

The constrained maximization of X yields optimal production conditions. These conditions can be derived without reference to resource prices. However, for purposes of relating welfare economics to age, it is more useful to introduce these prices. It can be shown that in a competitive market economy the necessary conditions for maximization of X can be written

$$\frac{M\,(a_{iq})}{M\,(a_{ir})} = \frac{P\,(a_{iq})}{P\,(a_{ir})} \tag{4}$$

where

$M\,(a_{ij})$ = the marginal physical product of the jth resource in the production of the ith commodity,

$P\,(a_{ij})$ = the price of the jth resource employed in the production of the ith commodity.

Equation (4) states that if we consider any two resources (say q and r) in any employment (say production of the ith good or service), then the ratio of their marginal products in that employment must equal the ratio of their prices in that employment.

Satisfaction of the optimal production conditions guarantees that the economy will be on a production frontier. That is, the conditions do not establish a unique combination of goods and services that must be produced. Rather, they specify an entire set of combinations of goods and services, each combination being consistent with efficient production. Demand and supply in the market will determine where on the production frontier the economy will settle as long as the optimal production conditions are satisfied. Violation of these conditions, however, will force the economy inside this frontier. It is then possible, by satisfying the optimal production conditions, to increase the production of at least one commodity, and possibly more than one, without decreasing the production of any other commodity.

Given that the economy is somewhere on the production frontier, the actual outputs must be distributed among consumers on some basis. The basis used in welfare economics is maximization of the joint utilities or "satisfactions" of consumers. An individual's utility is assumed to increase as he consumes more of at least one commodity, given no decrease in any other. Let

$$(5) \qquad u^k = u^k(x_1^k, x_2^k, \ldots, x_I^k) \quad \frac{\partial u^k}{\partial x_i^k} > 0 \;\; i = 1, 2, \ldots, I$$

denote the utility of the kth individual as an increasing function of the amounts of commodities he consumes, x_i^k. Suppose there are K consumers ($k = 1, 2, \ldots, K$). Then maximization of the joint utilities of all consumers is tantamount to maximization of any one's utility, given constant utilities for all others. Formally, the problem is stated as maximization of

$$(6) \qquad u^k = u^k(x_1^k, x_2^k, \ldots, x_I^k)$$

subject to the constraints

$$(7) \qquad u^t(x_1^t, x_2^t, \ldots, x_I^t) = \bar{u}^t \qquad\qquad t \neq k$$

$$(8) \qquad \sum_{k=1}^{K} x_i^k = \overline{x}_i \qquad\qquad i = 1, 2, \ldots, I$$

Constraint (7) holds constant the utilities of other consumers, $\bar{u}^t$, while constraint (8) simply states that the actual amount of any commodity produced, $\overline{x}_i$, is exhausted in its distribution among the K consumers.

Once more utilizing prices in a competitive market economy, the necessary conditions for maximization of joint utilities can be written

$$(9) \qquad \frac{U_n^k}{U_m^k} = \frac{P_n}{P_m}$$

where

U_i^k = the marginal utility of the ith commodity to the kth consumer, i.e., the increase in his total utility with respect to an increase in the amount of the ith commodity he consumes.

P_i = the market price of the ith commodity, common to all consumers.

Equation (9) states that if we consider any two commodities (say n and m) for any one consumer (say consumer k), then the ratio of marginal utilities of the two commodities must equal the ratio of their prices.

Like the optimal production conditions, the optimal exchange conditions do not yield a unique distribution of goods and services among consumers. Satisfaction of the optimal exchange conditions guarantees that the economy will be on a utility frontier. There is an entire set of distributions, each one satisfying the optimal exchange conditions. This means that violation of the optimal exchange conditions leaves the economy inside the utility frontier. Then, by satisfying the conditions, the utility of at least one consumer can be increased without a decrease in the utility of any other. Once the economy is on the utility frontier, however, it is possible to increase the utility of one or more consumers only by decreasing the utility of at least one other.

In other words, there are many personal income distributions that are optimal. Welfare economics asserts that nonoptimal income distributions are inferior to optimal distributions in the sense that some consumers can be made better off without others being made worse off in terms of utility. Among the various optimal income distributions, however, economics cannot conclude that one is better than another. For an income redistribution (a change from one optimum point on the frontier to another) entails a gain in utility for some persons at the expense of others. Because utility is subjective and interpersonal comparisons of utility cannot be made, it is impossible to tell whether the gain in utility by those benefiting from the income redistribution is greater or less than the loss in utility on the part of those sacrificing income. At this point economics encounters ethical value judgments that are necessary to determine which optimal income distribution is over all the best.

Welfare Economics and Age

The efficiency criterion for production expressed in equation (4) can be put into the framework of different age groups. Suppose resource q is defined as labor supplied by workers aged 45 years and over, while resource r is defined as labor supplied by another age group called younger workers. Let i refer to any employment. Then $P(a_{iq})$ is the wage rate of older workers and $P(a_{ir})$ is the wage rate of younger workers.

If older workers are less productive than younger workers in this particular employment, $M(a_{iq})$ is less than $M(a_{ir})$ for equal quantities of older and younger labor. Efficiency in production requires one of two possibilities. If approximately equal amounts of younger and older labor are to be employed, since $M(a_{iq})$ is below $M(a_{ir})$, then $P(a_{iq})$ must be less than $P(a_{ir})$. The wage rate must be less for older workers. If, on the other hand, the wage rates are to be approximately equal, diminishing marginal productivity implies that less older than younger labor should be employed in order to equalize their marginal products. The most meaningful definition of the wage rate is the total or gross wage rate inclusive of pension contributions by the employer. Consequently, a higher gross wage rate for older workers entails even less employment of older labor if efficient production is to be achieved under existing relative productivities by age.

Therefore, efficiency in production entails the hard consequence of a lower wage or smaller employment for older workers wherever they are less productive. Because the evidence suggests that the demand for older labor is quite wage inelastic, the wage cut necessary to absorb all older workers and maintain full employment is likely to be very large indeed. A similar argument applies in the case of female labor if r denotes female labor instead of younger male labor. Inferior productivity on the part of older males implies a lower wage or substitution of female labor. Simply to seek greater employment of older workers at given wages and productivity would violate the conditions of efficient production.

By theoretical reasoning it can be shown that if an economy is purely competitive, if there are diminishing returns to scale in all industries, and if resources are perfectly mobile, then the free play of market forces will result in the attainment of the optimum production conditions. Of course, resources are not perfectly mobile. In particular, older workers are immobile. Even if other conditions are satisfied in a free market economy, the optimum allocation of resources will not prevail when resource immobility persists. The optimum production conditions are violated if older workers remain in employments where their marginal product is lower than alternative employments. By moving from jobs of relatively low to relatively high marginal product, their wage rates would increase at the same time that the economy as a whole enjoys an expansion of aggregate output (moves closer to the production frontier).

Reference to the optimum exchange conditions brings out another aspect of relative economic welfare for different age groups. Since older workers are at an economic disadvantage, their situation could be improved by means of direct transfers—redistributing income by taking from the young and giving to the old. This would presumably be done outside of the market mechanism, such as lump sum transfers, rather than by something like a minimum wage rate that would disturb the efficient production conditions.

But this route is not without its difficulties either. In our present day economy with degrees of monopoly and oligopoly, one could hardly argue that the economy is somewhere on the utility frontier. As a consequence, two questions arise: (1) If the existing income distribution is nonoptimal, would a redistribution move the economy closer to the utility frontier? (2) If the economy were on the utility frontier, would a pure redistribution of income from young to old be an improvement?

If it can be shown that an income redistribution would benefit older persons without decreasing the utility (not income) of younger persons, then the redistribution can be said unequivocally to be an improvement Or if the gain in utility on the part of older persons exceeds the loss in utility by younger persons (so the young could be compensated for the loss, still leaving a net gain for the old and for society), then the redistribution is an improvement. Unfortunately, individual utilities are subjective, and comparisons of utilities among persons cannot be measured. One can argue that the capacity for enjoying income is less for the old than for the young, or vice versa. But the argument remains speculative without demonstrable evidence on either side that would help to establish a general rule for action.

The upshot is that economics can say very little about the desirability of a pure income redistribution. This does not mean that there should be no redistribution. The important point is that one cannot afford to be cavalier about questions of income or wealth redistribution. Ultimately the question is an ethical one, and awareness of the ethical assumptions underlying any policy advocated is essential. In a democratic society there is no single standard that determines remedial action. A variety of values, standards, and opinions come into play to form a consensus in the population; and the formulation of public policies cannot afford to disregard this multiplicity of values.

Criteria for Public Policy

The survey of economic welfare theory and its application to the age structure of the labor force helps to bring out the difficulties faced by public and private agencies in forming well-conceived policies designed to affect income and employment by age groups. Moreover, considerations drawn from welfare economics help to establish broad guidelines for formulating such policies. The specific details bearing upon productivity and mobility will not be covered here—partly because they are matters better handled by psychologists, biologists, and educators, and partly because specific circumstances vary greatly with time and space. Specific details rely on prior fact finding. The discussion is therefore restricted to general economic criteria that should be taken into account in choosing goals and specifying means for improving the lot of older workers. Other economic problems faced by some of the youngest age group, such as the effects on high school dropouts, are disregarded for largely the same reasons.

Emerging from the previous analysis are two separate approaches to public policy. One approach is to focus upon the income-earning abilities of older workers and the remuneration they receive in the market due to the operation of the price mechanism. This is similar to the approach of the anti-poverty program of the federal government. The second approach is to focus upon pure income redistribution outside the price mechanism and is similar to the approach of the Medicare program.

The discussion of efficiency conditions in the previous two sections took as given a certain "state of the world," namely given productivity and given immobility by age. But it is the purpose of policy actions to change the state of the world. As an alternative to accepting a lower wage or restricted employment in the older worker's present job in order to promote over-all productive efficiency in the economy, policies can be designed to raise productivity itself. In the language of the previous section, if $M(a_{iq})$ for the older worker is raised relative to $M(a_{ir})$ for the younger worker—with a possible increase in both—then efficiency is maintained by raising $P(a_{iq})$ relative to $P(a_{ir})$. Earnings and employment can both be raised if productivity is enhanced. Although productive efficiency is not the only or the most important social good, it is not necessary to sacrifice efficiency in order to ameliorate the economic problems of older workers. In turn, increased productivity entails a program of continual retraining with changing technology as the worker ages. It is well known that workers resist retraining once they have reached an advanced age. Consequently, the retraining must be an on-going part of employment in the intermediate years, rather than a shock which requires sharp readjustment after the age of 45.

Industrial, geographic, and occupational immobility is a second major determinant of the income and employment problem of the older worker. Greater mobility would not only improve the economic status of older workers but would also contribute to more efficient production in the economy. Aside from raising prductivity on a given job, disbursement of information regarding the availability of income alternatives—even financial subsidies to offset the psychological and cultural barriers to mobility—would help to promote movements to employments where productivity and earnings are higher for older workers.

However, efforts designed to raise the productivity and to increase the mobility of older persons entail costs that are borne by the tax-paying population. The execution of policy must be funded. In real rather than monetary terms, some of the resources of the economy must be drawn from other uses (where they would otherwise be producing real output) and directed to the task of raising the output of the oldest age group. What are the benefits to be derived and what are the costs involved? This question is essential to the formulation of policy. Unless the gain in income accruing to the older workers, and thus to the population as a whole, exceeds the cost of achieving this result, a policy cannot be justified on grounds of efficiency in resource allocation. It is clear that policies having as one goal the improvement of older-worker income and employment may conflict with another goal of efficiency in resource allocation, thereby dampening the economy's over-all growth rate in order to ameliorate the situation for a segment of the population.

Even if efforts to promote productivity and mobility do result in a net loss to the economy as a whole, the raising of income for the older population may still be regarded as desirable. But then a second question arises. Could not this rise in their income be achieved in a better way by means of a pure income redistribution? Assuming the benefit is the same in either case, the real cost of raising productivity and mobility may be greater than the real cost of simply transferring income from the rest of the population to the older group. That is, the real income (output) forgone by absorbing resources in the effort to raise productivity and mobility may well exceed the income forgone by keeping these resources where they are employed and redistributing part of the national income in favor of the older population.

The analytical framework developed in this chapter permits us to raise two questions that have seldom been taken into consideration in discussions of policy regarding age. First, what is to be the goal of policy? Presumably, the goal is the elimination of poverty among the older members of the population. But in defining this goal, we must not lose sight of other social goals and the possibility of conflict among them. Second, what are the means, and how are they to be ranked in preference? A complete answer to the second question requires a cost-benefit comparison of each contemplated means in order to determine its net social benefit or loss. A complete answer also requires a comparison of the various means in order to determine which yields the greatest benefit to society.

CHAPTER FOURTEEN

Issues of Public Policy

GIVEN the present state of knowledge about the effects of age, ironclad answers to questions of costs and benefits cannot be made. A detailed cost-benefit analysis of each alternative policy action judged to be relevant would be an enormous research project in itself (and the costs might not be justified by the benefits obtained). Certainly, for policy actions involving a large diversion of resources such cost-benefit analyses are desirable, and before much more time passes perhaps they will also be feasible. But, as we indicated in Chapter 3, the fact of the matter is that more and better data are needed. Also, a more systematic method of explanation, accounting for the simultaneous operation of more causal variables, is required in order to make best use of more refined data.

What this study has been able to do is push back the frontiers of our ignorance by utilizing an approach heretofore untried in studies of aging, namely the construction of behavioral models and measurement of their quantitative properties. The models are not capable of accounting for all explanatory variables, and there exist limitations on the quantitative data. Nevertheless, such models point the way for future research that can lead to detailed cost-benefit analyses of policy.

In many areas of life we act with less than perfect certainty, and remedial action on the plight of the older worker is warranted. Using the analytical framework of Chapter 13 as a guide, evaluation of the pros and cons connected with concrete policy proposals is possible. By proceeding along these lines, public policies could be formulated on a more secure foundation. In using the term "public policy" we shall include not only the policies of government but also those of private agencies (business firms and welfare organizations) whose actions are motivated by the social well-being of the community as a whole.

Two Older Groups

A distinction should be drawn between the problems of workers in the 45–65 age category and those over 65 years of age. This distinction has seldom been recognized in discussions of public policy on aging. Whereas those over 65 have passed the normal retirement age, those in the 45–65 age bracket are potentially active members of the labor force. As a consequence, the issues of public policy are different. Demarcating the two groups by drawing the line at age 65 is to some extent arbitrary. We do so because in contemporary American society this age is accepted as the normal retirement age.

Of course, no two persons in either age group are identical. The designation "older worker" is less of a class or a group than a misfortune. A person can be regarded as an older worker when age, aside from other personal characteristics, becomes a barrier to employment and adequate income. One person can be an older worker at 40 whereas another is not an older worker at the age of 80. The differences are most clearly drawn across occupations. Professional people and the self-employed are likely to be able to carry on complete or partial careers well into advanced age. Lawyers, teachers, physicians, and other professionals can work effectively into the seventh decade of their lives, and may continue longer. In addition, they are most numerous among the group of people who have been able to accumulate the greatest savings over their past working lives. Professionals and the self-employed should be differentiated from manual workers, especially the semiskilled and unskilled in blue-collar or white-collar jobs whose ability to survive in their occupation, prospects for re-employment, and accumulated personal savings are significantly less. But even within one of these occupations, some workers at the age of 50 are inferior to others at the age of 60 or 70 years.

Another variable is the normal retirement age. In another ten years the normal may be 60 rather than 65, and in twenty years the normal retirement age may be 50. The question of whether a given retirement age is desirable or not hinges on two considerations.

First, can the economy provide a total number of jobs which is sufficient to employ all those willing to work? If not, it may be necessary to match the job applicants to the jobs available by means of earlier retirement. Second, can retirement be accompanied by a useful, reasonably enjoyable, and financially secure life?

Ideally, the definition of an older worker should be functional rather than annual. If age, aside from nonage related personal qualifications, is a significant hindrance to employment and income, then a worker faces the older worker problem regardless of his precise age in years. In the actual day-to-day execution of any broad policy that might be adopted, such a functional criterion must be applied. Nevertheless, when we are dealing with large numbers of persons, the formulation of broad policy cannot take account of individual variations. In effect, policy discussion deals with an ideal type when reference is made to *the* older worker. On the average older persons are not as efficient as their younger colleagues and job competitors. Allowing for individual exceptions, experience in all areas of work confirms this view. Strength, agility, powers of concentration, memory, and adaptability decline as any one particular person ages. The decline is gradual. It occurs at uneven rates, but it is still there.

As a consequence, policies bearing upon the economic problems of the older workers should proceed with an ideal type of older worker in mind. Otherwise, we are forced to the helpless conclusion, "it all depends." Moreover, for practical reasons we distinguish between older workers in the 45–65 age category and those over 65. The distinction is pragmatic rather than absolutely precise and functional in every individual instance. For the distinction permits us to separate, at least conceptually, policies on retirement from policies on conditions of employment.

Policies on Retirement

It is not too difficult to put one's finger on the central question for those over 65 years of age. Is their retirement voluntary? But this question really opens Pandora's box. Another question follows: what does "voluntary" mean? We suggest that the word "voluntary" be taken to mean that retirement is preferred to the alternative of participation in the labor force and that retirement carries with it at least a socially acceptable minimal income. Naturally, a third question emerges: what is a "socially acceptable minimal income"? Let us put this question aside for the moment.

Voluntary retirement is a matter of individual preference. The alternatives are work or leisure. A person's choice between these alternatives is obviously based upon income. However, it is also based upon his conception of work, his willingness to spend the entire day at home, his capacity for a personally enriching (non-boring) use of leisure, his health, etc. These are the noneconomic, or nonincome, aspects of retirement. Once again, individuals vary a great deal in their personal preferences, and we cannot hope to account for individual differences. In elaborating on a meaning of voluntary retirement we can put questions of income aside and classify older persons as preferring one or the other alternative. Here, we shall consider only those who would prefer leisure to work if they could ignore income. For these the problem then reduces to an economic one of financing retirement. Are they denied the possibility of fruitful retirement because of inadequate retirement income? This is simply another way of asking, what is a socially acceptable minimal income?

Obviously, if the answer is given in dollars and cents, objections can be found. More theoretically precise is a definition of real income in terms of utility (or the capacity for "enjoying" income). A minimum level of personal utility is a precise notion of real minimum income. However, since utility is subjective and immeasurable, we are forced to quote a dollar and cents figure out of practical necessity. In connection with the federal antipoverty program, eligibility is based upon an annual income below about 3,000 dollars (with allowances for dependents). A similar rule of thumb is required in the case of the aged, even though the particular dollar amount is arbitrary to some extent. What that dollar amount shall be is a matter of political consensus.

A careful examination of the meaning of retirement would reduce to questions of pure semantics if it did not raise real, concrete problems in the evaluation of policy. It might be asked, what proportion of workers over 65 are involuntarily retired? The question has been put to older people in the form of reasons for retirement. Their answers to such questionnaires are unreliable for the reasons spelled out in Chapter 3. In terms of our definition, the question can be put another way. How many satisfy the conditions for voluntary retirement? Using the poverty program breakoff of 3,000 dollars annual income, the answer is indicated in Table 14-1.

It is apparent that the differences among age groups, all of which are 65 or more, are not great. For all those 65 or over who did not work, 90.6 per cent had incomes below 3,000 dollars. If we were to apply this dollar figure to define a socially acceptable income and use our suggested definition of voluntary retirement, we must conclude that 90.6 per cent are involuntarily retired. Even if the cutoff income is placed at 2,000 dollars, about 80 per cent are involuntarily retired.

Table 14–1. MALES WHO DID NOT WORK IN 1959
(PERCENT OF TOTAL AGE GROUP IN EACH INCOME BRACKET)

	Income					
Age	*Zero*	*$1 to $999*	*$1,000 to $1,999*	*$2,000 to $2,999*	*$3,000 to $3,999*	*$4,000 and over*
65–69	6.4	27.4	35.3	17.7	6.4	6.7
70–74	5.5	33.2	37.4	14.2	4.5	5.3
75 and over	10.1	45.5	29.3	8.1	2.8	4.1
65 and over	7.8	36.6	33.5	12.7	4.4	5.2

Source: *Sources and Structure of Family Income,* Subject Report PC (2)–4C, U.S. Census of Population, 1960.

A second question that may arise is the role of social security retirement benefits. We have already argued in Chapter 2 that these benefits, together with private pension income and income from past savings, are simply not sufficient to prevent poverty among the aged. Table 14-1 provides further evidence. It may be true that some individuals receive a nonpoverty income from sources other than currently earned income, but the figures of Table 14-1 speak for themselves. In the aggregate, that is, for our ideal older-worker type, it is obvious that retirement income (including social security) is not sufficient to designate retirement as voluntary on a wide scale.

There is danger of losing perspective when we examine such income figures. The aged are not all of the poor, neither are they the only claimants for assistance. One recent study [1] showed that 70 per cent of the abject poor are found among those living in rural farm areas, nonwhites, families headed by a female, or the

[1] O. Ornati, *Poverty Amid Affluence* (New York: The Twentieth Century Fund, 1966).

aged—or others with some or all of these characteristics in common. The remaining 30 per cent do not include the aged.

We submit that the policy problem connected with poor people over 65 years of age is primarily one of pure income redistribution. The statistics of Table 14-1 are income figures and do not cover financial aid from children, other family members, or friends. However, these are transfer payments. It is only a question of whose income is reduced in order to provide this aid. Should the redistribution be from the population generally to the aged? Or should the redistribution be from relatives and friends of the aged to the aged?

It is unrealistic to suppose that the aged poor can be reinstated in the labor force on a large scale, given present trends in technological change, without reducing the over-all efficiency of the labor force and retarding the growth rate of the economy. This does not mean that they can do no work. Some are undoubtedly willing to work and capable of respectable performance on certain types of jobs. Sheltered workshops appear to have been effective with the mentally retarded and those in need of vocational rehabilitation for psychiatric reasons. The workshops contract with private firms to have simple tasks done at whatever pace the sheltered workers can attain. Why not have sheltered workshops for the aged as well? Earnings would certainly be low, but the income of the aged could be supplemented while they retain the dignity of earning income and the mentally healthy environment of "something useful to do."

Nevertheless, sheltered workshops will not completely solve the poverty problem. Pure income transfers are necessary to raise income above a poverty level. There have been societies that simply left the older folks to die when they could not carry their own weight. Parricide has been found to exist among some primitives. Presumably, we are more humanitarian. But the issue is one of poverty, not age in itself. As we have indicated, there are others who fall into the poverty category for a variety of reasons. Some of these can be aided by means other than pure income redistribution, such as the present antipoverty program, or measures of improving employment conditions to be discussed in the next section. Nevertheless, there will doubtless be others for whom poverty can be alleviated only by income redistribution.

A crucial aspect of income redistribution is the question of how much income in total is to be transferred and how that total is to be allocated among those who qualify for assistance. Obviously we cannot give a final answer to this question. It is much too important to be decided by the authors of this study. What is needed is broad representation from a variety of disciplines in order to advise the public authorities. Rather than provide final answers at this point, we have been able to clarify the issues and point out the alternatives that should be taken into account in the formulation of policy. Without this clarification and without exploration of the implications of alternative goals and means, it is unlikely that public policy will be well conceived and well executed.

There is already a movement underway at the federal level of government to provide further assistance to the aged. In 1933 Francis E. Townsend, a California physician, proposed the famous Townsend Plan under which every old person was to be given 200 dollars a month out of funds derived from a tax on business transactions. The plan gained numerous followers. But partly because his economic reasoning was suspect and partly because of the radical nature of the proposal at the time, the program remained a dream. Today, however, the federal government is speaking about a guaranteed annual income of 3,000 dollars for all families, including the aged. The aims of this and the Townsend plan are not basically different. In January 1966 President Johnson sent to Congress a report of his Council of Economic Advisers which affirmed that the guaranteed income idea is worthy of further study. Possible prospects are an expansion of public assistance coverage and steady escalation of social security in terms of scope and financial benefits.

Providing income transfers to the aged through social security (including Medicare and other programs) is likely to be the most practical route. If the minimal guaranteed income is to be 3,000 dollars, the program will be costly. The total cost of the social security program in 1966, including the new health insurance for the aged, is 5 billion dollars greater than the cost in 1965. The total tax share amounts to 22.4 billion dollars. The estimated cost of benefits, cash payments, and health services, is estimated to rise to 21.2 billion dollars. This is about 2.6 billion dollars more than in 1965, even though the health insurance program is funded for only half of the 1966 calendar year.

A crucial question is our ability to support income transfers of this magnitude. The answer depends upon the rate of growth of national income and the nation's productive capacity. Another question is our willingness to do so. Some have pointed to the dangers of bigger government and the challenge to our traditional freedom and sense of personal responsibility. Others have emphasized the effect of a guaranteed income on those earning slightly in excess of that minimum. Why should these persons work when they can be given a dole amounting to almost what they earn? This latter question is not likely to be relevant for the aged poor, but it is seriously relevant for the nonaged poor.

Management of the income redistribution by means of social security has advantages. It forces those who are now young to pay as they go in anticipation of retirement. Their social security taxes must undoubtedly increase, so to some extent they help provide for a greater future retirement income. For those presently over 65 who have not been taxed over their working life the magnitude of the pure income redistribution is greater. The aspect of a social security tax paid by the worker as he ages raises another issue that has not been publicly considered, namely other measures directed toward the 45–65 age group which would improve their employment conditions and make them less dependent on income supplements once they pass the age of 65.

Policies on Employment Conditions

Workers in the 45–65 age group are regarded as potentially active members of the labor force. Some do indeed enjoy stable employment and an income well above a poverty level. Others retain employment that permits them to rise somewhat above the poverty income level. The most serious cases are those with poverty or near poverty incomes because of partial or complete nonparticipation in the labor force. It has been argued in earlier chapters that this nonparticipation is not voluntary. Certainly, by the definition of "voluntary" introduced in the previous section, their retirement is not voluntary because it does not carry adequate income. Departure from the labor force is motivated by a failure to find employment that would bring an earned income substantially above their meager retirement income. Underlying this failure to retain employment or find re-employment as shifts occur in the economy are three primary causal factors: declining productivity with advancing age, limited work horizons, and immobility. The interpretation of these factors, especially declining productivity, has been presented in Chapter 13.

As in the case of workers over 65 years of age the policy issue is one of eliminating or reducing poverty wherever it may be found. However, there is a difference to be drawn in considering workers in the 45–65 age bracket *vis-à-vis* those over 65. The former are below the normal retirement age, yet they cannot maintain employment with adequate income. In addition, workers in their forties, and even in their fifties, have needs and responsibilities that are, on the average, likely to be greater. Their children may not be fully educated, and their mortgage or other debts tend to be greater.

The employment difficulties of workers in the 45–65 age group raise the question of two routes to a solution pointed out in the analytical framework of the previous chapter. On the one hand, efforts can be made to raise productivity and/or increase mobility. On the other hand, low incomes can be supplemented by pure income transfers from the rest of the population.

In previous approaches to public policy a strong emphasis has been placed upon discrimination against the older worker by employers. It is implied that discrimination based on age is similar in nature to racial discrimination, i.e., that it has no foundation in economic efficiency.

The arguments claiming discrimination are based upon studies already reviewed in Chapter 3, in which older and younger workers appeared equal in productivity on a given job, or workmen's compensation insurance costs were no greater for the old because of equal accident rates. The findings of these studies have been discounted. Lower productivity among the older workers is founded on weaker adaptability to change. It is clear that *some* workers in their forties, and even in their fifties and early sixties, do not suffer serious diminution in physical productivity. There may be some slackening in the ability to produce as the worker approaches his sixties, but such diminution may be offset by better attendance rates, attention to duties, and greater reliability than younger workers. But even for workers whose productivity does not perceptibly diminish, workmen's compensation costs, pension costs, and even plans providing medical and hospitalization benefits, increase as workers attain higher age levels.

Carriers of workmen's compensation insurance call attention to the longer recuperative periods required by people in older age groups. While statistics have been presented showing favorable accident rates among older-age groups, the answer is that these are a selected group, and also that supervisors are not likely to assign employees in the higher age groups to jobs which are more than normally dangerous or which require greater than normal agility and risk. In other words, the accident experience of older workers on the job is not convincing evidence that an expansion in the employment of this age group in a particular establishment would not adversely affect the accident experience of the plant. The effect of employment of workers in their late forties, fifties, and sixties upon pension costs is less disputable.

Proposals that assume pure age discrimination would presumably appeal to business firms to hire older job applicants. Private firms are motivated by profits. If from humanitarian motives a firm were to hire less productive older workers, it would soon feel the effects upon the cost per unit of product, and thus upon its profit in a competitive market. The evidence of this study leads to the conclusion that firms do indeed discriminate. But this discrimination is based upon considerations of efficiency. At a given wage rate the firm employs the most productive workers. Preference for younger workers is not like racial discrimination; it is the outcome of productivity comparisons. Moreover, as has been mentioned previously, the employment problem of the older worker is not entirely a matter of hiring practices by employers.

Rather than attempting to convince employers that they ought to hire older job applicants, policy should be directed toward making older workers more attractive as job applicants. The actions necessary to accomplish this objective fall into three categories: (1) efforts to raise productivity, (2) compensation for unchangeable limited work horizons, and (3) efforts to stimulate greater mobility.

PRODUCTIVITY. Continuous retraining appears to be the key to improving productivity. On-the-job training normally occurs at the apprenticeship stage of employment. Constant retraining along the way, as the worker ages, is necessary if the worker is to keep pace with technological innovations and changing production methods. Successful retraining programs require the consent of the trainer and the trainee. It is well known that workers resist sudden retraining efforts by the time they are 45 or 50 years of age. Continuous retraining would eliminate the shock effect of new learning at an older age. A psychological attitude of acceptance toward change and relearning would probably have to be an integral part of retraining programs.

The aim of retraining is to assist the worker to survive in a well-paid job or in a growing occupation. Obviously, retraining is irrelevant in the unskilled occupational categories or in a dying occupation. If financing of the retraining costs cannot be justified by private firms in terms of the benefits they receive, then a public subsidy from general tax revenues would undoubtedly be necessary. However, the new computer-based technology is creating a number of jobs for which the older worker can be trained at relatively low cost to the firm. To the extent that these jobs do expand in the future, they provide one attractive possibility for contributing to an expansion of an over-all retraining program. At the present time, it is impossible to say whether technological developments will continue in this direction.

Offsetting limited work horizons. Compensation for limited work horizons could be achieved by creating an equalization fund out of which employers would be compensated for the increased costs of workmen's compensation and pensions attributable to newly hired older workers. Problems of financing and restriction of the payment to newly hired older workers could arise. The financing aspects may in fact be the more manageable. An equalization fund could be set up by taxing private pension funds and premiums paid to private and public carriers of workmen's compensation insurance; or the equalization fund could be set up from general revenues. It would be used to equalize costs of pensions and workmen's compensation between newly hired younger and older workers. It should be noted that it is hiring rather than employment which would entitle an employer to draw upon the equalization fund. In other words, equalizing of costs would not be allowed for older workers who have been on the payroll, as this fund would be intended to compensate for the newly hired and not for all increased costs attributable to the age of workers above 40 or 45 years.

It might be argued that such differentiation would encourage the dismissal of older workers already on the payroll, and might even lead to collusion between employers, unions, and workers to transform the status of an older worker, already employed, into a new hire. Such aims cannot be easily achieved, but steps to prevent such practices could be taken.

Since limited work horizons restrain the re-employment of displaced older workers, a different attack upon the problem might be to reduce the number seeking re-employment. A recent development is the encouragement of early retirement. Such a policy is designed to clear out workers with high seniority, who have reached the age of 55 or over, but have not attained an age at which they can be compelled to retire under a compulsory system. Early retirement cannot be regarded as a solution to the problem of employment of the older worker. Implicit in these programs is the assumption that the work force of a particular firm or plant is "overloaded" with higher-age employees and that early retirement would help to relieve the situation. The reason why firms are willing to commit large sums to early retirement is that they believe it is advantageous to freshen up their work force with younger people. However, not only does such early retirement shorten the work life of the retiree, but the longer period of pension payments means that the over-all amounts drawn by the pensioner from retirement to death are greater. Such increased costs are borne by industry and are over time shifted to consumers of their products and services.

While early retirement may well be desirable in specific instances, especially for those who have lost some of their working capacity, it is by no means evident that it would be expedient *as a general social policy*. Earlier retirement, if generally practiced, would in fact mean lowering the age of retirement for all workers regardless of productive ability, and the issue should be discussed in those terms. When unemployment is widespread and many younger workers are involuntarily idle, the retirement of the aged seems one of the minor methods of alleviating a serious employment problem. However, as employment recovers, employers are likely to discover, (as one of the automobile companies did in 1965) that it had allowed too many of its skilled workers to fade out of their plants via the road to early retirement. Society thereby loses the skill and work ability of many men who are still quite productive. Were such a system to become general, or were there an explicit reduction in the age of retirement, thousands of workers would be lost to industry annually. If retirement brings with it special problems, early retirement would tend to increase them, and many who had left the security of their jobs might return to the labor market under less favorable circumstances.

Aside from loss of skills and experience of many workers, early retirement on a large scale is likely to be accompanied by problems of personal adjustment. In addition to the increased costs of retirement, the retiree will have to spend a longer period of his life away from work, and many will be deprived of employment during a period of their lives when they are in excellent physical and mental condition. Many of those compelled to leave the labor market will be spending years in idleness or the artificial entertainment of the golden age clubs.

It is difficult to find answers which may satisfy all the criteria that might be used in determining an optimal age of retirement. Ideally, an individual worker should remain employed as long as he is physically and mentally able to compete successfully in productivity and wishes to continue in remunerative employment. On one side, society must not only consider the needs and satisfactions of the older person. In a world of limited resources and opportunities, the new entrant, inexperienced youth, and those in their thirties and early forties also have claims on the public interest. It is perhaps an anomaly that, in an age when the life span is being slowly extended, those individuals who can maintain their physical and mental capacity into old age should be facing early retirement. Yet, if a choice between older and younger workers has to be made, equity and interest both demand that it be made in favor of the young. The latter have not had their chance, their life expectancy as well as their family obligations are greater, and certainly they should not be sacrificed for the benefit of the aged. If justice cannot convince, prudence might. The young will not stand idly by while they are denied an opportunity to marry, raise families, and lead a reasonably good life. To provide opportunities to the aged at the expense of their children and grandchildren is to stimulate discontent.

MOBILITY. Part of the older-worker problem is attributable to the particular labor market in which older workers find themselves and their inability or unwillingness to move in the direction of other markets where income prospects are better. Granted that employment opportunities expand less for the old than the young as the over-all economy grows, failure to respond to such opportunities contributes to the income problem of the older worker.

This implies that remedial policies should also focus upon promoting greater mobility among older groups. What specific programs might be adopted? Dispersement of information is a partial attack upon immobility. In many instances older workers may not be aware of the alternatives open to them. Low-interest, or interest-free loans to finance movement might also help. But since moving costs are a relatively small component of net returns to migration, it is unlikely that these loans would promote much more mobility. A third possibility is government-sponsored subsidies that exceed moving costs and help to offset the lower pecuniary returns to migration on the part of the old as compared to the young. Assistance in relocation by professional social workers should help to offset the nonpecuniary restraints upon migration, so that older people find a congenial new environment and attach less importance to their presently established community ties.

Of course, such efforts to promote greater mobility cannot be regarded as independent of the other routes to improved economic status. It makes little sense to encourage older workers to move to growing labor markets if they cannot find employment there because of relatively low productivity and limited work horizons.

One indirect assistance to job survival and re-employment is a high level of total employment in the economy. Re-employability of older workers, although it has elements which are separate and distinct (associated with structural unemployment), is also closely intertwined with events in the over-all economy (cyclical unemployment). Low general employment due to a shortage of aggregate demand increases the obstacles to maintaining employment or finding employment in other labor markets, not only for the older worker but for all others as well. A judicious use of monetary and fiscal policy in order to promote high employment and growth contributes indirectly to the solution of the older worker problem. Indeed, "full" employment is a necessary condition for successful execution of the programs mentioned above. It is not, however, a sufficient condition. Such programs, or others similar to them, must be added, although full employment smooths the way for their successful execution.

Costs and Benefits Once More

Undoubtedly this discussion has raised more questions than it has answered. But it is vitally important that these questions be raised. Too often in the past policy actions have emerged out of fragmentary evidence, vague goals, "off the top of my head" thinking, and random political pressures. Questions have not been asked—at least the right questions have not been asked—before action has been taken. Modern society has evolved to a stage of scientific achievement and wealth at which we need to ask some very serious questions about where we want to go and how we want to get there.

Otherwise, the year 1984 may bring upon us a Brave New World that is the result of forces over which we have lost control.

Among our goals are social goals. Traditionally the goals of freedom, efficiency, prosperity, and equality of opportunity have been part of our social objectives. It is in this context that the problem of poverty and the plight of the aged should be considered. With some exceptions, policy recommendations with respect to aging have failed to conceive of policy in terms of alternative social goals and alternative means to achieve any one goal. Emphasis on this approach to policy will be needed in the future.

Once our goals are defined, the extent to which they may conflict and the possibilities of satisfying two or more goals simultaneously are the relevant issues. The process of defining goals is a political one, but exploration of their implications is an "academic" process. The means for attaining given goals also deserves investigation, for some may be superior to others. In principle, a cost-benefit analysis of each alternative should be undertaken in order to judge the relative desirability of optimal measures to improve the economic status of the older worker. If future research can be carried in this direction, our present efforts to grapple with the economics of age will be justified.

Index

Absenteeism and older workers, 69
Accident rates and older workers, 39, 228–29
Adult education programs, fostering, 10
Age groups
  demand-supply model of labor market and, 51, 55
  distinguishing older, 221–22
  education by, 8
  employment problems by, 206, 232
  employment status by, 6
    occupations, 133, 136, 142, 146, 150
    regression-analysis results, 162–75
  female employment by, 150
  geographic mobility by, 108–13
  income by, 6–8, 224
  job-survival rate by, 134–36
    measuring, 140
  labor force by, *see* Labor force, age structure of
  length of employment by, 175–76
  nonparticipation in labor force by, 15
  population trends by, 12–13, 204
  productivity by, 206–8
  regression-analysis results for, 162–72
  retirement and, 221–22
  self-employment by, 146
  trends in median of, 12–13
  unemployment by, 15, 30, 75–76, 142
  welfare programs for, 203
  See also Older workers; Younger workers
Aged
  income of, 224
    decline, 14–15
    redistribution, 226–27
    retired, *see* Pension plans, private; Retirement; Retirement benefits
  increasing proportion of, 5
  historical trend, 12–13
  nonparticipation in labor force by, 6, 15
  public policies on, 221–23, 225, 234
    aid programs, 10–11, 203, 226–27
    surveys, 9
  sheltered workshops for, 225
  social goals and, 234
  See also Older workers
Agriculture, *see* Farmers
Aluminum Corporation of America, 79–81
Antipoverty program
  focus of, 10, 203
  income of poor defined by, 223
  See also Welfare economics
Apparel industry
  in demand-supply model of labor market, 51
  older workers in, 53
Area market hiring, 82
Automobile industry
  older workers in, 64–65
    union policies, 81–85

Automobile industry (*continued*)
  skills lost through retirement from, 231
Avien Company, 78

Bates, Harry, 85
Birth rates, declining trend in, 13–14
Blacksmiths, older workers as, 33
Blue-collar workers, 191
  aged, 221
  educational level of, 147–48
  female workers among, 150
  full-time workers among, 151
  geographic migration by, 152
  job-survival rates for, 134–36
  median incomes of, 153
  nonwhites among, 143–44
  occupational growth-rates for, 138–39
  productivity of, 155
  regression-analysis results for, 162–76
  self-employed among, 146
  seniority systems and, 70
  unemployed among, 141–42
  union members among, 158
  See also specific blue-collar occupations
Bookbinders' Union, policies on older workers of, 88–89
Borden Chemical Company, 78
Bricklayers, Masons, and Plasterers' International Union of America, policies on older workers of, 85
Building trades, union policies on older workers in, 85–87, 89
"Bumping" system, 67, 79
Bureau of Labor Statistics, 9
Business concentration, 156–57
Business cycles
  decline of, 3–4
  older workers and, 19–20
  retirement, 231

Camps, youth, 10
Capital, geographic migration of, 106
Census data, 107, 131–34
Central Hudson Gas and Electric Company, 87–88
Chemical industry
  demand-supply model of labor market and, 51
  older workers in, 68, 78
Children
  decreasing mortality rate of, 13
  geographic mobility and, 99–100, 104
  regression analysis and, 173
  welfare programs for, 10, 203
  See also Heads of households
Chrysler Corporation, 83–84
Clark, F. L., 32–33
Clerks, 191
  educational level of, 147
  employment prospects for, 204
  female workers among, 150
  full-time workers among, 151
  geographic migration by, 152
  increase in, 17
  job-survival rates of, 134–36
  median income of, 153
  nonwhites among, 143–44
  occupational growth-rates for, 139
  regression-analysis results for, 162–76
  self-employed among, 146
  unemployed among, 142
Climate and geographic mobility, 99
Closed shop, limitation of, 76
Collective bargaining, *see* Unions
Commissions on Aging, 9
Community culture and geographic mobility, 99–100, 104
Community programs for aged, 9–10
Compulsory retirement
  income factors in, 224
  largeness of occupation and, 154
Concentration, industrial, 156–57
Concord Electric Company, 88
Conservatism of older workers, 69
  See also Mobility, older workers and
Cost-benefit analysis of alternative welfare policies, 220, 234
Council of Economic Advisors, 226
Craftsmen, 191
  educational level of, 147
  female workers among, 150
  full-time workers among, 151
  geographic migration by, 152
  nonwhites among, 144
  occupational growth-rates among, 139
  older workers as, 18
  productivity of, 155

regression-analysis results for, 162–76
self-employed among, 146
unemployed among, 142
union members among, 158
See also Skilled workers; Skills

Data, limitations of, 31, 59
See also Surveys
Death rates, historical decrease in, 13–14
Delaware Power and Light Company, 88
Demand-supply model of labor market, 44–58
data for, 47–52
evaluation of, 55–58
evidence for, 43–44
results of, 52–55
theoretical framework of, 44–47
Department of Health, Education, and Welfare, 9
Department of Labor, 9
Diet, improvement in, 4, 205
Discipline of older workers, 69
Discrimination against older workers, 18–20, 29–30, 227–29
Dorfman, Robert, 34–35
Drop-outs, youth, 10

Earnings, *see* Income
East-North Central States, migrants to, 110–11
East-South Central States, migrants to, 110–11
Econometric models, *see* Models
Economic concentration, 156–57
Economic research, current emphasis in, 3–5
Economic theory
geographic mobility and, 105
income redistribution and, 216
traditional, 215
welfare, *see* Public policies; Welfare economics
Economy
growth of, 3–4
unevenness, 115
income redistribution and, 226
older workers and, 233
Education
adult, 10
by age groups, 8
employment and, 4, 129
current need, 204
job-survival rate, 147
occupational categories, 147–48
occupational change, 125–26
older workers and
disadvantages of older workers,
retraining programs, 229–30
variations, 8, 24
regression-analysis results for, 162–76
Eisenhower, Dwight D., 10
Elderly people, *see* Aged; Older workers
Electrical Workers' Union, policies on older workers of, 86–90
Employer attitudes toward older workers
discrimination in, 18–20, 29–30, 227–29
factors in, 207
growth and, 53
pragmatic approach in, 71
seniority system and, *see* Seniority systems
surveys of, 9, 60–73
Employment
age and, 6, 204
public policies, 227–33
by age groups, *see* Age groups
economic research on, 4
education and, *see* Education, employment and
factors affecting, 129–30, 227–33
full, 4
older workers and, 233
measurements of, 131–34
by occupations, 153–54
retirement and, 231
trends in, 204
See also Labor force; Occupations
Employment horizons of older workers, 208, 210
offsetting limitations of, 230–31
Employment statistics, limitations of, 59
Environment and geographic mobility, 99

Fabricated metal products industry, and demand-supply model of labor market, 51

Family ties and geographic mobility, 99, 113
Farmers, 191
  educational level of, 147–48
  female workers among, 150
  full-time workers among, 151
  geographic migration by, 152
  job-survival rates of, 134–36
  median income of, 153
  nonwhites among, 144
  occupational growth-rates of, 138–39
  older workers among, 16–17, 91
  poor among, 224
  regression-analysis results for, 173
  self-employed among, 146
  unemployed among, 142
Federal Council on Aging, 10
Federal government and aged, *see* Public policies
Federal Security Agency, 9
Females
  age structure of, 13
  employment of, *see* Women workers
  as heads of households, poor, 224
Food industry, and demand supply model of labor market, 51
Ford Motor Company, 82–85
Foreign-born, age structure of, historical, 13
Freedom and income redistribution, 277
Full employment, 4
  older workers and, 233
Full-time workers
  by occupations, 149, 151
  regression-analysis results for, 162–76

General Motors Corporation, 81
Geographic mobility, *see* Mobility
Great Depression
  older workers in, 19
  problems of, 3–4
Grinnell Corporation, 78–79
Growth rates by occupations, 138–39
  regression-analysis results for, 162–76
  See also specific occupations

Heads of households
  geographic migration by, 113
  poor among, 224
Health
  of aged, 9, 23–24
  of older workers, 6
    retirement reasons, 23, 35, 223
  over-all improvement in, 24, 205
  See also Medical care; Medicare
Health, Education, and Welfare, Department of, 9
Hiring halls, 76
Hiring practices
  area market, 82
  older workers and
    discrimination, 18–20, 29–30, 227–29
    employer attitudes, *see* Employer attitudes toward older workers; Surveys, of hiring practices
    pension plans, 59, 64, 68–69, 71, 91
  unionized, 76
Hospitalization and insurance programs, 10–11

Immigration, historical pattern of, 13
Income
  of aged, *see* Aged, income of
  employment and, 129
  job-survival rates and, 152
  occupational choice and, 119–20
    theoretical model, 120–24
  of older workers, 12
    geographic mobility, 95–106, 109
    industries, 57
    pension plans, 20, 23, 205
    percentage variations, 6–8
    retirement, 29, 153, 223–27
  poverty level of, 223
  real, defined, 223
  regression-analysis results for, 162–76
  of tenant farmers, 3
  See also Pension plans; Retirement
Income redistribution
  economic theory and, 216
  importance of, 225–27
  quantity to be transferred by, 225–27
  retirement and, 223–27
Income-tax exemptions, 203
Industrial concentration, 156–57, 210
Inflationary pressures, 4
Intelligence tests, inferiority of older workers on, 39

International Brotherhood of Bookbinders, policies on older workers of, 88–89
International Brotherhood of Electrical Workers, policies on older workers of, 86–90
Interviews, *see* Surveys

Job corps, 10
Job-survival rates
  by age groups, 134–36
    measuring, 140
  educational level and, 147
  females in labor force and, 148
  geographic migration and, 152
  income and, 152, 163
  industrial concentration and, 156
  occupational change and, 126
  predicting occupational employment and, 180–81
  regression analysis for, *see* Regression analysis, occupational
  trends in, 158
  unemployment and, 147
  unions and, 157
Job training, 4
  continuous, 229–30
Johnson, Lyndon B., 10, 226

Keynesian theory, 4

Labor, Department of, 9
Labor force
  age structure of
    education, 8
    employment status, 6
    income, 6–8
    social problems, 9
    trends, 5, 12–15
  diversity of, 4–5
  nonparticipation in, 6, 15
  occupational composition of, *see* Occupations
  quality of, 4
  See also Older workers; Women workers; Younger workers
Labor market, demand-supply model of, *see* Demand-supply model of labor market
Laborers, 191
  educational level of, 147
  female workers among, 150
  full-time workers among, 151
  geographic migration by, 152
  industrial concentration and, 157
  job-survival rate of, 134–36
  median income of, 153
  nonwhites among, 143–44
  occupational growth-rates of, 138–39
  productivity of, 155
  self-employed among, 146
  union members among, 158
Labor unions, *see* Unions
Lawyers in advanced age, 221
Local government policies for aged, 9–10
  See also Public policies
Long, Clarence D., 29–32
Lumber industry, and demand-supply model of labor market, 51

Machinists, International Association of, policies on older workers of, 78
Managers, 191
  educational level of, 147
  female workers among, 150
  full-time workers among, 151
  geographic migration by, 152
  job-survival rates of, 134–36
  median income of, 153
  nonwhites among, 143–44
  occupational growth-rates of, 139
  older workers as, 17
  regression-analysis results for, 162–76
  retirement income of, 205
  self-employed among, 146
Manufacturing industries, older workers in, 57, 77–81, 89–90
  See also specific branches of manufacturing
Market forces, 204
  free play of, 215
Medical care, 4
  for aged, *see* Medicare
Medicare, 203, 217, 226
  provisions of, 10–11
Mentally retarded, sheltered workshops for, 225
Metal products industry
  demand-supply model of labor market and, 51
  older workers in, 64–65, 67

Mid-Atlantic states, migrants to, 110–11
Mining industry, older workers in, 65, 68
Mobility
  by age groups, 105, 107–16
  current need for, 204
  by heads of households, 113–14
  job-survival rates and, 152
  of nonwhites, 113
  by occupations, 151–52
  older workers and, 60, 205, 209–10
    automobile industry, 84–85
    census evidence of immobility, 107–16
    economic theory and, 215–16
    public policies, 232–33
    theoretical models, 95–107
  by race, 113
  regression-analysis results for, 162–76
  by sex, 113
  welfare economics and, 218
Models
  of demand-supply factors in labor market, 44–58
    data, 47–52
    evaluation, 55–58
    evidence, 43–44
    results, 52–55
    theoretical framework, 44–47
  of geographic mobility of older workers, 95–107
    age as factor, 103–6
    equilibrium migration flows, 101–3
    expected gross returns from migration, 96–98
    nonpecuniary determinants of migration, 99–101
    pecuniary costs and net returns, 98–99
    problems, 95–96
  for occupational change, 120–26
  for predicting occupational employment, 179–99
    conclusions, 197–99
    decomposition of measures of inaccuracy, 189–98
    empirical results, 188–97
    goal, 179–80
    judging predictive accuracy, 182–88
    methods, 180–82
  regression analysis, *see* Regression analysis, occupational
  ultimate aims of, 198
  for welfare economy, 211–14
Mortality rates, historical increase in, 13–14
Mountain states, migrants to, 110–11

National Conference on Aging, 9
National Electrical Association, 87
National Health Survey, 9
National Labor Relations Board, 83
Negroes, poverty of, 3
  See also Nonwhites
Neighborhood Youth Corps, 10
New England, migrants to, 110–11
New York Electrical Contractors Association, 87
Nonparticipation in labor force, 6
  by age groups, 15
  See also Retirement
Nonwhites
  geographic mobility of, 113
  by occupations, 141, 143
  poor among, 3, 224
  regression-analysis results for, 162–76

Occupations
  change in
    education, 125–26
    income, 120–24
    technological innovation, 128
    theoretical model, 120–26
  educational level and, 125–26, 147–48
  female workers by, 148–50
  full-time workers by, 149, 151
  geographic migration by, 151–52
  growth rate by, 138–39
    regression-analysis results, 162–76
  historical changes in, 16–18
  nonwhite workers by, 141, 143
  number of wokers by, 153–54
  of older workers
    farming, 16–17, 91
    job-survival rates, 32–33
    labor force compared with, 35
    nonagricultural work, 17–18, 53, 57, 62–73
  predicting, 179–99

conclusions, 197–99
decomposition of measures of inaccuracy, 189–98
empirical results, 188–97
goal, 179–80
judging predictive accuracy, 182–83
methods, 180–82
productivity by, 155–56
self-employed workers by, 143–46
structure of, factors, 119–20
survival rates in, 32–33, 134–38, 140
unemployment by, 139–41
See also Employment; Labor force; *and specific occupations*
Office of Economic Opportunity, 10
Oil industry, older workers in, 62
Old Age and Survivors' Insurance, 9, 29, 49
See also Social security
Older workers
accident rates of, 39, 228–29
age categories among, 221–22
age groups compared with, 206
business cycles and, 19–20
retirement, 231
definition of, 222
demand-supply model of labor market and, 44–58
data, 47–52
evaluation, 55–58
evidence, 43–44
results, 52–55
theoretical framework, 44–47
educational level of
disadvantages, 25, 30
retraining programs, 229–30
variations, 8, 24
employment of, *see* Employment
full employment and, 233
health of, 6
retirement reasons, 23, 35, 223
hiring of
discrimination, 18–20, 29–30, 227–29
employer attitudes, *see* Employer attitudes toward older workers; Surveys, of hiring practices
pension plans, 59, 64, 68–69, 71, 91
income of, 12
geographic mobility, 95–106, 109
industries, 57
pension plans, 20, 23, 205
percentage variations, 6–8
retirement, 29, 153, 223–27
increasing proportion of, 5
on intelligence tests, 39
mobility of, 60, 205, 209–10
automobile industry, 84–85
census evidence of immobility, 107–16
economic theory and, 215–16
public policies, 232–33
theoretical models, 57, 95–107
occupations of
farming, 16–17, 91
job-survival rates, 32–33
labor force compared with, 35
nonagricultural work, 17–18, 53, 57, 62–73, 221
pension plans and, 29
attitudes of workers, 23
benefits, 20, 205
effects, 22–23
hiring practices, 59, 64, 68–69, 71, 91
increasing benefits, 20
surveys, 34–35
union-negotiated, 21–22
productivity of, 30, 38–39, 56, 72, 91, 204, 210
public policies, 229–30
public policies on
costs and benefits, 233–34
employment conditions, 227–33
existing programs, 9–11, 203, 226–27
medical care, 10–11, 203, 217, 226
mobility, 232–33
retirement, 223–27, 231–32
two older age groups, 221–23
race and, 210
racial and age discrimination compared, 229
re-employment of, 60
seniority system and, *see* Surveys, of hiring practices
union policies on, 76
research on
method of approach, 26–29
studies determining presence or absence of particular factors, 36–40
studies explaining observed phenomena, 29–36

Older workers (*continued*)
retirement of, *see* Retirement
retraining of
aim, 230
continuous, 229–30
employer attitudes, 63, 66
seniority and, *see* Seniority systems
skills of
hiring practices, 63, 66, 231
importance, 70
surveys of
hiring practices, 60–73
reasons for retirement, 34–35, 223–24
technological innovation and
effects, 11, 18, 29–30
geographic mobility, 105
occupational mobility, 105
retraining, 230
unemployment of, 15, 19, 30, 71–72, 75–76
unions and, *see* Unions, older workers and
wages of
employment and, 58–59
industries, 57–58
women workers and, 18–19, 30, 47, 53, 56–59, 72, 91, 208–9
work habits of, 69
work horizons of, 208, 210, 230–31
workmen's compensation and, 91, 228–29
On-the-job training, 4, 229–30
Operatives, 191
educational level of, 147
female workers among, 150
full-time workers among, 151
geographic migration by, 152
industrial concentration and, 157
job-survival rates among, 134–36
median income of, 153
nonwhites among, 143–44
occupational growth-rates of, 139
productivity of, 155
regression-analysis of, 162–76
self-employed among, 146
unemployed among, 142
union members among, 158

Pacific states, migrants to, 110–11
Paint products industry, older workers in, 69–70
Painters' union, policies on older workers of, 86
Parricide, primitive, 225
Part-time workers, regression-analysis results for, 162–76
Pension plans, private
development of, 21, 205
older workers and, 29
attitudes of workers, 23
benefits, 20, 205
early retirement provisions, 22
effects, 22–23
hiring practices, 59, 64, 68–69, 71, 91
surveys, 34–35
union-negotiated, 21–22
Personal freedoms and income redistribution, 227
Personal utility and real income, 223
Physicians in advanced age, 221
Poor
aid programs for
aged, 10–11, 203, 226–27
focus, 10, 203
basic categories of, 223–25
income of, defined, 223
income redistribution for, 225–26
social goals and, 234
Population trends
age structure and, 12–13, 204
birth rates and, 13–14
future and, 14
Portland General Electric Company, 88
Poverty
causes of, 5
income level for, 223
persistence of, 3
See also Poor
Predicting occupational employment, 179–99
conclusions, 197–99
decomposition of measures of inaccuracy and, 189–98
empirical results of, 188–97
goals of, 179–80
judging predictive accuracy in, 182–83
methods for, 180–82
Primitive peoples, parricide among, 225
Production levels, growth of, 3

Productivity
by age groups, 206–8, 228
by occupations, 155–56
of older workers, 30, 38–39, 56, 59, 72, 91, 204, 210
public policies, 229–30
welfare economics and, 217–18
Professionals, 191
average number of workers as, 154
careers in advanced age, 221
educational level of, 147–48, 163
employment prospects for, 204
female workers among, 150
full-time workers among, 151
geographic migration by, 152
increase in, 17
job-survival rate of, 134–36, 163
median income of, 153
nonwhites among, 143–44
occupational growth-rates of, 139, 163
regression-analysis results for, 162–76
retirement income of, 205
self-employed among, 146
unemployed among, 141
union members among, 158
Psychiatric problems, vocational rehabilitation in, 225
Public policies
on aged, 221–23, 225, 234
aid programs, 10–11, 203, 226–27
surveys, 9
on older workers
costs and benefits, 233–34
employment conditions, 227–33
existing programs, 9–11, 203, 226–27
medical care, 10–11, 203, 217, 226
mobility, 232–33
retirement, 223–27, 231–32
two older age-groups, 221–23
on poor, focus, 10, 203
Public relief, 203

Questionnaires, unreliability of answers to, 23–24
See also Surveys

Race
employment and, 129
older workers and, 210
racial and age discrimination compared, 229
See also Nonwhites
Real income, definition of, 223
Recessions, *see* Business cycles
Re-employment of older workers, 60
seniority systems and, *see* Surveys, of hiring practices
union policies on, 76
See also Employer attitudes toward older workers; Hiring practices
Regression analysis, occupational, 31*n*
empirical results of, 162–78
age groups, 162–72
1900–1950 period, 175–76
occupational groups, 176–78
patterns concluded from, 176–78
for predicting occupational employment, 179–99
conclusions, 197–99
decomposition of measures of inaccuracy, 189–98
empirical results, 188–97
goal, 179–80
judging predictive accuracy, 182–83
methods, 180–82
regression equation for, 160–62
Relief, public, 203
Research on older workers
method of approach in, 26–29
studies determining presence or absence of particular factors in, 36–40
studies explaining observed phenomena in, 29–36
Retirement
age of
future changes, 221–22
"normal," 203
optimal, 232
compulsory
income factors, 224
largeness of occupation, 154
early, 6
forced, 19
public policies, 231–32
economic fluctuations and, 231
income and, 223–27
public policies on, 223–27, 231–32
reasons given for, 23
unreliability of explanations, 34–35, 223

Retirement (*continued*)
voluntary
factors, 223–24
income and, 153
See also Retirement benefits
Retirement benefits
employment income compared with, 23
of private pension plans, 20, 205
social security, 22, 205, 224
Retraining
aim of, 230
continuous, 229–30
employer attitudes toward, 63, 66

Sales workers, 191
educational level of, 147
female workers among, 150
full-time workers among, 151
geographic migration among, 152
job-survival rates among, 134–36
nonwhites among, 144
occupational growth-rates of, 139
regression-analysis results for, 162–76
self-employed among, 146
Schools for adult education, 10
See also Education; Retraining
Self-employed, 210
by age groups, 146
careers in advanced age, 221
decline in, 16–17
by occupations, 143–46
regression-analysis results for, 162–76
Semiskilled occupations
increase in, 17
older workers and, 17, 70
advanced age, 221
Seniority systems
dual effect of, 72
geographic mobility and, 100
hiring practices and
conclusions, 71–73
little or no effect of seniority system, 62–66
partial effect of seniority system, 70–71
re-employment restricted by seniority system, 66–70
survey design, 60–62
lay-offs and, 19
long-tenure workers and, 75
plant-wide, 81, 83–84
scope of, 70
trends in, 77
union policies toward, 77–92
automobile industry, 81–85
building trades, 85–87
manufacturing industries, 77–81, 89–90
over-all effects, 88–92
utilities, 87–89
Service workers, 191
educational level of, 147
female workers among, 150
full-time workers among, 151
geographic migration by, 152
job-survival rates of, 134–36
median income of, 153
nonwhites among, 143–44
occupational growth rates of, 138–39
older workers as, 57
wage rates, 18
regression-analysis results for, 162–76
scarcity of opportunity for, 209
self-employed among, 146
union members among, 158
Sex and employment, 129
See also Women workers
Sheldon, Henry D., 14, 32–33
Sheltered workers, 225
Skilled workers
employment practices for, 204
loss through retirement of, 231
See also specific skilled occupations
Skills
of older workers
hiring practices, 63, 66, 231
importance, 70
poverty and, 5
programs for improving, *see* Retraining
Slum dwellers, 3
Smelting industry, older workers in, 68
Social Science Research Council, 9
Social security
income redistribution and, 226–27
medical provisions under, 10–11
retirement benefits from, 22, 205, 224
Social Security Administration, 23

South Atlantic states, migrants to, 110–11
Spengler, Joseph J., 14
States
  aged and, 9
  migrants between, 110–12
  See also Mobility
Steel industry, older workers in, 65, 78
Steiner, Peter O., 34–35
Surveys
  of hiring practices, 60–73
    conclusions, 71–73
    little or no effect of seniority system, 62–66
    partial effect of seniority system, 70–71
    re-employment restricted by seniority system, 66–70
    survey design, 60–62
  or reasons for retirement, 34–35, 223–24
  of unemployed workers, 36
Survival rates, *see* Job-survival rates

Taft-Hartley law, 76
Taxation and welfare economics, 218
Teachers in advanced age, 221
Technological innovation
  older workers and
    effects, 11, 18, 29–30
    geographic mobility, 105
    occupational mobility, 105
    retraining, 230
  requirements of, 204
Temporary Extended Unemployment Compensation program, 76
Tenant farmers, income of, 3
Theil, H., 180
Townsend Plan, 226
Trade unions, *see* Unions
Transportation costs of migration, 98–99, 104, 108
  government-financed, 232–33
Troy, L., 157
Truman, Harry S, 9

Unemployment
  by age groups, 30, 75–76, 142
    historical trend, 15
  job-survival rate and, 140–41
  long-term, 76
  by occupations, 139–41
  of older workers, 15, 19, 30, 71–72, 75–76
  regression-analysis results for, 162–76
  surveys of, 36
Unemployment rate and employment, 129
Unions
  demand-supply model of labor market and, 50, 52
  employment and, 130
  job-survival rates and, 134, 136, 157
  occupations in, 157–58
    regression-analysis results, 174–75
  older workers and, 210
    automobile industry, 81–85
    building trades, 85–87, 89
    influence on employment, 59–60
    job listing and transfers, 78–81
    job seniority, *see* Seniority systems, union policies toward
    manufacturing industries, 77–81, 89–90
    over-all effects, 88–92
    pay adjustments, 88–89
    pension plans, 21–22
    re-employment, 76
    resistance of younger workers, 90
    utilities, 87–89
United Automobile Workers of America, policies on older workers of, 81–85
United Steel Workers of America, policies on older workers of, 78–81
Unskilled workers
  in advanced age, 221
  decline in, 17
  See also specific unskilled occupations
Utilities, union policies on older workers of, 87–89

Voluntary retirement
  factors in, 223–24
  income and, 153

Wage rates, 49
  definition of, 215
  of older workers
    employment and, 58–59
    industries, 57–58
  of women, 30

Welfare economics
  age and, 214–17
  goals of, 219
  model for, 211–14
  public policy criteria and, 217–19
  See also Public policies
Welfare programs, current, 9–11, 203, 226–27
West-North Central states, migrants to, 110–11
West-South Central states, migrants to, 110–11
White collar workers, 191
  educational level of, 147–48
  female workers among, 150
  full-time workers among, 151
  geographic migration by, 152
  job-survival rates among, 134–36
  median incomes of, 153
  nonwhites among, 143–44
  occupational growth-rates of, 138–39
  regression-analysis results for, 162–76
  self-employed among, 146
  seniority systems and, 70
  unemployed among, 141–42
  union members among, 158
  See also specific white-collar occupations
Wolman, L., 157
Women workers
  abilities of, 70
  by age groups, 150
  job-survival rate and, 148
  lower wage-rates of, 30
  occupations by, 148–50
  older workers and, 18–19, 30, 47, 53, 56–59, 72, 91, 208–9
  regression-analysis results for, 162–76
  younger workers and, 58
Wood products industry, and demand-supply model of labor market, 51
Work habits
  of older workers, 69
  of poor, 10
Work horizons of older workers, 208, 210
  offsetting limitations of, 230–31
Workmen's compensation and older workers, 91, 228–29

Younger workers, 24
  accident rates of, 39, 228
  flexibility of, 12, 18
  income of, 7
  job-survival trend among, 159
  in labor force, historical trend, 15
  mobility of, 114
  rights of, 232
  seniority system and, 74
  unemployment rate of, 75
  union policies and, 90
  women workers and, 58
Youth, programs to aid, 10